AFRICAN HISTORICAL DICTIONARIES
Edited by Jon Woronoff

HISTORICAL DICTIONARY
OF SENEGAL
Second Edition

by
Andrew F. Clark
and
Lucie Colvin Phillips

African Historical Dictionaries No. 65

The Scarecrow Press, Inc.
Metuchen, N.J., & London
1994

British Library Cataloguing-in-Publication data available

Library of Congress Cataloging-in-Publication Data

Clark, Andrew Francis.
    Historical dictionary of Senegal / by Andrew F. Clark and
Lucie Colvin Phillips.—2nd ed.
        p.   cm.—(African historical dictionaries ; no. 65)
    Rev. ed. of : Historical dictionary of Senegal / Lucie Gallistel
Colvin. 1981.
    Includes bibliographical references.
    ISBN 0-8108-2747-6 (acid-free paper)
    1. Senegal—History—Dictionaries.   I. Phillips, Lucie
Colvin, 1943–.   II. Phillips, Lucie Colvin, 1943–   .   Histori-
cal dictionary of Senegal.   III. Title.   IV. Series.
DT549.5.C57   1994
966.3′003—dc20   93-27031

CONTENTS

LIST OF MAPS

EDITOR'S FOREWORD—SENEGAL

Although Africa consists of about 50 countries, some of them stand out more than others. Senegal is one, due to its strategic location, its geographical dimensions and the size of its population. Despite some sluggishness in the economy, it does possess considerable potential. And it has maintained its position as a cultural and educational center. By joining various smaller and larger regional groupings, of which it was often a leading member, it has taken advantage of its assets and promoted broader unity. During the early post-independence period, Senegal's status was enhanced by the prestige of its first president, Léopold Sédar Senghor. Yet even today, what Senegal says and does carries considerable weight.

In the past, Senegal's role was even more prominent, and it is impossible to study the colonial period without encountering it at every turn in French policy. As Dakar was the capital of the vast French West Africa Federation, decisions adopted there affected the largest bloc of territories in the continent, and many aspiring leaders were educated there. Senegal was the homeland of Senghor, one of the trio of militant black poets who launched a call for respect of *négritude,* paving the way for independence. As the process of decolonization began, most of the successive reforms affected Dakar, strengthening or weakening that crucial link, until ultimately the Federation fell apart and Senegal had to choose its own path.

Thus a Historical Dictionary of Senegal is not only of use to those studying about, travelling to or doing business with that country, it is of general interest to anyone concerned with events in France's erstwhile colonial empire or West Africa at the present time. The book will prove particularly helpful to students, who will find the substantial chronology to be an excellent reference tool. Even accomplished scholars should appreciate the clear and precise entries and the appended tables. A comprehensive bibliography can then take each reader further into more specialized subjects.

The first edition of the Historical Dictionary of Senegal was written by Dr. Lucie Gallistel Colvin, whose knowledge, insight and experience greatly enriched the text. This second edition builds on that solid foundation. It comes from another notable scholar, Dr. Andrew F. Clark, assistant professor of African history at the University of North Carolina at Wilmington. He has gotten to know the country well through extended stays and careful research, some of it for a dissertation on "Economy and Society in the Upper Senegal." He has also written articles and papers as well as the book *Comparative Perspectives on Slavery: Pulaar Traditions from Bundu.*

Jon Woronoff
Series Editor

NOTE ON SPELLING AND PERSONAL NAMES

The major indigenous languages of Senegal belong to the Niger–Congo family of African languages. *Wolof, Serer, Pulaar, Mandinka, Jola, Soninke* and other African words as well as personal and place names are generally spelled phonetically, in a simplified version of the international phonetic system. Where spelling could cause readers to miss historic connections, as between modern Diops and their Jop ancestors, a cross-reference is included. Where modern Senegalese personal and place names have standard spellings recorded in print and in familiar usage, they are not phoneticized.

Arabic words and names are transliterated from the Arabic, except where an anglicized or French term has gained historic usage and the Arabic form is little known (e.g., *Almoravid* instead of *al-murabitun, marabout* instead of *murabit*).

Precolonial rulers and other outstanding figures are normally known only by their given names. Their patronyms, which today serve as last names in Senegal, are generally known to oral historians, but not mentioned. A person's given names usually consisted of a personal name followed by the given names of the mother and/or the acquired names and titles symbolic of the person's chosen career. For example, Lat Jor Jop is the well-known name of a hero of the resistance. His mother's name was Ngone Latir Fal, and his father was Saxewar Soxna Mbay Job (Diop). In this Dictionary he is listed under Jop, and a cross-reference would be found under Lat Jor. Other varieties of a person's name are listed in parentheses after the name, and titles he bore are mentioned in context in the entry. Titles, except those in English, are underlined.

ACRONYMS AND ABBREVIATIONS

AOF   Afrique Occidentale Française
     (French West Africa)

BCEAO Banque Centrale des Etats d'Afrique de l'Ouest
     (Central Bank of West African States)

BDS   Bloc Démocratique Sénégalais
     (Senegalese Democratic Bloc)

BMS   Bloc des Masses Sénégalaises
     (Bloc of the Senegalese Masses)

BPS   Bloc Populaire Sénégalais
     (Senegalese Popular Bloc)

CEAO   Communauté Economique de l'Afrique de l'Ouest
     (Economic Community of West Africa)

CEDEAO Communauté Economique des Etats de l'Afrique de
     l'Ouest
     (Economic Community of West African States;
     ECOWAS)

CFA   Communauté Financière Africaine (between 1946–
     1962, CFA referred to Colonies Françaises d'Afri-
     que)

CFAO   Compagnie Française de l'Afrique de l'Ouest

CILSS Comité Interétats pour la Lutte Contre la Secheresse Sahelienne
(Interstate Committee to Combat the Sahelian Drought)

CNTS Confédération Nationale des Travailleurs Sénégalais
(National Confederation of Senegalese Workers)

CRADs Centres Régionaux de l'Assistance pour le Développement

ECOWAS Economic Community of West Africa States (see CEDEAO)

FIDES Fonds d'Investissement pour le Développement Economique et Social (Investment Fund for Economic and Social Development)

IFAN Institut Fondamental d'Afrique Noire (formerly Institut Français d'Afrique Noire; now IFCAD)

IFCAD Institut Fondamental de Cheikh Anta Diop (formerly IFAN)

OCA Office de Commercialisation Agricole
(Office of Agricultural Marketing)

OCAMM Organisation Commune Africaine, Malagache et Mauricienne
(African, Malagasy and Mauritian Common Organization)

OERS Organisation des Etats Riverains du Sénégal
(Organization of Senegal River States)

OMVG   Organisation pour la Mise en Valeur du Fleuve Gambie
(Organization for the Development of the Gambia River Basin)

OMVS   Organisation pour la Mise en Valeur du Fleuve Sénégal
(Organization for the Development of the Senegal River Basin)

ONCAD   Organisation National des Centres de l'Assistance pour le Developpement (National Office of Development Assistance Centers)

ORTS   Office de Radiodiffusion-Télévision du Sénégal (Radio and Television Broadcasting Agency of Senegal)

PAI   Parti Africain de l'Indépendance (African Independence Party)

PDS   Parti Démocratique Sénégalais (Senegalese Democratic Party)

PIT   Parti de l'Indépendance et du Travail (Party for Independence and Work)

PRA   Parti du Regroupement Africain (Party of African Regroupment)

PS   Parti Socialiste (Socialist Party)

PSS   Parti de la Solidarité Sénégalaise (Party of Senegalese Solidarity)

RDA   Rassemblement Démocratique Africain (African Democratic Assembly)

RND   Rassemblement National Démocratique (National Democratic Assembly)

SCOA   Société Commerciale de l'Ouest Africain (Commercial Cooperation of West Africa)

SFIO   Section Française de l'International Ouvrière (French Section of the Worker's International)

SONADIS Société National de Distribution au Sénégal (National Distributing Company of Senegal)

UAM   Union Africane et Malagache (African and Malagasy Union)

UMOA   Union Monétaire de l'Ouest Africain (West African Monetary Union)

UNESCO United Nations Economic and Social Council

UNTS   Union Nationale des Travailleurs Sénégalais (National Union of Senegalese Workers)

UPS   Union Progressiste Sénégalaise (Senegalese Progressive Union)

INTRODUCTION

The Republic of Senegal is Africa's westernmost state, bordered by Mauritania to the north, Mali to the east and Guinea-Conakry and Guinea-Bissau to the south. Except for a short stretch of Atlantic coastline, Senegal surrounds the Republic of the Gambia. The country covers 196,840 square kilometers (76,000 miles), making it about the size of South Dakota. Senegal has 700 kilometers of Atlantic coastline. The 1988 census counted 6.9 million people, 62 percent of whom live in rural areas.

Senegal's history has been profoundly affected by its unique location bordering both the Sahel, or the southern edge of the Sahara Desert, and the Atlantic Ocean. The region's long involvement in the trans-Saharan trade exposed it to strong Islamic traditions originating in North Africa, and people in the Senegal River region were among the first in West Africa to adopt Islam. Because of its maritime position, Senegal became one of the first West African areas to develop direct commercial ties with Western Europe and to send large numbers of slaves to the New World. Senegal was also among the first regions in sub-Saharan Africa to be conquered and colonized by Europeans, and the strong links established between France and the oldest of its former French African colonies remain. In addition to Islamic and European influences, Senegal's history has also been determined by events in the Western Sudan and in other parts of Africa.

The origins of the inhabitants of modern Senegal, including the Wolof, Serer, Lebu, Fulbe, Soninke, Mandinka and Diola, are unclear, but they organized themselves into chiefdoms and larger political units that flourished during the period of the great Ghana and Mali Empires. Three African civilizations in particular have woven patterns into the fabric of early Senegalese history. Tekrur,

1

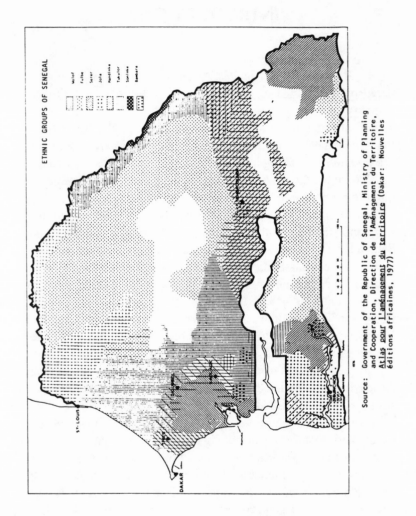

ETHNIC GROUPS OF SENEGAL

Source: Government of the Republic of Senegal, Ministry of Planning and Cooperation, Direction de l'Aménagement du Territoire, Atlas pour l'aménagement du territoire (Dakar: Nouvelles éditions africaines, 1977).

one of the oldest and most prominent precolonial states in the area, evolved in the middle valley of the Senegal River during the first millennium CE. Because of its riverine location reaching to the edge of the desert, Tekrur benefitted from the trans-Saharan trade between North and West Africa, and its inhabitants converted early to Islam. During the thirteenth century, Tekrur became a vassal of the Mali Empire to the east. The Mande of Mali settled the Gambia River basin and the area between the upper Senegal, Gambia and Niger rivers. They exerted commercial, cultural and sometimes direct political influence over all of modern-day Senegal. At the same time, the Wolof united central Senegal into the Jolof Empire. Eventually, the empire expanded to include the predominantly Serer kingdoms of Sin and Salum.

Precolonial Senegalese societies were generally divided into three main social categories or estates: freeborn, artisan castes and slaves. Freeborn consisted of nobles belonging to royal lineages, and peasant farmers or commoners. Artisans, who belonged to hereditary endogamous castes based on occupational specialization, consisted of gold, silver and iron smiths, woodworkers, weavers, leatherworkers and griots, or musicians and praise singers. Slaves, who occupied the lowest strata of society, were further divided into trade or first-generation slaves; domestic or later-generation slaves who generally could not be sold; and crown slaves, or *cedo.*

Portuguese ships arriving off the northern coast in 1444 were the harbingers of the era of European contact and expansion, which would bring first the trans-Atlantic slave trade and then colonial conquest. The Jolof Empire and some kingdoms on the upper Senegal River already had a flourishing trade in slaves with Arabs crossing the Sahara. The Portuguese quickly became another outlet for this trade, making the Senegambia region their foremost West African market throughout the fifteenth and sixteenth centuries.

The rapid escalation of the slave trade fragmented Senegambian societies both geopolitically and socially. Geographically, the Portuguese use of water routes offered an advantage to

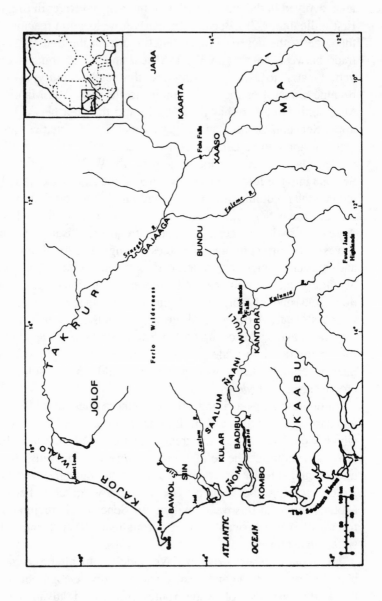

SENEGAMBIAN STATES ABOUT 1700

kingdoms with ocean and river ports. Galam or Gajaaga, situated on the upper Senegal River, became the dominant kingdom in the upper valley, largely because of its active participation in the slave trade. The Jolof Empire had been oriented toward the interior, with its capital on the central plains between the Senegal and Gambia Rivers. By the mid-sixteenth century, after only a century of European contact, the empire was rent into its constituent parts, as former provinces declared and fought for their independence. The successor kingdoms included Futa Toro in the middle Senegal valley, Niani and Wuli on the north bank of the Gambia River and the Wolof and Serer states stretching along the coast (from north to south): Walo, Kajor, Bawol, Sin and Salum. Jolof retained the same dynasty, but was from then on a weak and isolated kingdom.

This radical disruption did not destroy the Senegambia as a distinct historic region, but the area was fundamentally reoriented. The successor states established a stable balance of power and a commercial focus on the coast and the Senegal and Gambia rivers. Kingdoms like Kajor and Salum, with good ports and well-organized militaristic elites, attacked and raided their neighbors for slaves, but usually did not conquer them. Weak kingdoms, such as Walo, that could not protect their people from Moor raiders or European traders, were preyed upon by their neighbors and internal factions.

European traders very rarely made war on local African kingdoms, since they were unable to operate militarily on the land. They usually built their bases on islands, paying tribute to local rulers. Relations were not so cordial among Europeans as competition for trade resulted in a chronic state of hostility and frequent seizures. After the Portuguese, the Dutch and later British and French interlopers moved in on the Senegambian trade. By the peak of the slave trade in the late seventeenth and eighteenth centuries, England was well-established on the Gambia River while France dominated the Senegal River from its base on Saint-Louis island. The Dutch were forced out and the Portuguese retreated south to the Casamance region.

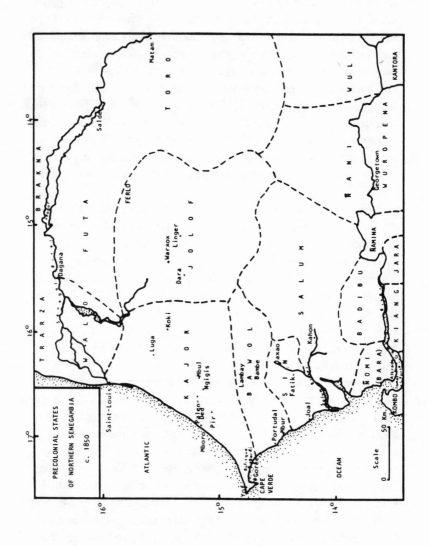

PRECOLONIAL STATES
OF NORTHERN SENEGAMBIA
c. 1850

Dependence on slave exporting also transformed the internal processes of Senegambian societies. The kings' domestic servants gradually became bodyguards and then standing slave armies. The best and most loyal slaves became the kings' bureaucrats, usurping functions that were formerly the prerogatives of noble families. The nobility and their crown slaves theoretically served as protectors of the poor dependent castes and estates. If the latter were disobedient or troublesome, however, they became the victims instead of the benefactors of that "protection." Women captured in slave raids tended to be retained in the Senegambia, dramatically increasing the number of domestic slaves in the region. In addition, there was never any pretense that the Wolof, Fulbe or Malinke kingdoms benefitted non-Muslim minorities, who huddled in enclaves subject to regular raiding.

Islam spread throughout the region, and the dynamics of its spread and its precepts became fundamental to the area during the slave-trade era. Islam provided the rationale for the constant warfare that generated slaves; it also offered a vision of an egalitarian, peaceful, law-abiding society, which coalesced into the internal opposition to the slave trade. The slave trade was the rallying cry of Muslim clerics, who frequently attacked the corruption and greed of existing rulers. When they occasionally seized power, however, they found themselves likewise disposing of prisoners by trading in slaves.

The export of slaves ceased to be the dominant activity of the Senegambia by the late eighteenth century, when an industrializing Europe turned to other forms of labor. It did not stop, however, until the latter half of the nineteenth century, when emancipation in the New World ended the demand for illegal slaves. The first French attempt to find an economic substitute for the slave trade in Senegambia was the agricultural colonization scheme of 1817 to 1827. Although it failed, local traders were simultaneously developing a commercial alternative in the rapidly growing gum arabic exports. Gum had been harvested in the forests of the Senegal River basin for centuries and was used in small quantities to fix textile dyes. As textile production in Europe expanded through industrialization, the gum trade grew large enough to replace the slave trade among French merchants in Senegal. The upper Senegal valley was a focus of the gum arabic trade throughout the nineteenth century. In the 1840s and 1850s, groundnuts or peanuts, used increasingly in Europe to supply oil for soap, cooking and light industrial uses, rivaled and then surpassed gum as the dominant export from the Senegambia. The expansion of the groundnut crop contributed to the initial shift in the region's center of gravity from the coast and river valley to central and western agricultural areas.

The colonial conquest of Senegambia, occurring between approximately 1850 and the 1920s, followed directly out of European commercial interests. The region experienced a particularly long and violent period of invasion and resistance, owing to European rivalries and the strength of interior kingdoms. Africans had known many conquests before, but none could have prepared them for the devastation, warfare and irreversible consequences of machine-age European colonialism. *Al-Hajj* Umar Tal, the most influential of the religious leaders in the Senegambia, launched his holy war on the upper Senegal river kingdoms in 1852, just as the French were embarking on an aggressive policy throughout the River basin. The two clashed directly in the upper Senegal valley from 1855 through 1858.

Both clerics and Europeans sought to topple the traditional nobilities, whose leadership was rooted in slave raiding and trading. These dynasties, however, proved more vital than either of their enemies had expected. When one ruler was defeated or killed, another came to the fore. Frequently, the second generation were men like Lat Jor Jop of Kajor, Alburi Njay of Jolof and Abdul Bokar Kan of Futa Toro, who combined Islamic zeal with hereditary legitimacy, which the clerics lacked.

Islamic reform in the Senegambia acquired widespread ideological unity under the leadership of *al-Hajj* Umar. It lacked practical unity, however, as numerous clerics founded their own movements. Many did so with *al-Hajj* Umar's blessings, explicit or implicit. Ma Ba emerged in Salum and Rip, Amadu Shaixu in Futa

Toro and Jolof, *Fode* Kaba Dumbuya and *Alfa* Molo Balde in the Casamance and Mamadu Lamine Drame in Bundu. From the 1860s through the 1890s, military alliances and campaigns shifted inconclusively. The only clear tendency was that the French on the Senegal and the British on the Gambia made slow but significant inroads, building fortified posts, telegraphs and railroads through still-turbulent territory. Eventually the European technological advantage in weapons and communications won out.

As the twentieth century dawned, combat exhaustion settled over the area, and the colonial government expanded its control. Each of the clerical jihadists mentioned above lay dead, and many of the traditional nobility as well. Those who survived and still posed a threat were captured and deported to faraway places. Wolof, Fulbe and Moorish traders were forced out of their markets by European and Lebanese agents. Many Africans flocked to new clerical leaders, especially Amadu Bamba Mbacke and *al-Hajj* Malik Sy, who founded the two most influential Islamic brotherhoods in Senegal today, the Muridiyya and the Tijani lodge at Tivawan. Initially, these two men publicly kept their distance from the French, but they soon made their peace with the colonial state.

After the conquest, Senegal occupied a privileged place in France's colonial empire. The federal capital of French West Africa was established at Dakar, and Senegal was the only colony in Black Africa where France tried to apply assimilationist ideals. Residents of the urban *communes* of Senegal (Dakar, Saint-Louis, Gorée and Rufisque) were granted full citizenship rights and had greater access to Western education and employment. Yet there were sharp differences in status between the few citizens of the Four Communes and the majority of subjects of the protectorate, or rural Senegal. The disparity gave rise to considerable resentment in the rural areas, as well as contributing to the development of two radically different styles of political leadership. In the communes, the Western-educated Senegalese intellectual dominated politics, whereas in the protectorate the religious marabouts held power.

These marabouts not only preached obedience to colonial authorities, they also encouraged their followers to grow ground-nuts for the market in the new areas they were settling. The French enthusiastically approved of this practice, which promoted the foundation of the economy. In return, the colonial authorities granted many Murid and Tijani marabouts large tracts of land. By World War I, Senegal's economic prosperity was inextricably linked to the groundnut. Moreover, the colony's center of gravity had shifted irreversibly from the Senegal River region to the central groundnut basin. Migrants flocked to the new agricultural lands, with many adopting the Wolof language and embracing the Murid brotherhood.

In 1914, urban African voters elected Blaise Diagne the first black African deputy to the French Assembly. He championed the *citoyen* cause throughout the war, eventually winning the principle that place of birth, not color, should determine the rights of commune residents in Senegal. Residents in the protectorate and the Islamic brotherhoods supported and helped finance his work, although they could neither vote for him nor exercise the other rights he secured for commune inhabitants. Diagne and the French administration soon reached a rapprochement. The government supported him in elections, and he enlisted African cooperation with colonial policies, most notably leading a massive recruitment drive during World War I. Neither concerned themselves with the resentments of nonvoters in the protectorate.

Socialism as a political doctrine appeared in Senegal in the 1920s and 1930s, and was very attractive to intellectuals. Even though it came first as a direct European import, it seemed superior to capitalism. African intellectuals could find nothing attractive about capitalism—to them it was responsible for coloni-alism, an appallingly deadly world war and then, in the Great Depression of the Thirties, total economic collapse. Lamine Guèye, one of Senegal's earliest lawyers, founded the Socialist Party of Senegal in 1927, and a Senegalese branch of the French Section of the Socialist International (SFIO) in 1937. Colonial government opposition and then the suspension of electoral

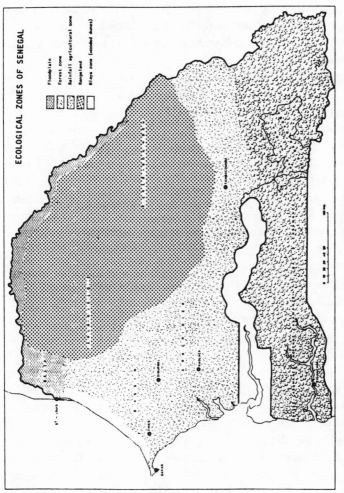

ECOLOGICAL ZONES OF SENEGAL

Floodplain
Forest zone
Rainfall agricultural zone
Rangeland
Niaye zone (wooded dunes)

Source: Government of the Republic of Senegal, Ministry of Planning and Cooperation, Direction de l'Aménagement du territoire, Atlas pour l'aménagement du territoire (Dakar: Nouvelles Éditions africaines, 1977).

politics in the colonies during World War II kept them out of office for nearly two decades. But in 1946 Guèye was the acknowledged unofficial political leader of Senegal. The Constitution of the Fourth French Republic, issued that year, gave him the opportunity to be elected deputy. It also extended the franchise to the protectorate, eliminating finally the discriminatory status of rural residents. It also enhanced the power and influence of the marabouts.

Léopold Sédar Senghor, then a teacher and poet in Paris, was Guèye's nominee for the protectorate deputy's seat. Although then a political neophyte, Senghor soon moved into the commanding position that he held for many years afterward. An early master of realpolitik, he stumped in the countryside to win the 1946 election, capitalizing on the subjects' resentment of past urban privileges and securing the support of Muslim leaders. Senghor broke with Guèye in 1948, founding his own political party, the Bloc Démocratique Sénégalais. In 1951 he defeated Guèye, and then went on to build a unified political machine capable of carrying Senegal through the first stages of political decolonization.

Senghor, with support from Senegalese marabouts, rejected immediate independence and endorsed General de Gaulle's 1958 plan for a French community. Within a year, however, Senegal began negotiations to obtain independence as part of the Mali Federation, which also included the former French Sudan. The Mali Federation became independent on April 4, 1960, but divisions quickly arose between the two colonies, and the federation was dissolved on August 22. Senegal declared its unilateral independence immediately afterward.

Senegal owed much of its political stability in the first two decades of independence to the rule of Senghor. The first two years were marked by a power struggle between President Senghor and Prime Minister Mamadou Dia, which ultimately resulted in the ascendancy of Senghor and the arrest and imprisonment of Dia. In 1963 a new constitution established a strong presidential regime, and an election shortly thereafter gave Seng-

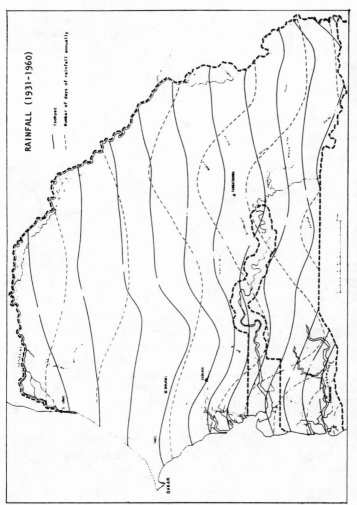

RAINFALL (1931-1960)

_____ Isohyet

- - - - - Number of days of rainfall annually

DAKAR

○ DIOURBEL

○ KAOLACK

○ TAMBACOUNDA

Source: Government of the Republic of Senegal, Ministry of Planning and Cooperation,. Direction
          de l'Aménagement du territoire, Atlas pour l'aménagement du territoire (Dakar: Nouvelles
          Éditions africaines, 1977).

hor an overwhelming majority. Until the mid-1970s, Senegal was transformed into a virtual one-party state with Senghor treated as the "father of the nation" and the ruling Socialist Party as the only viable political organization in the country.

The new republic went through difficult economic circumstances with the Sahelian drought of 1966–1973, France's abandonment of colonial price supports in 1967, the rise in oil prices in the early 1970s, and worldwide inflation. Halfhearted efforts at diversification of the monocrop (groundnut) economy had to contend with entrenched political and religious interests and French dominance of Senegal's foreign aid. A marked decline in peanut prices in the mid-1970s, and a resultant drop in production, had a severe impact on the country's economy. Senegal also inherited the bulk of the bureaucracy of the former AOF, which proved a decidedly mixed blessing. The country did experience a moderate level of commercial and industrial growth between 1960 and 1980, estimated variously at 2 to 7 percent per year. Population growth greatly outstripped economic growth, however, and constant inflation contributed to a declining real per capita income. When Senghor resigned in December 1980 in favor of his prime minister, Abdou Diouf, the country's political stability was threatened by worsening economic stagnation and deterioration.

Abdou Diouf, labelled a brilliant technocrat during his term as prime minister, quickly set about instituting political and economic reforms. He liberalized the political process by allowing an increased number of opposition parties. Thus 14 political parties were recognized by the elections of 1983. Diouf also restructured his administration in an effort to increase efficiency and to eliminate corruption and nepotism. Yet increased urban unemployment, rising inflation and falling groundnut production, in addition to strict structural adjustments imposed by the International Monetary Fund, caused an economic downturn. Diouf was also criticized for his intervention in the attempted coup in the Gambia in 1981. The resulting Senegambian Confederation was beset by difficulties and ultimately dissolved in 1989.

The 1983 elections, the first test for Diouf and his reforms, gave the ruling Parti Socialiste an overwhelming majority and the president an 82 percent approval rating. In 1988, Diouf received 73 percent of the vote, although the absentee rate surpassed 40 percent. Charges of vote rigging and other irregularities sparked serious rioting in Dakar. The city was placed under a three-month state of emergency, and opposition leaders were arrested, tried and convicted. Amnesty was eventually granted to all political detainees. Diouf pursued constitutional reforms and reshuffled his cabinet. His economic policies have made little impact, however, and Senegal, like many other African countries, has experienced a declining real per capita income. The country remains dependent on groundnuts and foreign aid, mainly from France and the United States. A series of drought years, spiralling inflation and rapid population growth have thwarted efforts to improve Senegal's economic situation.

In 1989, Senegal faced a serious crisis with its Arab-dominated neighbor, Mauritania. Long-standing hostility and border disputes between the two countries erupted into a massacre of Senegalese in Mauritania, and revenge attacks against Mauritanians in Senegal. In the aftermath of the killings, several thousand Senegalese and Mauritanians were repatriated, property and assets were confiscated and all borders were closed. The situation has remained tense, although mediation efforts have been under way recently.

CHRONOLOGY OF IMPORTANT EVENTS

Time	Senegal River Valley	Geographical Areas of Senegal Central Western	Casamance and Senegal Oriental
Paleolithic 1500–800 B.C.		Mousteroid culture in Cape Verde-Thies area	
Neolithic 6500 B.C.–0	Arrival of new populations. Sites with pottery, polished hematite axes, and tumuli, from Cape Verde to the Falémé River in the Upper Senegal Valley.		
Protohistoric period:			Beginning of the metal age. Iron-smelting sites throughout the eastern area.
c. 4th cen. A.D.	Beginning of the metal age in the Senegal River Valley.		
590–800 A.D.		Megalithic burial sites in upper Gambia and Saloum basins.	
c. 5th cen. A.D. into historic period		Sand burial mounds without megaliths throughout central western Senegal.	

| | | Geographical Areas of Senegal | |
Time	Senegal River Valley	Central Western	Casamance and Senegal Oriental
c. 4th cen.	Beginning of Tekrur in the middle valley; trans-Saharan trade develops. Slaves and gold exchanged for luxuries.		Namandirou (Kingdom of Du in Arab sources) on the upper Senegal and Falémé, founded and ruled by Ndao patrilineage, tributary to Ghana.
11th cen.	War Jabi, King of Tekrur converts to Islam, launches jihad against non-Muslim neighbors. Invites charismatic Berber cleric Abdullah ibn Yasin into his kingdom; Serer begin emigrating to Bawol-Sin area, resist Islam.		Most of upper Senegal tributary to Ghana.
1042–1087	Almoravid movement, initiated by cleric ibn Yasin, conquers and rules all western Sudan, Sahara, Morocco, and Spain.		
12th–14th cent.	Tekrur absorbed by Jolof.	Jolof empire is founded by Njajan Njay, ruled by Njay dynasty. Kingdom of Walo, tributary to Jolof, is founded by his legendary half-brother Barka Mboj.	Upper Senegal tributary to Mali Empire.

Date	Events	
	Wagadu matrilineage establishes kingdom of Bawol, also tributary to Jolof.	Tirimaxan Trawore conquers large area, consolidates it as the Kabu Empire, pays tribute but retains autonomy from Mali. Successive waves of Malinke settle eastern Senegal and the river valleys, forcing indigenous Bañun into lower Casamance. There Bañun found kingdom of Kasa.
	Malian invasion, led by general Tirimaxan Trawore, defeats Jolof, imposes tribute. Trade between Mali and Jolof also grows.	
	Gelwar matrilineage, offshoot of royal family of Kabu, establishes kingdom of Sin, tributary to Jolof.	Ñani and Wuli kingdoms establish their independence from Jolof, pay tribute to Kabu.
1444	Portuguese captain Dinis Diaz first sights Senegal River, learns of Jolof Empire. Slave trade develops; horses, brass manillas, and iron bars imported.	
c. 1490	Koly Tengela Ba conquers middle valley, founds Deñanke dynasty and kingdom of Futa Toro.	Mbegan Ndur establishes Gelwar matrilineage, kingdom of Salum.
c. 1550		Jolof Empire collapses after Amary Ngone Sobel Fal wins independence for Kajor and

Time	Senegal River Valley	Geographical Areas of Senegal — Central Western	Casamance and Senegal Oriental
early 1600s		Bawol. Walo, Sin, and Salum also gain independence.	Initial contacts between Europeans and states in the upper Senegal.
		Dutch factory established on Gorée Island, then fort built.	
1638	French factory established on Island of Bocos, in the mouth of the Senegal River.		
		Coastal kingdoms trade with Dutch, French and British; Jolof, isolated, cannot.	
1659	French factory built on Saint-Louis island.		
1673–77	Tubenan religious revolution led by Nasir al-Din overthrows traditional rulers of Futa Toro, Jolof, Kajor, Brakna Moors and Walo; establishes loyal rulers in their places. Nasir and three of his successors are killed in battle before their rule can be consolidated. Traditional dynasties, with French traders' help, defeat the clerics and reestablish themselves. Only in Jolof does king continue loyal to Tubenan.		Galam (Gajaaga) involved in trans-Atlantic slave trade.
1677–79		French Compagnie du Sénégal drives out Dutch, establishes by force a monopoly of trade on the	French explorations in upper Senegal valley, especially in gold-producing areas of Bambuk.

	coast. Expeditions led by Admiral d'Estrées and Sieur Ducasse. British trade on Gambia.	
1690s		Malik Dauda Sy founds clerical dynasty in Bundu.
		The Sissibe lineage rules until 1840s.
1697–1720	Lat Sukabe Fal establishes Gej matrilineage in Kajor, and the new patrilineal House of Ce Yasin in Kajor and Bawol. Firearms are adopted.	
	Matrilineal claims of the Logar, Jos and Tejek families are asserted in Walo, increasingly dominate court politics.	
1758–63	Seven Years' War; British eliminate French from the Senegambia briefly.	
1763	Gorée is returned to the French.	
1770s	Clerical revolution in Futa Toro overthrows Deñanke dynasty, weakened by Trarza, Brakna, and Moroccan raids. Establishes elec-	Decline in slave exports from Galam.
	Rulers of Kajor, Bawol, Walo and Jolof are invited to endorse the Islamic reform movement and its new leaders; they accept.	

Time	Geographical Areas of Senegal		
	Senegal River Valley	Central Western	Casamance and Senegal Oriental
	tive Almamate over a clerical confederacy. Sulaiman Bal initiates the revolution, Abdul Qadir Kan consolidates it.		
1776	*Almamy* Abdul Qadir embargoes trade with the British, forbids export of Tukulor slaves, imposes tolls, but sells his own POWs.		
1778	Saint-Louis returned to French, whose trade on the River resumes.		
c. 1790	Futa Toro seeking hegemony in the area, defeats Walo and Trarza.	New ruler in Kajor refuses to renew predecessor's endorsement of *Almamy* Abdul Qadir, quarrels with clerics of Kajor. Conflict in Kajor becomes civil war, clerics lose. One group of defeated clerics, under Jal Jop, flees to Cape Verde, establishes clerical Lebu republic independent of Kajor.	

1789–1815	French Revolution and ensuing wars disrupt Atlantic trade.
1793	Slavery declared abolished in France, but decree never promulgated in Senegal.
1796	*Almamy* Abdul Qadir, allied to *Bur-ba* Jolof, invades Kajor. Is defeated and held captive until replaced as Almamy. Then released, resumes office.
1802	Napoleon reinstates slavery.
1803	Gorée falls to the British.
1806	Britain outlaws slave trade.
1809	Saint-Louis falls to the British. Abu Nacām Kunta comes as missionary to the court of Kajor, founds Qadiri lodge.
1814–15	Treaties of Paris and Vienna return Saint-Louis and Gorée to France, require prohibition of the slave trade.

Time		Geographical Areas of Senegal	
	Senegal River Valley	Central Western	Casamance and Senegal Oriental
1819–27	French agricultural colonization scheme is tried in Walo, to replace old slave-trade economy. Fails. Export of gum-arabic develops as the first alternative to the slave trade.		French fort established at Bakel in Galam.
1827–30	*Seriñ Koki* Njaga Isa and his deputy Dile Cam conquer Walo by jihad. French allied to Walo nobility defeat and kill Cam.		Expansion of gum arabic trade from the upper valley.
1828–29	Another of Njaga Isa's disciples Hamet (Mahdiya) Ba, proclaims himself the *Mahdi* and prophesies the end of the world. Nearly overthrows the Almamate of Futa Toro.		
1832	Queen Mother of Walo marries King of Trarza. French oppose alliance.		
1833–35	French make war on Walo and Trarza seeking annulment of marriage.		

1835	Treaties end war, leaving marriage intact, but promising that their child(ren) will not claim both thrones.	
1840s	Groundnuts prove valuable export. Peasant production revolutionizes colonial commerce and indigenous economy.	
1845–64	*Al-Hajj* Umar Tal's militant Islamic reform movement, based first in Dinguiray, Futa Jalon, and then on the upper Senegal, dominates the politics of the mainland. Popularizes Tijani brotherhood.	Civil wars in Bundu and Gajaaga, ending with conquest by Umar Tal in mid-1850s.
1848	Slavery abolished in Saint-Louis and Gorée, during revolution of 1848 in France.	
1848–51	Senegal allowed to elect a Deputy to Second Republic's new Assembly.	
1852	Louis Napoleon abolishes colonial representation.	*Al-Hajj* Umar Tal begins move into upper Senegal region.

Time	Senegal River Valley	Geographical Areas of Senegal Central Western	Casamance and Senegal Oriental
1854–61; 1863–65	Louis Faidherbe, Governor of Senegal, with support of large merchants and Second Empire, launches first campaigns for colonial domination.		Faidherbe recognizes Bokar Saada Sy as *almamy* of Bundu.
1855–58	Faidherbe fights the Trarza in Walo and Trarza during dry seasons; in high river seasons attacks *al-Hajj* Umar. Annexes Walo; keeps Umar east of Bakel.		*Fode* Kaba Dumbuya conquers Kombo and Foñi, establishing new clerical state.
1859		Unsuccessful clerical revolt in Kajor.	
1859–65	Recruitment drives for Umarian jihad, now being waged in the Niger River Valley.	Faidherbe invades Sin, Salum, Bawol and Kajor, taking kings of first three into "Protectorate," annexing latter. Builds telegraph from Saint-Louis to Gorée through Kajor. Lat Jor Jop emerges as hero of the resistance in Kajor, Albury Njay in Jolof.	Recruitment drives for Umarian jihad to the east.

1859–91	Abdul Bokar Kan emerges to dominate the politics of Futa Toro. Opposes *al-Hajj* Umar's annual recruitment drives, which drain manpower from Futa. Tries to defend Futa from the French.		Bokar Saada Sy consolidates and extends rule in Bundu. Area around Bakel annexed. Increasing French military and administrative presence in the region.
1861–67		Ma Ba launches jihad in Badibu, attracts allegiance of Lat Jor and Albury.	
1867			*Alfa* Molo Balde launches jihad in upper Casamance, founds Fuladu.
1868–69	Shaixu Ahmadu Mahdiyu Ba son of Hamet, emerges to lead jihad during cholera epidemic. Helps Lat Jor defeat French invasion.		
1871		French give up annexation of kajor, recognize Lat Jor Jop as *Damel*. Shaixu Ahmadu Ba conquers Jolof, alienating Lat Jor and his protégé Albury Njay.	

Time	Senegal River Valley	Geographical Areas of Senegal Central Western	Casamance and Senegal Oriental
1869/70–			*Fode* Kaba Dumbuya launches jihad in lower Casamance, begins three decades of conflict with Fuladu.
1874		Shaixu Ahmadu Ba and Abdul Bokar Kan invade Kajor, defeating Lat Jor Jop and Albury Njay.	
1875		Lat Jor and Albury call on French help, defeat and kill Shaixu Ahmadu. Albury reestablished in Jolof.	
1879	French plan conquest of western Sudan, to be linked to its Algerian domain by Senegal-Niger-trans-Saharan railway.	French sign treaty permitting railroad construction through Kajor, marking beginning of final campaigns of conquest. Lat Jor Jop renounces treaty, as he learns it does not give him the throne of Bawol.	Construction of Kayes-Bamako railroad begins.
1883		French begin a railroad through Kajor. Albury Njay helps Lat Jor harass unauthorized builders.	Upper Senegal used as staging area for advances into the Western Sudan.

1883–86		French force Lat Jor into exile, install Samba Yaya Fal as *Damel*.	
1885–87		Samba Laobe Fal defects from Lat Jor to French, made *Damel*, allows railroad.	Death of Bokar Saada Sy (Bundu). Mamadu Lamin Drame leads Soninke jihad against Fulbe of Bundu and French, who finally defeat and kill him.
1886		Lat Jor and Sambe Laobe killed. Kajor annexed definitively.	
1887		French invade Salum, but Saer Maty Ba, with help of Abdul Bokar Kan and Albury Njay, defends his rule.	Gallieni establishes *villages de liberté* in upper Senegal.
1889	British-French treaty delimits Gambia-Senegal borders, after abandoning idea of exchanging Gambia for Ivory Coast.	Defeated courtiers of Wolof states flock to cleric Ahmadu Bamba Mbake. Many also join Tijani cleric *al-Hajj* Malik Sy.	

Time	Senegal River Valley	Geographical Areas of Senegal Central Western	Casamance and Senegal Oriental
1890	Major French expedition Albury Njay and Abdul Bokar Kan flee to join *al-Hajj* Umar's son Ahmadu on the upper Niger. Abdul Bokar killed, Ahmadu defeated. Ahmadu and Albury retreat across the Sudan. French Protectorate declared over interior, borders similar to today's except eastern and southern poorly defined, not conquered. Urban *communes* (Saint-Louis, Gorée, Dakar and Rufisque) have separate administration.		Creation of colony of *Soudan français*. Includes parts of the upper Senegal. Decline in gum arabic trade from the upper Senegal.
1890–1920			French expeditions to individual villages "pacify," the Casamance, impose head tax.
1895–1902	French West Africa organized, with its capital at Dakar.	Ahmadu Bamba exiled by the French to Gabon. Received as saint on his return.	
1901	Saint-Louis remains capital of Senegal		*Fode* Kaba's domain conquered, he is killed in his *tata*.

	Communes	Protectorate
1903		Fuladu (Casamance) conquered, Musa Molo forced into exile in Gambian half of Fuladu.
1903–07		Ahmadu Bamba's second exile to Mauritania. He founds new Murid brotherhood, offshoot of Qadiriyya.
1906		Dakar-Bamako railroad construction begun.
1907–12		Ahmadu Bamba allowed third exile in Jolof closer to his native Bawol. Followers stream to him.
		Migration from eastern regions to Dakar, Murid areas and to the British Gambia.
1910–13		"Association" replaces "assimilation" as official French policy for the Protectorate. Commune residents are still to be assimilated.
1912		Ahmadu Bamba circulates a letter calling on his adherents to abandon all hope of armed resistance to the French, urging cooperation in the temporal domain. He is allowed to return to Bawol. He aids French military conscription campaigns for WWI.

	Communes	Protectorate
1913–14		Drought and famine throughout Sahel.
1914	Blaise Diagne, first African elected Deputy to French Assembly from Senegal.	
1914–18	World War I. Diagne asserts commune residents' rights to serve in army only if treated as full French citizens. Wins his point.	Massive recruitment drives for WWI. After winning privileged conditions of military service for urban commune residents, Diagne leads major French conscription drive in the rural Protectorate. Rural residents, especially Murids, serve in large numbers, but many are bitter over discrimination.
1912 on		French grant vast tracts of land to marabouts, especially Murids, to reward loyalty and expand peanut production. Lands along new railroad very lucrative. Increased migration to Murid areas and groundnut basin.
1918/19	Diagne founds first political party, the Republican Socialist Party of Senegal.	
1922		*Al-Hajj* Malik Sy dies, is succeeded as Tijani *Xalifa* by his son Abu Bakr.
1923		Dakar-Bamako railroad completed. Proposed trans-Saharan link abandoned.

1927	Ahmadu Bambu dies, is succeeded as Xalifa of the Murids by his son Mamadu Mustafa. Grand Mosque and tomb construction already begun at Touba is renewed.
1929	Lamine Guèye founds Parti Socialiste Sénégalais.
1930s	Great Depression. Senegal's monocrop economy severely hurt by dramatic drop in groundnut prices and trade.
1934–41	Galandou Diouf serves as Deputy. Négritude movement among Parisian African and West Indian students.
1937	Lamine Guèye founds a Senegalese branch of the French Socialist Party, SFIO. Trade Union CGTS also is founded. Senghor developing ideas of ''Négritude.''
1939–45	World War II. France falls to Hitler, who installs Vichy Nazi regime. French West Africa rejects de Gaulle's Free French attempt to make Dakar its base, siding initially with Vichy. In 1942/43 it switches to de Gaulle. Massive recruitment drives. Many Senegalese fight and die in Africa, Europe, and Asia.

1940s   Accelerated growth of Dakar.

1946   Constitution of the Fourth French Republic enfranchises rural Senegalese, allows one rural, one urban deputy. Lamine Guèye is elected urban deputy. He sponsors Léopold Senghor for the rural seat, and Senghor wins easily.
Commune vs. Protectorate distinction loses relevance as civil rights are extended to all Senegal.

1947   Senghor breaks with Guèye, founds his own party, the BDS.

1951   Elections to the French National Assembly. Senghor swings rural areas, Guèye holds only a few urban precincts.

1952   Territorial Assembly elections confirm Senghor's advantage. Senghor's platform includes improved French aid to education, economic development and elimination of discrimination.

1956   *Loi cadre* extends universal adult suffrage to French West Africa as step toward internal autonomy.
BPS replaces BDS as a result of a unity movement among political parties led by Senghor.

1957   Majhmout Diop founds Marxist PAI, rejects unity movement.

1958   Constitution of the Fifth French Republic dissolves French West Africa, offers referendum on self-government within the French Union. Senegal votes 98 percent *yes,* following Senghor. France and Ivory Coast oppose idea of unified self-governing French West African federation. UPS replaces BPS, Guèye joins, dissolves SFIO.

Republic of Senegal

1960   Independence. Mali Federation, comprising Senegal and former Sudan, is granted independence April 4. Breaks up before elections in August. Senegal and Mali each proclaim separate independence. Senghor is elected President, Mamadou Dia Prime Minister. African socialism and négritude are the official philosophies. April 4, 1960, declared Independence Day in Senegal. PAI banned.

1961   BMS founded by Cheikh Anta Diop.

1962   Constitutional Crisis, due to falling out between Senghor and Dia. Dia tried and imprisoned until 1974. Senghor quickly consolidates power.

1963   Constitution of the Second Senegalese Republic is on strong Presidential model. Approved in referendum. Senghor elected unopposed, UPS sweeps Assembly elections with 94.2 percent of the vote. BMS dissolves.

1964   Cheikh Anta Diop founds FNS.

1965–66   FNS and other small opposition parties banned. UPS absorbs PRA, is sole legal party.

1966   Dakar hosts First World Festival of Negro Arts.

1968   General elections in February, Senghor and UPS elected unopposed. Student strike at University of Dakar and High Schools in May, followed by national strike called by UNTS May 31–June 4. Army puts down, with injuries but no deaths. Leaders imprisoned and released. University closed for the remainder of the term. Lamine Guèye dies.

1969   Student strikes beginning in March again result in closing of the University. Various unions strike in May, UNTS calls a general strike for June 11, but government declares a State of Emergency. Classes do not resume until November term. CNTS formed, with government sponsorship, to replace UNTS. Peasants, suffering from four years' drought and loss of French price supports for peanuts, refuse to pay their debts to the government marketing agencies.

1970   Constitutional reform introducing a weak prime minister's office is approved by voter referendum. Senghor appoints Abdou Diouf. Peasant dissatisfaction with ONCAD and peanut prices leads to widespread refusal to grow peanuts, reversion to millet and sorghum.

1971   Official visit by French President Pompidou in February is preceded by student and worker unrest. Student strikes in March result in closing of the University for the month, banning of UED and UDES. Student leaders are imprisoned, deported and/or conscripted. Drought continues, peasant debts written off.

1972   Severe drought continues, livestock die, peasants flee to urban relatives and/or ration food to survive.

1973   Student disturbances begin in January, culminate in May. Drought continues, requiring importation of emergency food relief. Inflation severe. Administrative reform in some regions.

Republic of Senegal

1974   Amnesty of political prisoners, including Mamadou Dia. Legal opposition party, the PDS, is founded by Abdoulaye Wade, with Senghor's blessings. Rains return to normal, but crops still deficient due to locust and rodent damage.

1976   PS replaces UPS, joins Socialist International. General amnesty of political offenders restores civil rights to Mamadou Dia and Majhmout Diop. Constitutional reform allows for three legal political philosophies, each to be represented by a single legal political party. Abdoulaye Wade's PDS, Majhmout Diop's PAI and Senghor's PS are recognized.

1978   General elections. Senghor elected with 81.7 percent, against Wade's 17.7 percent. PS takes 82 seats in the Assembly; PDS and PAI opposition win 18. Senegal hosts Socialist International congress. Administrative reform completed throughout country.

1980   Senghor resigns on December 31, in favor of Prime Minister Abdou Diouf.

1981   Diouf becomes Senegal's second president on January 1. Economic and financial adjustment plan is launched by the IMF and supported by France and USA (the country's largest aid donors). Diouf legalizes all political parties without ideological stipulation or restrictions. In August, Senegalese troops move into the Gambia to suppress an attempted coup against President Jawara. In December, Senegal and the Gambia announce plans for a Senegambian Confederation with Diouf as president and Jawara as vice president.

1982   Separatist unrest in the Casamance leaves several dead and injured.

1983   First meeting of the Senegambian Confederation Assembly. By March, 14 political parties are officially recognized in Senegal. April elections, the first test for Diouf and the new openness, give Diouf 82 percent of the presidential vote. PS wins 111 seats in the Assembly; PDS wins 8 seats; RND takes 1 seat. Absentee rate very high. After the election, Diouf abolishes the post of prime minister. Retired President Senghor elected to the *Academie Française*. In December, serious riots in the Casamance leave 25 dead and 80 wounded.

1984   Sekou Toure of Guinea-Conakry dies, and some Guinean refugees in Senegal return home. Relations between Senegal and Guinea improve steadily.

1985   Diouf becomes chairman of the Organization of African Unity for one year. Drought throughout Senegal, resulting in food shortages. Groundnut production severely curtailed. Student and worker unrest in Dakar.

1986   Scholar-politician Cheikh Anta Diop dies, and the University of Dakar and IFAN research institute are renamed after him. Diouf launches new economic adjustment and recovery program aimed at liberalizing the economy through a range of measures, including privatization of many state enterprises. Beginning of talks on granting the Casamance region some autonomy and more say in local affairs.

1987   Confrontations in the Casamance claim 10 lives. In April, students launch a protest movement at the University, which spreads throughout Dakar. University closed for remainder of term. Dakar police go on strike briefly; Diouf responds forcefully, but is clearly disturbed by unrest. Post of prime minister reinstated with appointment of Habib Thiam. Several creditor governments agree to further rescheduling of Senegal's debt. Some drought, but crops mainly deficient owing to locust and rodent damage.

1988   Elections in February give Diouf 73.5% of the vote, with opposition leader Abdoulaye Wade receiving 25.8% of the votes cast. PS wins 103 seats; the PDS takes 17 seats. Absentee rate over 40 percent. Charges of vote rigging and election fraud lead to riots in Dakar. Diouf declares a three-month state of emergency, closes university, imposes a curfew on Dakar and arrests all opposition leaders. Wade and others tried and convicted, but released when Diouf declares general amnesty for all political detainees.

1989   Far-reaching administrative reforms include firing Jean Colin (finance and interior minister since independence) and Dauda Sow, longtime president of the National Assembly. Prime Minister Habib Thiam dismissed from government, and the post of prime minister is abolished. In April, outbreak of ethnic violence between Mauritanians and Senegalese in both countries. Many dead and wounded, especially in capital cities and in Senegal River region. Mass exodus of Senegalese and Mauritanians to their home countries; property confiscated and destroyed. Relations between the two countries severed and all borders closed. The Senegambian Confederation finally dissolved in September.

Republic of Senegal

1990   In December, renewed separatist violence in the Casamance.
Several demonstrators killed; separatist leaders tried and imprisoned in Dakar.

1991   The post of prime minister is reinstated. Opposition leader Abdoulaye Wade enters government as minister of state, instituting period
of "cohabitation." In April, Senegalese troops, having fought in
the anti-Iraq coalition, killed in plane crash in Saudi Arabia.
Casamance separatists released and sent back to Casamance after
pledging support for Diouf and his government. A late and sparse
rainy season increases the threat of drought and food shortages.

TABLES

TABLE 1. GOVERNORS OF SENEGAL[1]

I. Under the first Compagnie du Sénégal, 1673–1694.

1677   Compte d'Estrées commanded fleet, which took Gorée from the Dutch.

1678–84   Sieur Ducasse commanded the company fleet in the area, unsuccessfully sought monopoly along the coast.

1685   Moreau de Chambonneau.

1685   Jajolet de la Courbe, Michel. Interim governor, the employees having arrested Chambonneau and sent him to Gorée.

1686–87   Chambonneau, reestablished at Saint-Louis.

1687   François, Director-General of the Company, on inspection visit.

1688–90   Jajolet de la Courbe, interim.

1690–93   Chambonneau. English occupied Senegal from January to July 1693.

1695   Jajolet de la Courbe named Governor of Senegal by the Minister of the Navy, but never takes his post.

1695–97   Bourguignon, Jean. Interim Governor of Gorée, 1693 on.

II. Following bankruptcy of first company, a second Compagnie du Sénégal is organized in 1696.

1697–1702   Brue, Andre. In 1702 called to France to become Administrative Director-General of the Company.

---

[1]Source: *Journal officiel.*

1702–06   Lemaítre.

1706–09   Jajolet de la Courbe.

III. Third Compagnie du Sénégal organized, 1709.

1710–11   Mustelier, d. 1711.

1712–13   Richebourge, de. Governor of Gorée, then of Senegal. Drowned 1713.

1714–20   Brue, Andre. Again named Director for Senegal.

III. The Compagnie du Sénégal sold its charter privilege to the Compagnie de l'Occident. Brue remained in charge.

1720–23   Desprée de Saint-Robert, Nicolas.

1723–25   Dubellay, Julien. Named Director and Commander-General. In 1725 Desprée de Saint-Robert returned to inquire into Dubellay's mismanagement. He arrested him and resumed direction himself until his death in 1725 or 1726.

1726   Plumet, Arnaud. Interim.

1726–33   Levens de la Rouquette, De.

1733   Lejuge, died at sea on the way.

1733   Devaulx. Interim.

1734–38   Judde. Named but did not assume the post.

1734   Devaulx. Interim until 1736, when officially named.

1738–46   David, Pierre Félix Barthélemy.

1746–1758   Estoupan de la Brue.

On April 29, 1758, Saint-Louis fell to the British. Gorée fell December 29, 1758. By the Treaty of Paris, 1763, Britain restored Gorée but kept Saint-Louis. France initiated direct royal administration under the Ministry of the Navy.

1763   Poncet de la Rivière. Recalled in November 1764.

1764   Esmenager, Chevalier. Infantry Brigadier. Recalled following complaints of embezzlement.

1767   La Gastière, de. Infantry Captain., d. 1768.

1768   Maizière. Interim.

1768   Rastel de Rocheblave, de. Infantry Captain.

1772   Des Maretz de Moncharton. Navy Captain. Did not assume the post.

1774   Le Brasseur, Commissioner in the Navy.

1777   Armèny de Paradis, Alexandre Davis. Military Engineer. d. 1778.

1778   Boucher. Captain in the African Volunteers. Interim.

In 1779 Saint-Louis is retaken from the British by Armand Louis de Gontaud-Biron, the Duke of Lauzun, who takes the title of Governor for two months from January to March 1779.

1779   Eyries, Jaques Joseph. Ship's Lieutenant. Departed 1781.

1781   Bertrand, J. B. Interim.

1781   Dumontet, Colonel Anne Gaston.

1783   The Treaty of Versailles confirms France's repossession of Senegal.

1783   Le Gardeur de Repentigny, Louis. Colonel.

1785   Boufflers, Chevalier Jean Stanislas de. Colonel. Arrived Feb., left June.

1786   Blanchot, François Emilie de Verly. Garrison Major. Interim until Boufflers's return in February 1787.

1787   Boufflers. February to November.

1787   Boucher. Interim, November–December, until Blanchot returned from France.

1787   Blanchot. Interim, 1787–89.

1789–1801   Blanchot officially named Governor.

1790–92   Boucher. Interim during Blanchot's absence.

1801   Charbonnie. Interim.

1801   Laserre, Louis Henri Pierre. Colonel.

1802   Blanchot returns, following turmoil in the colony.

1807   Levasseur, Captain. Interim following Blanchot's death.

1808   Pinoteau, Colonel. Did not assume the post.

On July 13, 1809, Senegal fell to the British. Gorée had fallen in 1803. Both were restored to France by the Treaty of Paris of 1814. In January 1815 Trigant de Beaumont was named governor, but Napoleon's return from the Isle of Elba prevented his departure. The Treaty of Vienna in 1815 reconfirmed Senegal's return to France, actually effected in January 1817.

1816   Schmaltz, Julien. Lieutenant Colonel in the Infantry.

Dec. 1817   Fleuriau, Frigate Captain. Interim during Schmaltz's stay in France, until March 1819.

1820   Lecoupé. Ships' Captain.

1821–27   Roger, Baron. Attorney, biologist and author.

1824   Hugon. Frigate Captain and Commandant for Gorée, assured the interim during Roger's stay in France until Nov. 1825.

1827   Gerbidon. Interim.

1827   Jubelin. Principal Commissioner, Navy.

1829   Brou, Ships' Captain.

1831   Renault de Saint Germain. Battalion Chief, Infantry and Navy. Died 1833.

1833   Cadest. Commissioner (Navy). Interim.

1833   Quernel, Germain. Frigate Captain.

1834   Pujol. Frigate Captain.

1836   Malavoie. Commandant of Gorée. Died end of 1836.

1836   Guillet. Interim.

1837   Soret. Retired Navy officer.

1838   Charmasson. Ships' Captain. Assumed office April 12, 1839.

1841   Montagnies de la Roque. Ships' Captain.

1842   Pageot-Desnoutieres. Commissioner (Navy), Chief of the Administrative Service. Interim.

1842   Bouet, *Capitaine de Corvette* (later Admiral Bouet-Willaumez). Provisional Governor.

1844   Laborel. Battalion Chief. Interim.

1844   Thomas. Interim.

1845   Ollivier, Ships' Captain. Committed suicide, March 1846.

1846   Hoube, Battalion Chief, Troop Commander. Interim.

1846   Bourdon-Gramont, *Capitaine de Corvette.*

1847   Caillé, Battalion Chief, Director of External Affairs of Senegal. Interim, from the death of Bourdon-Gramont August 24 until his own death two weeks later.

1847   Burtin-Duchateau, Battalion Chief, Troop Commander. Interim.

1847   Baudin, Ships' Captain.

1848   Burtin-Duchateau. Interim.

1848   Baudin, named a second time, assumed the post.

1850–54 Protet, Frigate Captain.

1850   Aumont, Frigate Captain, Commander of Gorée. Interim until Protet's arrival.

4/53–1/54 Verand, Chief of the Administrative Service. Interim during Protet's absence.

1854–61 Faidherbe, Louis Léon César. Battalion Chief, Construction Battalion.

6/56–11/56 Morel, Charles. Battalion Chief, Infantry and Navy. Interim during Faidherbe's absence.

9/58–2/59   Robin, A. Frigate Captain. Interim. During Faidherbe's absence.

6/1861   Stephan, Léopold François. Ordonnateur. Interim.

1861   Jauréguiberry, Jean Bernard. Ships' Captain. Assumed office in December.

1863   Pinet-Laprade, Jean. Lieutenant-Colonel in Construction. Interim, May 1863 awaiting Faidherbe's reinstatement.

1863   Faidherbe named again.

1865–69   Pinet-Laprade, Jean. Interim, then two months later named Governor.

1867   Trédos, Ferdinand Charles Alexandre. Commissioner (Navy), Interim during Pinet-Laprade's absence from May to October.

1869   Trédos, second interim, following Pinet-Laprade's death in yellow fever epidemic in August.

1869   Valière, François Xavier Michel. Colonel of Infantry and Navy.

1873   Gally-Passebosc, François Eugène Oscar. Lieutenant Colonel, Infantry and Navy. Interim during absence of Valière, 8–11, 1873.

1875   Bontemps, Albert Guillaume. Commissioner (Navy) Interim during Valière's absence, 7–10, 1875.

1876   Brière de l'Isle, Louis Alexandre Esprit Gaston. Colonel, Infantry and Navy.

1878   Le Guay, Léon. Commissioner (Navy) Interim during Brière de l'Isle's absence, 6–9, 1878.

1880   Lanneau, Louis Ferdinand de. Ships' Captain.

1881   Deville de Perière, Marie Auguste. Commissioner. Interim following Lanneau's death in August.

1881   Canard, Henri Philibert. Colonel de Spahis.

1882   Vallon, Aristide Louis Antoine. Ships' Captain.

1882   Servatius, René.

1883   Le Boucher, Adolphe Ernest Auguste. Director of the Interior. Interim.

1883   Seignac-Lessups, Alphonse. Assumed office in 1884.

1883   Bourdiaux, Henry. Artillery and Navy Colonel. Interim.

1884   Quintrie, Alexander. Director of the Interior. Interim, during Seignac-Lessups' absence.

1886   Genouille, Governor, third class.

1886   Ferrat, Henri Victor. Frigate Captain. Interim, during Genouille's absence 8/86–9/86.

1887   Quintrie, Alexander. Interim, during Genouille's absence, 6–9/87.

1888   Quintrie, Alexander. Interim.

1888   Clément-Thomas, Léon Emile. Governor, third class.

The decree of August 1, 1889, placed the southern rivers (Bissao and Casamance), the French establishments on the Gold Coast and the French establishments on the Gulf of Benin under the authority of the governor of Senegal.

1890   Lamothe, Henri Felix de. Governor, fourth class.

1890   Fawtier, Paul. Director of the Interior. Interim, two days.

The decree of December 17, 1891, placed French West African coastal possessions from Portuguese Guinea to the British colony at Lagos under a separate *Governor of French Guinea.*

1892   Roberdeau, Henri Victor Charles Amédée. Director of the Interior. Interim during Lamothe's absence, 6–11, 1892.

1893   Couzinet, Charles. Director of the Interior. Interim during Lamothe's absence, 9–12/1893.

1895   Moutiet, Louis. Director of the Interior. Interim.

The decree of June 16, 1895, created a Government-General of French West Africa. Senegal was placed under the direct authority of the Governor-General. (See list of names below.)

Decree of October 1, 1902, reestablished the post of Governor of Senegal, responsible to the Governor-General.

1902   Guy, Camille. Governor, third class, named Lieutenant-Governor of Senegal.

1903   Rognon, Charles. Secretary General. Interim, during Guy's absence, 5–11, 1903.

1905   Penel, Julien. Chief administrator, first class. Interim, Guy having been named interim Governor-General, 3–4/1905.

1905   Poulet, Georges. Secretary General, second class. Interim, 7/1905.

1905   Penel, resumes interim governorship until Guy's return, 8/05–1/06.

1907   Van Vollenhoven, Joost. Governor, second class. Interim.

1908   Gourbeil, Maurice. Governor, second class.

1908   Peuvergne, Jean Jules. Governor, third class. Interim awaiting Gourbeil's arrival.

1909   Peuvergne. Named Governor.

1909   Gaudart, Marie Antoine Edmond. Secretary General, first class. Interim, awaiting Peuvergne's arrival, 2–5, 1909.

1909   Gaudart, Interim during Peuvergne's absence, 7–11, 1909.

1911   Cor, Henri François Charles. Governor, third class.

1914   Antonetti, Raphael. Secretary General. Interim during Cor's absence 5/14–2/16 [sic].

1917   Levèque, Fernand Emile. Governor, first class.

1919   Didelot, Pierre Jean Henri. Secretary-General, first class. Interim during Levèque's absence, 3–9, 1919.

1920   Tellier, Théophile Antoine Pascal. Chief administrator, first class. Interim.

The decree of December 4, 1920, united the territories of Senegal under direct administration (the communes, q.v.) and the protectorate countries of Senegal into a single *Colony of Senegal.* A colonial council was created for it, and it was administered by a Lieutenant Governor responsible to the Governor-General.

1921 Didelot, Pierre Jean Henri. Governor, third class.

1923 Maillet, Camille. Chief administrator, first class. Interim during Didelot's absence, 10/23.

1925 Maillet, Camille. Interim.

1926 Cadier, Joseph Zebédée Olivier. Governor, third class. Detached, charged with administration of the Circumscription of Dakar.

1926 Jore, Léonce. Governor, third class.

1929 Beurnier, Maurice. Governor, third class. Interim.

1929 Beurnier. Named Lieutenant-Governor.

1930 Maillet, Camille. Interim during Beurnier's absence, 7–10/1930.

1931 Debonne, Benoît Louis. Chief Administrator. Interim during Beurnier's absence, 8–10/1931.

1933 Solomiac, Léon. Governor, third class. Interim during Beurnier's absence, 5–12, 1933.

1936 Martine, Félix Nicolas Constant. Chief Administrator. Interim.

1936 Lefebvre, Louis. Governor, third class.

1938 Parisot, Georges, Governor, second class.

1941 Rey, Georges Pierre. Governor, second class.

1942 Deschamps, Hubert. Governor, second class.

1943 Dagain, Charles. Governor, third class.

1945 Maestracci, Pierre Louis. Governor, third class.

1946 Durand, Oswald. Governor, second class.

1947 Wiltord, Laurent Marcel. Chief of Offices and of Secretaries General, Interim.

1947 Wiltord, promoted Governor, third class, named Lieutenant-Governor.

1950 Bailly, Camille. Administrator first class. Interim.

1951   Bailly, Camille. Promoted Governor third class, named Lt. Governor.

1952   Geay, Lucien Eugène. Governor, third class.

1954   Jourdain, Maxime Marie Antoine. Governor, third class.

1955   Colombani, Don Jean. Chief Administrator. Interim.

1957   Lami, Pierre Auguste Michel Marie. Governor, third class.

The decree of April 4, 1957, following the *loi cadre* (q.v.) of June 24, 1956, gave Senegal a Council of Government as its local executive authority.

On November 25, 1958, Senegal chose the status of Country belonging to the French Community and declared itself a Republic.

On January 17, 1959, Senegal and Sudan joined to form the Mali Federation.

On August 20, 1960, Senegal withdrew from the Mali Federation and proclaimed a separate independence. Independence Day is officially celebrated April 4, 1960, the day the grant of independence was signed.

GOVERNORS-GENERAL of FRENCH WEST AFRICA

The decree of June 16, 1895, created the Government General of French West Africa, comprising the territories of Senegal, French Sudan, French Guinea and Ivory Coast.

1895   Chaudie, Jean Baptiste Emile Louis Barthèlemy. Inspector-General of the Colonies.

1896   Ballay, Noël Victor. Governor of French Guinea, Interim during Chaudie's absence, 7–10, 1896.

1897   Ballay, Interim during Chaudie's absence, 7–10.

1898   Ballay, Interim during Chaudie's absence, 7–11.

1900   Ballay, Governor, first class. Named Governor-General.

1901   Lanrezac, Victor. Governor, third class. Interim during Ballay's absence, 4–10/01.

1902   Capest, Pierre Paul Marie. Governor, third class. Interim following Ballay's death, Jan. 26, 1902.

1902   Roume, Ernest. Councilor of State on Extraordinary Service, Director at the Ministry of Colonies, named Governor-General.

1902   Liotard, Victor Théophile. Governor first class. Interim during Roume's absence, 6–10/02.

The decree of October 1, 1902, detached Senegal from direct administration of the AOF, establishing a Governor of Senegal responsible to the Governor-General.

1903   Merlin, Martial Henri. Governor, third class. Interim during Roume's absence, 6–10/03.

1904   Merlin, Martial Henri. Governor, second class. Interim during Roume's absence, 7–11/04.

The decree of October 18, 1904, added Dahomey; the military territories of Upper Senegal-Niger, and Niger; and Mauritania to the AOF.

1905   Guy, Camille. Governor, third class. Lt. Gov. for Senegal. Interim Governor-General during Roume's absence, 3–4/05.

1905   Merlin, Martial Henri. Governor, second class, Interim during Roume's absence, 7–11/05.

1906   Merlin. Interim during Roume's absence, 8/06–2/07.

1907   Merleau-Ponty, Amédée William. Governor, third class. Lt. Gov. for Upper Senegal-Niger. Interim Gov.-Gen. during Roume's absence, 8–12/07.

1907   Merlin. Resumed the interim, 12/07–2/08.

1908   Merleau-Ponty. Governor, second class. Appointed Governor-General.

1909   Liotard. Governor, first class, Governor of French Guinea. Interim during Ponty's absence, 9/09–1/10.

1911   Clozel, Marie François Joseph. Governor, second class. Interim during Ponty's absence, 1–8/11.

The decree of September 7, 1911, put the Military Territory of Niger under the direct administration of the Government General.

1915   Clozel. Governor, first class. Interim following Ponty's death, June 13, 1915.

1915   Clozel. Delegated for the period of the hostilities the functions of Governor-General.

1916   Angoulvant, Gabriel. Governor, first class. Interim during Clozel's absence, 6–11/16.

1917   Van Vollenhoven, Joost. Governor, first class. Gov.-Gen., May to December.

1917   Carde, Jules Gaston Henri. Governor, third class. Interim following Van Vollenhoven's enlistment for active military duty.

1918   Merlin, Martial Henri. Governor-General of Madagascar. Appointed Governor-General of the AOF, assumed his post September 1919.

1918   Angoulvant. Governor-General of the AEF, responsible for both the AEF and the AOF until Merlin's arrival.

1919   Brunet, Charles Désiré Auguste. Governor, second class, took over the interim.

The decree of March 1, 1919, divided the colonies of Upper Senegal and Niger, and created the colony of Upper Volta.

1920   Brunet. Interim during Merlin's absence, 8–12/20.

The decree of September 4, 1920, reorganizes Mauritania, Niger and Senegal.

1922   Olivier, Marcel. Governor, second class. Lt.-Gov. of French Sudan. Interim during Merlin's absence, 5–12/22.

1923   Carde, Jules Gaston Henri. Governor, first class. Assumed his post as Governor-General March 18 and left the same day for France.

1923   Olivier. Interim until Carde's return, July 21.

1924   Dirat, Auguste Alphonse Henri. Governor, third class. Interim during Carde's absence, 5–10/23.

1926   Dirat. Interim during Carde's absence, 4–11/26.

1927   Dirat. Interim during Carde's absence, 6–10/27.

1929   Dirat. Interim during Carde's absence, 3–10/29.

1930   Brévié, Jules. Governor, first class.

1931   Dirat. Interim during Brévié's absence, 4–11/31.

By the decree of September 5, 1931, the colony of Upper Volta is suppressed.

1933   Fournier, Alberic Auguste. Governor, first class. Interim during Brévié's absence, 4–12/33.

1935   Boisson, Pierre François. Governor, second class. Interim during Brévié's absence, 5–12/35.

1936   Coppet, Jules Marcel de. Governor, second class.

1936   Vadier, Joseph. Governor of the colonies. Interim awaiting Coppet.

1938   Geismar, Léon. Governor of the colonies. Interim.

1938   Boisson. Governor, first class, Commissaire of the Republic for the Cameroons. Interim.

1939   Cayla, Léon Henri Charles. Governor-General of Madagascar, appointed Governor-General for the AOF.

The decree of June 25, 1940, created a High Commission of French Africa, having authority over the AOF, the AEF and the mandated territories of Cameroons and Togo.

1940   Boisson, Pierre François. Governor-General of the AEF, named High Commissioner of French Africa. When Admiral Erlan arrived to become High Commissioner, Boisson became Governor-General of the AOF.

1943   Cournarie, Pierre Charles. Governor-General of the colonies, named Governor-General of French West Africa.

1946   Barthes, Bené. Inspector-General of the colonies is designated High Commissioner of the Republic serving as Governor-General of the AOF.

The decree of September 4, 1947, creates the colony of Upper Volta.

1948   Bechard, Paul Leon Albin. Deputy. Temporarily appointed High Commissioner, Governor-General of the AOF.

1951   Chauvet, Paul Louis Gabriel. Governor-General of Overseas France. Interim.

1952   Cornut-Gentile, Bernard. Governor-General of Overseas France, High Commissioner of the Republic of AEF, named High Commissioner of the Republic of AOF.

1956   Cusin, Gaston. Inspector-General of the National Economy, appointed High Commissioner of the Republic in AOF.

The decrees of April 4, 1957, applying the *loi cadre* (q.v.) of June 23, 1956, modified the structures of the Government-General of the AOF, "with a view to transforming it into an institution for cooperation." They created a Council of Government as the local executive authority and extended the prerogatives of the territorial assemblies. The functions of the former Government-General were divided among the High Commissioner of the Republic and the Territorial Group (organization responsible for coordinating the territories' actions in economic and financial matters, and for managing their shared infrastructural equipment).

1958   Messmer, Pierre Auguste. Governor, second class. High Commissioner of the Republic for the Cameroons, named High Commissioner of the Republic for the AOF.

1960   Independence (q.v.).

TABLE 2. POPULATION OF SENEGAL (BY REGION), 1988

Resident Population by Region

Dakar	1,500,459
Diourbel	616,184
Fatick	506,844
Kaolack	805,447
Kolda	593,191
Louga	489,529
Saint-Louis	651,206
Tambacounda	383,572
Thies	937,412
Ziguinchor	398,067
Total Population of Senegal	6,881,911

Source: Senegal 1988 Population Census; USAID/Senegal/ADO, *Senegal Agricultural Sector Analysis* (1991).

TABLE 3. KEY ECONOMIC INDICATORS, 1987–1990

($US millions on fiscal year basis unless otherwise indicated)

	1987	1988	1989 (e)	1990 (e)
Population (millions)	6.7	6.9	7.1	7.3
Population Growth (%)	2.7	2.7	2.7	2.7
Per Capita GNP ($U.S.)	520	650	648	663
DOMESTIC ECONOMY				
GDP (billions of CFA)	1,338	1,433	1,470	1,565
Nominal GDP (% change)	9.4	7.1	2.6	6.5
Real GDP (% change)	4.2	4.4	0.6	4.5
GDP Deflator (% change)	5.0	2.5	1.9	2.0
Consumer Price Index (% change)	0.4	−2.6	−1.9	2.0
PRODUCTION AND EMPLOYMENT				
Labor Force (millions)	3.4	3.5	3.6	3.7
Industrial Production Index (1976 = 100)	109.1	113.7	119.0	NA
Government Operations Surplus/ Deficit as % of nominal GDP (cash basis)	−4.6	−5.2	−4.3	−4.3
BALANCE OF PAYMENTS				
Exports (fob)	631	749	778	862
Imports (fob)	902	1004	987	1057
Merchandise Trade Balance	−271	−255	−209	−195
Current Account Balance	−254	−258	−211	−158
Foreign Debt	3,106	3,768	3,723	4,079
Debt Service Paid (after rescheduling)	267	336	277	249
Debt Service Owed (before rescheduling)	350	425	446	431
Debt Service Ratio (after resched, pct)	23	25	19	18
Average Exchange Rate (CFA/ $US) (FY)	319	292	315	300
FOREIGN INVESTMENT				
U.S. Direct Investment (stock)	27	29	29	29

TABLE 3. KEY ECONOMIC INDICATORS, 1987–1990 *(cont.)*

($US millions on fiscal year basis unless otherwise indicated)

	1987	1988	1989 (e)	1990 (e)
U.S. MERCHANDISE TRADE				
U.S. Exports to Senegal (fas) (CY)	49.0	69.1	68.7	NA
U.S. Imports from Senegal (cif) (CY)	7.4	8.2	5.5	NA
U.S. Share of Senegal's Exports (%) (CY)	1.2	1.1	0.7	NA
U.S. Share of Senegal's Imports (%) (CY)	5.4	6.9	7.0	NA
U.S. Bilateral Aid	45.1	31.9	52.5	44.3
Economic Assistance	42.5	30.8	52.0	42.0
Military Assistance	2.6	1.1	0.5	2.3

Sources: Government of Senegal Ministry of Finance, IMF, World Bank, USAID/Senegal, U.S. Department of Commerce.

TABLE 4. AGRICULTURAL OUTPUT OF MAJOR CROPS,
1960/61-1988/89
(in tons)
(yearly average for subperiods)

Yearly Averages	Groundnuts	Millet/ Sorghum	Rice	Maize
1960/61–1964/65	942,180	442,960	91,620	29,280
1965/66–1969/70	918,450	544,520	116,340	42,720
1970/71–1974/75	761,237	474,401	83,304	33,066
1975/76–1979/80	962,187	569,147	100,321	46,501
1980/81–1984/85	746,820	537,980	106,840	73,260
1985/86–1988/89	778,425	744,675	144,150	122,825

Sources: World Bank, Operations Evaluation Department, *The World Bank and Senegal, 1960–1987* (Washington, DC: 1989); and Elliot Berg Associates, *Adjustment Postponed: Economic Policy Reform in Senegal in the 1980s* (Alexandria, VA: 1990).

TABLE 5. MAJOR EXPORTS BY VALUE, 1982–1987

(in millions of CFA)

Products	1982	1983	1984	1985	1986	1987
Peanut Products	51,474	66,817	61,349	28,508	23,499	24,082
Petroleum Products	53,812	55,558	69,760	64,496	40,415	34,298
Phosphates	18,348	18,741	25,815	22,687	18,132	10,187
Canned Fish	11,695	11,698	21,215	19,674	14,958	14,998
Unrefined Salt	5,146	5,126	6,017	5,946	4,716	2,892
Phosphate Fertilizer	1,198	3,872	2,788	3,561	1,373	1,311
Shoes	1,365	1,127	1,475	1,516	1,265	1,021
TOTALS						
NON-PEANUT PRODUCTS	93,250	96,747	128,650	119,142	80,859	64,707
OTHER PRODUCTS	55,081	71,912	87,022	104,842	110,435	93,457
TOTAL	199,805	235,476	277,021	252,492	214,793	182,246

Source: USAID/Senegal, *Statistical Bulletin*, June 1990.

TABLE 6. MAJOR IMPORTS BY VALUE, 1982–1987
(in millions of CFA)

Products	1982	1983	1984	1985	1986	1987
Food Products	47,929	52,065	62,306	53,032	40,547	33,718
Chemical Products	86,178	94,258	128,075	113,586	94,865	71,088
Wood and Textiles	23,807	23,625	22,619	21,842	22,779	21,987
Machinery and Equipment	71,138	96,901	84,298	72,267	72,808	89,284
Other Products	108,013	123,874	131,304	110,244	101,930	91,521
TOTAL	337,065	390,723	428,602	370,971	332,929	307,598

Source: USAID/Senegal, *Statistical Bulletin*, June 1990.

THE DICTIONARY

- A -

ADMINISTRATION. Senegal has a highly centralized and bureaucratized form of governmental administration largely inherited from France. The President of the Republic appoints ministers. Currently there is a presidentially appointed prime minister, although the post has frequently been abolished. The minister of the interior, with the president's approval, generally appoints officials of the territorial administration. There are currently four ministers of state, 14 other ministers, and eight secretaries of state.

The country is currently divided into 10 regions: Dakar, Diourbel, Fatick, Kaolack, Kolda, Louga, Saint-Louis, Tambacounda, Thiès and Ziguinchor. Regions are named after their administrative capital. Before 1985, the regions were: Cap Vert (Dakar); Casamance (Ziguinchor and Kolda); Diourbel; Fleuve (Saint-Louis); Louga; Senegal Oriental (Tambacounda); Sine-Saloum (Fatick and Kaolock); and Thies. Each region consists of three *departements,* which are divided into *arrondissements.* The population is further organized into *circonscriptions urbaines* (urban communes) and *communautés rurales* (rural communities), initiated after the administrative reform of 1972, and now operative throughout the country. There are 314 rural communities and 33 urban communes. Some rural communities include groups of villages, others a single large village. The limits and names of all units are fixed by decree. Regions are headed by appointed governors and an elected assembly; departments are headed by *prefets,* and *arrondissements* by *sous-prefets,* both advised by elected councils. *Communautés rurales* are usually headed by a village chief with an autonomous budget, but actual administration remains in the hands of the *sous-prefets.*

During the colonial period, the four *communes* (q.v.) of Saint-Louis, Gorée, Rufisque and Dakar were administered directly by the French, while the rural areas formed the protectorate under less direct control of the colonial bureaucracy. The protectorate and communes together constituted the Colony of Senegal, with its capital at Saint-Louis. The colony belonged to the Federation of French West Africa (q.v.), with its government-general headquartered at Dakar. After independence in 1960, Dakar was named capital of the Republic of Senegal.

AFRICAN SOCIALISM. The official economic and political doctrine of Senegal since independence in 1960, instituted by Léopold Sédar Senghor (q.v.) and continued by Abdou Diouf (q.v.). African socialism has been more of an ideology than a practical policy, however. Many theories of African socialism were advanced in the 1950s and 1960s, most notably by Kwame Nkrumah (Ghana), Julius Nyerere (Tanzania) and Gamal Abdel Nasser (Egypt). Most African leaders espoused some form of socialism, eschewing capitalism because of its colonial and imperialistic connotations and distrusting the totalitarianism and interventionism of Communism. The appelation ''African'' socialism distinguished the doctrine from ''European,'' or Western, socialism, which was supposedly based on a different sociological heritage. African leaders also insisted that they did not want to be dominated by socialist countries in Europe.

Senghor's theory of African socialism was first articulated in the late Forties while he was a deputy in Paris, and was closely associated with his concept of *négritude* (q.v.). His version was published shortly after independence as *Nation et voie africaine du socialisme* (see Bibliography). Senghor rejected Western concepts of capitalism, materialism, bourgeois values, individualism and competition. Instead, he favored cooperative work based on traditional African values of kinship, community and cooperation. Nationalism and religion, whether traditional, Muslim or Christian, also played important roles. Senghor envisioned peasants as dynamic agents of development. Compared to Nkrumah and Nyerere, Senghor's version of African socialism was considerably more idealistic, less pragmatic and, ultimately, less dogmatic and less rigorously enforced. Senghor and Diouf have both used the ideology of African socialism as window dressing rather than as a basis for their rules. President Diouf has generally embraced Senghor's concepts but has sought closer ties with European socialist governments, most notably the Mitterand administration in France.

In practice, Senegal's economic policies have combined nationalization and the continuance of capitalist and private institutions. In the early 1960s, groundnut marketing was nationalized, rural cooperatives initiated and a national system of agricultural credit, extension services and cooperative administration started. Since the mid Sixties, several semi-governmental, semi-private cooperations have also been formed in the areas of rural development, housing, manufacturing, commerce, banking and the national daily newspaper. In the 1980s, in response to the deteriorating economic situation in the country, there was considerable restructuring of nationalized agencies. (See, e.g., OCA, ONCAD, LE SOLEIL.)

AGRICULTURE. Farming has always been the dominant economic activity of most ethnic groups in the Senegambian region. In 1990, approximately 66 percent of the population were dependent exclusively on cultivation, with another 8 percent dependent upon some combination of agriculture and stockraising. The agricultural sector accounted for 21 percent of real GDP, with overall economic output closely linked to the amount of rainfall received during any given year. The total food crop production for the 1989–1990 crop year was 1.1 million metric tons.

The chief staple food crops are millet (q.v.) and sorghum, grown chiefly in association or in competition with groundnuts (q.v.), since all three crops require similar soils and climate. More than 90 percent of land under cultivation in the late 1980s was devoted to these three crops. Official estimates include approximately 2.5 million acres under groundnuts and 2.5 million acres under sorghum and millet. Other crops include cassava, rice, maize and cotton. These field crops are supplemented by kitchen garden crops of niebe beans, yams, sweet potatoes and assorted vegetables and condiments, especially along rivers and streams. Truck gardening of vegetables has developed around the main towns, notably Dakar, and sugar cultivation is being actively promoted by the government.

Since independence, the government has continued, on a revised and accelerated basis, the efforts initiated by French authorities to achieve increased agricultural productivity by more widespread dissemination and higher average input of such improvements as better seed, fungicides, fertilizer and animal traction. The Senegalese government actively promotes agricultural production and research, especially of rice and other food crops. In some areas, the effects of permanent cultivation and overcrowding have prevented increased yields. The severe drought of the late 1960s and early 1970s dramatically curtailed agricultural production, but a series of good rainfall years in the early 1980s permitted increased production. The mid-1980s and then 1990–91 have witnessed a period of reduced and erratic rainfall, however, causing a decline in overall agricultural production per capita. (See also WALO.)

AIR TRANSPORT. The national parastatal airline, Air Senegal, is based in Dakar and provides scheduled service to Bakel,

Banjul (the Gambia), Kaedi (Mauritania), Kedougou, Kolda, Linguiere, Matam, Podor, Richard-Toll, Saint-Louis, Simenti (in Niokolo-Koba National Park), Tambacounda and Ziguinchor. Senegal belongs to the Air Afrique consortium. The international airport at Yoff in Dakar is serviced by Air Afrique and various airlines based in Europe, the Middle East and Africa.

ALFA MOLO, ALFA MOLO EGUE. See BALDE, ALFA MOLO EGUE.

ALMAMY. Sometimes transcribed as *al-maami*. Pulaar (Fulfulde) term for the head of state in Futa Toro (q.v.) and Bundu (q.v.). It was also used by the rulers of Futa Jalon (Guinea) after 1725. The title is derived from the Arabic *al-Imam*, the leader in prayer, and hence the leader of the religious community. The area ruled by an *almamy* was usually called an *almamate*.

ALMORAVID. (from Arabic, *al-Murabitun*). Eleventh-century Islamic movement of reform, proselytization and conquest in the western Sahel and Sahara, and the Iberian peninsula. The movement began with a Sanhaja Berber cleric, Abdullah ibn Yasin, who founded a religious retreat, or *ribat,* on the Senegal River near Podor about A.D. 1040, under the protection of the Tekrur (q.v.) king War Jabi. By proselytization and jihad (q.v), they introduced Islam to the peoples along the Senegal River.

   In 1042–43, the focus of the movement shifted north into the Sahara Desert, and military leadership devolved on two Lamtuna Berber chiefs, Yahya and Abu-Bakr ibn Umar. They conquered the Saharan peoples living along the major trade route linking Sijilmasa and Awdaghost. Next came Morocco and eventually Spain. Shortly after the death of Yahya the empire split, with Abu-Bakr dominating the southern (Saharan and Sahelian) half, and a cousin, Yusuf ibn Tashfin, controlling Morocco and Spain. Abu-Bakr apparently invaded the Ghana Empire in 1076–77, razed the capital and installed a converted king. When Abu-Bakr died in 1087, the Saharan-Sahelian empire of Ghana gradually disintegrated. The lasting effects of the Almoravid movement included the conversion of the courts of ancient Tekrur and Ghana to Islam, and a wider, if superficial, extension among the kingdoms' people. It also became a historic model and source of theological justification for later jihads.

AMIR. Sometimes transcribed as *emir*. Arabic title, equivalent to Commander, frequently used by the Muslim communities of precolonial Senegambia for military leaders. The rarer title, *Amir al-mu^{c}inin,* or Commander of the Faithful, was taken by a few leaders of holy wars, or jihads (q.v.), who modeled their careers on the militant asceticism of the seventh-century Arab Caliphs. The most notable military leader who took the title Commander of the Faithful was al-Hajj Umar Tal (q.v.) in the mid-nineteenth century.

ARCHIVES. The National Archives of Senegal (*Archives Nationales du Sénégal*), located in the Administration Building in Dakar (q.v.), are the main national repository of records. It is one of the most important repositories for original French colonial documents in Africa. Copies of many of the colonial documents can also be found in the *Archives Nationales de la France, Section Outre-Mer,* formerly in Paris and now located in Aix-en-Provence in southern France. Because parts of eastern Senegal were attached to the colony of *Soudan français*, many colonial documents on eastern Senegal can also be found in the *Archives Nationales du Mali,* located in Koulouba near Bamako, Mali.

The archives in Dakar contain extensive written documents in European languages, primarily French, from the earliest period of European contact with the region up to the present. In addition, there are some Arabic materials. The archives seek to collate all works published on Senegal, as well as recorded oral materials on Senegalese history. Other archives are located in the old capital of Saint-Louis (q.v.). Touba, the site of the main Murid mosque, has an archive of documents pertaining to the Islamic Murid brotherhood (q.v.). A few historic documents can occasionally be found in towns that served as administrative posts during the colonial era.

ARDO. Pulaar term for the leader of a pastoral, or transhumant (q.v.), community. In the Wolof, Serer and Futanke (each q.v.) states with sizable pastoral Fulbe populations, an *ardo wodaabe* (q.v.) was appointed to be head of the pastoral Fulbe community and a liaison with the ruler.

ARMED FORCES. Senegal currently has armed forces numbering about 9,400 (exact figures are difficult to determine), up from 2,700 at independence in 1960. This comprises an army of 8,500, a navy of 700 and an air force of 200. There are also a 1,600-member Gendarmerie Nationale and 3,600-member National Police (Sûreté Nationale). It is estimated that about $60 million is spent annually on defense. The military absorbs approximately 10 percent of the national budget, plus an unpublished French subsidy. In the late 1970s, the United States began to contribute small-scale military aid, in response to appeals by President Senghor (q.v.) to counter Soviet assistance to neighboring Guinea, Mali and Guinea-Bissau. By 1990, however, Soviet military aid to Senegal's neighbors virtually ceased, and the United States curtailed military assistance to Senegal.

The armed forces are organized on the French model, trained and advised by French officers, but now mostly officered by Senegalese. Yet, France still stations more than 1,000 troops in the country and provides weaponry and much technical assistance. In 1974, France transferred one of its major Dakar bases to the Senegalese government, and in that same year, Senegal's armed forces were reorganized and a Ministry of Armed Forces was created. About 1,500 volunteers are accepted annually for a five-year stint. They are mostly eighteen to twenty-two years old, literate (85 percent), and over half are Wolof.

Senegal, which faces no genuine external military threat, is primarily concerned with preventing any internal unrest or a coup d'état. Unlike other West African nations except the Ivory Coast, Senegal has maintained a civilian government since independence. Both Senghor and his successor, Abdou Diouf (q.v.), have kept the armed forces from becoming powerful influences in domestic policies. Both presidents have continued extremely close ties with the French military, which would undoubtedly be summoned in the event of an internal uprising.

American transports, in cooperation with France, airlifted Senegalese troops to Zaire during the Shaba invasion of 1978. Senegalese troops entered the Gambia (q.v.) to suppress an attempted coup d'état in August 1980, against President Dauda Jawara. This intervention led to the formation of the Senegambia Confederation (q.v.), which ultimately failed. France used its Dakar bases to support the Chad government in its war with Libya in the late 1980s. In the 1990 civil war in Liberia, Senegal refused to join the West African peacekeeping force sent to mediate the conflict. Senegalese troops are serving in Lebanon as United Nations peacekeeping forces, and 500 Senegalese soldiers were sent as part of the anti-Iraq alliance in the Persian Gulf in late 1990. In early 1991, shortly after the Persian Gulf war, 90 Senegalese soldiers, serving in the anti-Iraq alliance, were killed in a plane crash in Saudi Arabia.

ASSASSINATION. A rare crime in Senegalese history, it did claim the life of the prominent Union Progressiste Senegalaise (q.v.) deputy, Demba Diop, in 1967. Apparently a result of intra-party rivalry, two UPS deputies were imprisoned. In

March 1967, there was an assassination attempt on President Senghor (q.v.) while he was attending Friday prayers at the Grand Mosquée in Dakar. The perpetrator was rumored to have been a partisan of the then-imprisoned former Prime Minister Mamadou Dia (q.v.), but no link was established in court, and the lone convict was executed.

ASSIMILATION. The cultural goal, and occasionally explicit policy, characterizing most French-African relations during much of the colonial period. Assimilation remained a colonial ideology, however, never becoming a widespread practice or having much impact in French territories. The only area of Senegal where assimilation was practiced was in the Four Communes (q.v.), and even there its impact was minimal.

Beginning with the rationalist, individualist themes in eighteenth-century French Enlightenment thought, French colonialists assumed Africans could and should be educated to assimilate French culture and become "black Frenchmen." The implicit assumption was that French culture was the highest ideal for everyone. Many Western-educated Africans, used to explicit racial contempt from Europeans, embraced the more subtly racist doctrine of assimilation.

During the French Revolution, the revolutions of 1848 and throughout the late nineteenth century, assimilation permeated French colonial thought. At the turn of the century, however, when France conquered large parts of West and Central Africa and Southeast Asia, the prospect of France trying to assimilate considerable numbers of African and Asian peoples vastly outnumbering its own population caused a radical swing in official policy. In the period immediately preceding World War I, association (q.v.) replaced assimilation as the cultural goal of French imperialism.

The first systematic African philosophical rejection of the implied cultural superiority in assimilation was the doctrine of *négritude* (q.v.), espoused in the 1930s in Paris by Senghor (q.v.), Aimé Césaire and Léon Damas.

ASSIMILE. During the colonial period, someone who had assimilated to French culture sufficiently to qualify for citizenship. The actual number of *assimilés* remained exceedingly small. Anachronistic. (See also EVOLUE; SUJET.)

ASSOCIATION. The French colonial policy that replaced assimilation (q.v.). The basic tenet was that African peoples and cultures would, through the colonial relationship with France, gradually evolve from their backward state toward the highly civilized French ideal. Islamic civilization was seen as an intermediate status, which might assist Africans in their "progress" toward the French ideal. Eventually, traditional African and Islamic cultures would be supplanted by superior European values, life-styles and technology. Association can be compared to the British policy of indirect rule. The French used association with either direct or indirect administration, depending on local circumstances.

The assumptions underlying association theory can be traced to European slave traders' and trading-post administrators' writings throughout the precolonial period, side by side with assimilation theory. It became official doctrine only in the twentieth century, after France had conquered more African and Asian people than its leaders could ever imagine assimilating. It became a rationale for having conquered Africans in the first place, and for methods of rule that would have been unacceptable in France, including forced labor, legislation by administrative decree, lack of electoral politics and wholesale military conscription.

Association policy and, more particularly, the *indigénat* (q.v.) system for which it provided the rationale were bitterly resented in French West Africa. Many French-educated Africans preferred assimilation, until Léopold Senghor (q.v.) and others in the 1930s pointed out that racism was implicit in both and offered instead *négritude* (q.v.) as a celebration of African culture in and for itself.

- B -

BA, *AL-HAJJ* MAMADU SAIDU. (c.1900–1981) An important Fulbe cleric who was born in Futa Toro (q.v.) and settled in the Upper Casamance (q.v.) at Medina-Gonasse in 1936. Ba belonged to the Tijaniyya (q.v.) brotherhood and became its most important representative in eastern Senegal. Surrounded by several thousand *talibe*-farmers reminiscent of the Murid (q.v.) pioneer communities, Ba created a Tijani "holy city" with considerable autonomy from secular authorities. Medina-Gonasse had its own laws, reportedly based on Islamic traditions, and residents paid taxes directly to the marabout. Every year an annual gathering outside Medina-Gonasse attracted several thousand men, mostly of Fulbe descent and from Senegal, the Gambia, Guinea-Conakry and Guinea-Bissau. Ba was succeeded by his son, *al-Hajj* Abubakar Mamadau Saydu in 1981, who does not exert the influence of his father. The town ultimately lost its political autonomy, but has retained its religious significance. The annual pilgrimage continues to attract large crowds and to be an important event in the region.

BA, BABACAR. (1930–) First Senegalese to be named minister for finance and economic affairs, he replaced the Frenchman Jean Colin (q.v.) in 1971. During his seven years in that capacity, he became the senior minister in the cabinet and a close collaborator of then Prime Minister Abdou Diouf (q.v.). In March 1978, amid press speculation of a rift with Diouf, he was transferred to the Ministry of Foreign Affairs. In September, amid reports in the official newspaper that his poor financial management had nearly bankrupted the government, Ba was removed from the administration.

Ba began his administrative career in the Ministry of the Interior in 1959. After brief tours in the territorial administration, he served as director of the cabinet under former Prime Minister Mamadou Dia (q.v.) until the latter was arrested in 1962. From 1962 to 1966, Ba was director for economic and technical cooperation in the Ministry of Foreign Affairs; from 1966 to 1968, first consul in charge of relations with the European Economic Community at Senegal's Embassy in Brussels; from 1968 to 1969, director of foreign affairs; and from 1970 to 1971, director of the cabinet for President Senghor. He has been a member of the ruling party throughout his career, and since 1973 an elected deputy to the National Assembly.

BA, HAME. (also called Amadu Shaixu Madiyu; Hamet; Muhammad Amar). (late eighteenth century–1862) Futanke (q.v.) cleric who led an abortive religious movement in Futa Toro in 1828–1829. Inspired by the teachings of *Serin Koki* Njaga Isa Jop (q.v.), Hame gathered his followers to prepare for the end of the world and declared himself the *Mahdi* (q.v.) in 1828. When he prepared to sacrifice his eldest son, claiming God told him to imitate Abraham, people turned against him and forced him to leave Futa Toro. He joined Njaga Isa in the conquest of Walo, but when that movement was defeated, he returned to Futa where he founded a new village, Wuro Madiyu, near Podor, where he lived until his death in 1862. (See also his son, BA, SHAIXU AMADU.)

BA, KOLY TENGELA (late fourteenth–early fifteenth centuries) Legendary founder of the Denanke (q.v.) dynasty of Futa Toro (q.v.). Pulaar oral traditions identify him variously as a pagan who led a massive migration of Fulbe from Futa Jalon (Guinea), or as the son of a Muslim prophet from Masina in the middle Niger delta (Mali). The traditions agree that he and his followers arrived in the middle Senegal River valley in the early 1490s and carved out an independent state, including much territory formerly subject to Jolof (q.v.). This conquest became the first step in the dissolution of the Jolof Empire.

BA, MA. (baptized Amath; also called Ma Ba Jaxu or Maba Diakhou Ba). (1809–67) Futanke (q.v.) cleric who led a brief but important holy war in the 1860s, overthrowing the traditional dynasty of Salum (q.v.) and mobilizing the neighboring Wolof and Serer kingdoms against French attempts at hegemony.

Ma Ba was born in Rip on the northern shore of the Gambia River in 1809, the grandson of a Denanke (q.v.) leader who had fought at the side of *Almamy* Abdul Qadir Kan (q.v.) in the 1770s. Ma Ba joined the Tijani brotherhood (q.v.) and, according to traditions, met *al-Hajj* Umar Tal (q.v.). Both Ma Ba and Umar Tal shared a similar worldview, requiring the overthrow of traditional rulers who were ineffective against the Christian invaders and corrupt, drunken and licentious in their personal lives. At this time, the people of the Gambian states were divided into two factions—Soninke (q.v., generally non-Muslims and indifferent Muslims), and marabout Muslims (strict Muslims). Ma Ba, a member of the marabout faction, founded his own town, Kiramba, and gathered followers.

In 1861 he was attacked by a Soninke group. When he defeated them, other Muslim religious figures and their followers joined him, and the minor victory grew into a revolution. His charisma and belief in his divine mission appealed to Muslims in persecuted communities, whether Mandinka, Fulbe or Wolof. He was joined by ousted *Damel Kajor* (q.v.) Makodu Kodu Diouf and in 1864 by a more recent claimant to the Kajor throne, Lat Dior Diop (q.v.). Together they attacked Bawol (q.v.), and in 1865 invaded Jolof (q.v.). After conquering the Wolof states, he turned on the larger Serer states, which had no sizable Muslim minorities. By 1865, he had extended his control to the important state of Salum. Ma Ba was killed in 1867 in a battle with the *Bur* Siin. His empire disintegrated over a 20-year period, rent by a four-sided struggle for control. The French, British, traditional rulers and the clerical heirs of Ma Ba competed for land and followers until the British–French border treaty of 1889.

Even though Ma Ba failed to maintain his empire, his influence was lasting. His campaigns permitted a new Muslim elite to seize power in their societies. This elite was largely responsible for the Islamization of a large part of the Senegambia.

BA, SHAIXU AMADU MAHDIYU. (d. 1875) Better known as Shaxu Amadu or Amadu Madiyu. Leader of a religious movement in Jolof (q.v.), 1868–1875. The son of Hame Ba (q.v.), Shaixu Amadu derived his prophetic vocation from family tradition and *al-Hajj* Umar Tal's (q.v.) call to action. Inspired by a cholera epidemic in 1868 that decimated the population of Senegambia, he saw the apocalypse coming, with himself in the role of *Mahdi* (q.v.) and the Tijaniyya (q.v.) as the only community of true believers. Forced into exile from his native Futa Toro, he obliged the *Bur-ba* Jolof and his court to make public submission. He and his brother Ibra Mahdiyu dominated Jolof and the Njambur province of northwestern Kajor from 1871 to 1875. Allied to Abdul Bokar Kan (q.v.) of Futa Toro, he invaded Kajor in 1874 and defeated the combined forces of *Damel* Lat Dior (q.v.) and Albury Njay (q.v.). In 1875, the two defeated rulers called upon the French for assistance and defeated and killed Shaixu Amadu at the Battle of Samba Sajo near Koki (q.v.).

BADOLO. Wolof term for a poor but freeborn peasant. Historically, it meant a Wolof who was neither casted (q.v.) nor slave (q.v.), but without wealth or a claim to any political title. He held the right to farm his land and to pass it on to his sons, but he also owed a small share of the crop to the local

Laman (q.v.), and military service and other small duties to his patron. An equivalent status generally existed in other stratified Senegambian ethnic groups.

BAKEL. Situated in the Goy (q.v.) province of Gajaaga (q.v.) on the upper Senegal River, Bakel was initially founded by refugees from Jolof (q.v.) in the eighteenth century. According to oral traditions, the refugees, belonging to the Njay (Ndiaye) lineage, received a concession of land from the *tunka,* or king, of Gajaaga. In 1820, the French negotiated a treaty with the Njay ruling lineage and built a fort and trading post on a high point overlooking the river. Numerous overland and river exchange routes passed through Bakel, and the French hoped to divert trade from the British posts on the Gambia River. By 1850, Bakel, an important gum arabic entrepôt, had become the region's major trading center. The fort was isolated during the six-month dry season, and the commander had considerable autonomy from the governor at Saint-Louis (q.v.). The post suffered from boycotts and embargos during the Umarian jihad (q.v.), but regained its military and economic prominence after 1860. The creation of the office of the *commandant-supérieur dans le Haut-Fleuve* with headquarters at Medine in Khasso (Mali) in 1880, the decline in the gum trade after 1894 and the growth of Kayes (Mali) all contributed to Bakel's demise. When the borders between Senegal, Mali and Mauritania were drawn, Bakel was more isolated than ever. Today Bakel is one of the most remote towns in Senegal.

BAL, SULEIMAN. (Eighteenth century). Futanke (q.v.) cleric who led the early phases of a movement that ended the Denkanke (q.v.) dynasty in Futa Toro (q.v.) in the 1770s and installed a Torodbe (q.v.) clerical oligarchy. About 1769 he began rallying fellow clerics in central Futa, calling for religious, political and social reform. He promised to protect followers from enslavement, destroy the decadent and ineffectual Denanke dynasty and drive out the despised Moorish and Moroccan overlords. Bal was killed in battle against the Moors (q.v.) before his movement had accomplished much. Yet, under his successor, Abdul Qadir Kan (q.v.), the Denanke were overthrown and clerical rule was established in Futa. This revolution and its ideology affected the entire Senegambia, from Futa Jalon through Kajor, north among the Moors, and east to Masina and beyond.

BALDE, ALFA MOLO EGUE. (Nineteenth century). Alfa Molo was the founder and ruler of Fuladu (q.v.) in the upper Casamance (q.v.). Allegedly of slave origin, he led the Fulbe of the upper Casamance in a revolt against their Mandinka overlords who ruled Jimara, Tomani and Kantora. He received aid from the Fulbe *Alfa* (q.v.) of Labe (Futa Jalon), and once established, Alfa Molo continued to send him an annual tribute. At his death in 1881, he was succeeded by his brother Bakary, but within two years his son and most dynamic general, Musa Molo, had conquered most of the kingdom. From his base at Hamdallahi, Musa Molo ruled with an iron hand and kept his army active, under very loose French supervision until 1903. When the French set up a military post in his capital, he moved to the Gambian half of his territory, where he retained considerable autonomy from the British until his exile in 1919.

BAMBUK. Located between the Bafing and Faleme affluents of the upper Senegal River, Bambuk consisted of numerous dispersed settlements, primarily Mandinka (q.v.), with no central political authority. Local traditions claim that the Cissoko lineage, originally from the Mande heartland near Kita (western Mali), were the first Mandinka rulers of Bambuk. Other lineages sought the Cissoko's permission to establish villages. Each settlement had its own hereditary chief and complete autonomy, although a loose "confederation" developed, mainly to insure cooperation against raids from centralized adjacent states like Bundu (q.v.) and Khasso (Mali). Mountainous terrain isolated and further protected the uniformly small villages, predominantly Mandinka and often including refugee slaves. Farabanna (q.v.) was the largest slave haven in the area.

Bambuk was situated at an important crossroads of trade routes linking Futa Toro (q.v.), the Gambia River system and the Senegal River (q.v.) network. In addition, surface gold mining compensated for Bambuk's limited agricultural and pastoral potential. The principal alluvial gold deposits were located along the Faleme River and the Tambura escarpment, which rose 150 meters above the savanna and ran the length of Bambuk in a north–south direction. Though their output was limited, the gold deposits of Bambuk generated intense interest among Europeans as early as the sixteenth century. Relying more on fantasy than fact, foreigners envisioned a new El Dorado on the shores of the Faleme River with one eighteenth-century traveller christening the area "the Peru of Africa." The most concerted gold-mining scheme, devised by Governor Louis Faidherbe (q.v.) and undertaken at Kenieba between 1858 and 1860, failed owing to inappropriate technology and the harsh disease environment. A new effort in the 1890s suffered from similar problems. After French occupation, Bambuk was parceled into several administrative districts in the colonies of Senegal and *Soudan français*. As a result, the area of Bambuk is now divided between eastern Senegal and western Mali.

BANUN/BAINUK. Ethnic group believed to be the original inhabitants of the lower Casamance (q.v.), who formed the basic population of the extensive kingdom of Kasa (q.v.) in the fifteenth through eighteenth centuries. After the seventeenth century, they were increasingly subjected to their more powerful and populous Mandinka and Jola (both q.v.) neighbors. Today there is a tendency for Banun to adopt Mande or Jola culture and identity.

BASSARI. A small ethnic group of approximately 12,000 people in southeastern Senegal and northeastern Guinea-Conakry. They belong to the Tanda (q.v.) peoples and are more closely linked to groups in the Guinea rainforest than with the Muslims of the savanna. The Bassari were primarily hunters and gatherers, with only limited cultivation and no pastoralism. Their isolated villages generally afforded protection from slave raiders, mainly from the Fulbe states of Bundu (q.v.) to the north and Futa Jalon (q.v.) in Guinea to the south.

Until recently the Bassari maintained their traditional religious and acephalous political systems, with an isolationist attitude toward their stronger, centralized Muslim neighbors. The Bassari are one of the few Senegalese groups with an active plastic arts tradition and who utilize masked dancers in ceremonies. Today their extensive and colorful initiation ceremonies, centered in Salemata in southeastern Senegal in April and May, attract numerous tourists. Many Bassari have migrated to towns, especially Kedougou, Tambacounda (q.v.) and Dakar (q.v.) to seek wage employment.

BAWOL. A Wolof (q.v.) kingdom with a large Serer (q.v.) population, located in the heart of today's groundnut basin east of Dakar. According to oral traditions, the Serer moved into the area from the Senegal River basin in the eleventh and twelfth centuries. Wolof groups filtered in from the north continuously from then on. Political organization was imposed by the Wagadu matrilineage, believed of Soninke (q.v.) origin, which mixed with local ethnic groups and ruled Bawol as a vassal of the Jolof Empire (q.v.) from approximately the thirteenth century until Bawol's independence in the 1550s. *Damel-Ten* Amari Ngone Sobel Fal (q.v.), who belonged to the Wagadu matrilineage, led Bawol and neighboring Kajor (q.v.) to independence about 1550. It was then ruled as a joint monarchy with Kajor, although there were always separate administrations for each kingdom.

The political structure of the kingdom included a hierarchy headed by the great electors, a crown-slave bureaucracy subjected directly to the king and representatives of each of the dependent communities (pastoralists, fishermen, clergy, casted groups and women). The capital was at Lambay, while Sali Portudal and Mbour served as principal seaports. The opportunity to acquire cloth, liquor, jewelry, metal and firearms from European slave traders encouraged the military aristocracy to raid isolated Serer and Non communities and to quarrel with one another in quest of slaves.

The aristocracy was dispossessed by French conquest, which began with an invasion in 1859 and culminated with the division of the kingdom into two provinces in 1895. The majority of the aristocracy and their soldier-slaves then joined the Murid (q.v.) movement, which has dominated the Bawol countryside since the colonial period.

BAY FALL (BAY FAL). See FAL, SHAIX IBRA

BIDONVILLE. French term for a shantytown, a poor residential area with irregular construction of wood, sunbaked brick and corrugated iron. Although pockets of bidonvilles remain in all urban centers, expanding cities in Senegal have historically pushed these areas to the outer periphery. Many quarters in Dakar (q.v.) can be classified as bidonvilles.

BLOC DEMOCRATIQUE SENEGALAISE . (BDS, Senegalese Democratic Bloc). The BDS was the first political party formed by Léopold Senghor (q.v.) in 1948, after he broke with his sponsor, Lamine Guèye (q.v.). Mamadu Dia (q.v.) initially served as secretary general. Appealing to the newly enfranchised rural electorate, and especially to Muslim clerics (q.v.), the party won a sweeping victory in the 1951–1952 elections. The BDS, originally a federation of political clans (q.v.), voted in its 1954 congress to require individual membership, hoping both to cement its internal structure and appeal to modern intellectuals. Historians Abdoulaye Ly and Amadou Moctar Mbow (q.v.) joined the movement briefly in 1956, and helped engineer a larger coalition. The new united party, named the Bloc Populaire Sénégalais (q.v.), replaced the BDS in 1956.

BLOC DES MASSES SENEGALAISES (BMS, Bloc of the Senegalese Masses). Founded in 1961 by Cheikh Anta Diop (q.v.), who became its secretary-general, the BMS was comprised of older former socialists with important family connections and served more to launch Diop's political career than as an effective electoral organization. It was legally dissolved in 1963 when most of its leaders were absorbed into the dominant UPS (q.v.), but Cheikh Anta and a small group of intellectuals remained aloof. In 1977 a new coalition under Diop emerged as the Rassemblement National Démocratique (q.v.), but it never exerted much influence, holding its only seat ever in the National Assembly between 1983 and 1988. The party has been disbanded.

BLOC POPULAIRE SENEGALAIS . (BPS, Senegalese Popular Bloc). The dominant political party in Senegal from 1956 until 1958, led by Léopold Senghor (q.v.) and Mamadou Dia (q.v.). It was a middle step in the process of fusion toward a single party, which marked the years immediately preceding and following independence. Formed by the merger of Senghor's Bloc Démocratique Sénégalais (q.v.) and several smaller parties, it was renamed the Union Progressiste Sénégalaise (q.v.), in 1958, when the Socialists were finally brought into the fold.

BORDERS. Senegal is bordered by Mauritania on the north, with the Senegal River (q.v.) serving as the frontier. Mali is its eastern neighbor; the Faleme River is the border, except for the addition of a mineral-rich portion east of the river from Kidira south. Guinea-Conakry and Guinea-Bissau share Senegal's southern border, and a strip averaging 10 miles on either side of the Gambia River sets off an independent Republic of the Gambia within Senegal.

The decision to make the Senegal River a border, rather than a highway as it had been for 15 centuries, grew out of the French politics of conquest. Louis Faidherbe's (q.v.) 1855 plan for establishing French hegemony involved separating Moors (q.v.) and blacks both politically and geographically, making the river an artificial racial dividing line. During the colonial period, however, blacks from both Senegal and Mauritania settled the north bank of the river, where they are now numerically predominant. Some Senegalese residents own fields on the north bank of the river in Mauritania. Tensions between Senegal and Mauritania have occasionally risen over racial issues. Most recently, during the ethnic disturbances of April 1989 (see MOORS), people on both sides of the Senegal River were killed, and the border between Senegal and Mauritania was officially closed. It remained closed through 1991, although there were negotiations under way to reopen the border at Rosso.

The Gambia River was the second major waterway linking the Senegambia economically to the interior French Sudan in the precolonial period. British–French rivalries in the partition era doomed it also, making it an enclave rather than a trade artery. The British–French treaty of 1889 awarded the river banks along the navigable portion to the British, and left in French hands the entire network of overland and feeder streams forming its economic hinterland. This border ignored traditional political and socioeconomic frontiers, partitioning each of the precolonial kingdoms along its length. This unique border is central to local politics today, involving both cooperation and conflict. The Senegalese government views the Gambia as an irksome historical accident and obstacle to development because it cuts off Dakar from the Casamance (q.v.) region. In addition, owing to disparities in prices paid for groundnuts and other items, there is heavy smuggling across the border. The attempt at creating a Senegambia Confederation (q.v.) in the 1980s did not substantially change the situation. Despite the dissolution of the Confederation in 1989, the Gambia and Senegal are obliged to cooperate closely on trans-Gambian highway plans and river development. This has resulted in one of the few harmonious Anglophone-Francophone relationships in Africa.

The borders with Mali and Guinea-Conakry both originated in French administrative convenience with the partition of precolonial states, ethnic groups and trade routes. Since independence, the borders seem to have become even greater economic and political obstacles. The border with Mali was closed in the early 1960s after the breakup of the Mali Federation (q.v.), and since then the roads, railroads and border provinces linking the two countries have been allowed to deteriorate. The Dakar–Bamako railroad is the only bridge between the two countries, and border formalities for rail passengers are extensive and time-consuming. Because of disagreements between Senghor and Sekou Toure of Guinea, the border with Guinea-Conakry was closed during the late 1960s through 1977. Yet, Guinean migrants, especially Fulbe, continued to flow illegally into Senegal. After the death of President Sekou Toure in 1984, relations between Senegal and Guinea-Conakry improved markedly, but the border remains an obstacle to regional development.

The border with Guinea-Bissau made Senegal a neighbor of one of Africa's recent colonial wars, from 1961 through 1975. Senegal accepted Bissauan refugees during the struggle for independence from Portugal, with estimates ranging from 70,000 (United Nations) to 300,000 (Senghor). Most were resettled in the Casamance (q.v.), while others moved into Sine-Saloum and the cities. Independence did not end immigration from Bissau, which has a far weaker economy than Senegal. Cordial diplomatic relations exist between the two countries.

BOUFFLERS, STANISLAS JEAN. (LE CHEVALIER DE). Governor of the trading posts in Senegal in 1786–1787, this flamboyant personality has left a greater mark on the romantic colonial history of Senegal than his political impact merits. A minor literary figure at the Court of Versailles, he left a diary detailing his dream of founding a private princedom on Cape Verde (q.v.) where he and his fiancée, the Comtesse de Sabran, could retire. His courtly manners impressed the *Damel* of Kajor (q..v.), initiating an exchange of formal diplomatic receptions and the beginnings of treaty negotiations. Boufflers left Senegal just a year and a half before the outbreak of the French Revolution and never returned. A small but popular hostel and restaurant on Gorée Island (q.v.) are named for him.

BRIERE DE L'ISLE, COLONEL LOUIS-ALEXANDRE. Governor of Senegal from 1876 through 1881, Brière, then a captain, revived the French master plan for the conquest of the Western Sudan that had been initiated by Faidherbe (q.v.) in the 1850s but had since stagnated. The keystone to Brière's plan, both for the military invasion of the countries involved and for persuading the French government to finance it, was the construction of two railroads. One was to link Dakar and Saint-Louis (both q.v.) via the peanut basin, while the other would connect the navigable portions of the Senegal and Niger Rivers. Brière sent envoys to negotiate treaties with Lat Dior Diop (q.v.), the *Damel* of Kajor, and Amadu Sheku Tal (q.v.), son of *al-Hajj* Umar Tal (q.v.) and head of an empire in the Western Sudan, permitting the construction of railroads through their territories. The rulers realized that the negotiations were to prepare for conquest, not to avoid it, and they mobilized against the treaties. Brière was recalled to France in 1881, losing his opportunity to follow through on the military aspect of his project. Over the next decade the diplomatic negotiations he initiated ultimately had the desired effect, although with less ease and

much greater cost in lives, money and time than he or the
French administration had foreseen.

BUNDU. The relatively large landmass of Bundu in eastern
Senegal consisted of the dry savanna area south of the Ferlo
Desert (q.v.) and west of the Faleme River. To the south were
Bambuk (q.v.) and several Mandinka polities; to the west
were the small states of Niani-Wuli (q.v.). Oral traditions
suggest that Futanke, or Fulbe emigrants from Futa Toro, led
by a Muslim cleric named Malik Dauda Sy (q.v.), moved into
the area, with the permission of the *tunka,* or king, of Gajaaga
(q.v.) in the 1690s. The area was sparsely inhabited by
indigenous Fulbe, Soninke (q.v.) and Mande speakers. The
Futanke migrants soon established Bundu's Muslim Fulbe
identity, however. Agriculture, pastoralism, trade and craft
manufacture dominated Bundu's economy.

Malik Sy, whose leadership rested primarily on religious
prestige, took the title of *almamy* (q.v.) as did his descendants. Theoretically, power alternated between the Bulebane
and Kussan branches of the Sissibe lineage, with the succession passing from elder to younger brothers before returning
to the eldest son of the eldest brother. By the 1840s, however,
the Bulebane house, led by Almamy Saada Sy, had allied
with the Massassi Bambara of Karta and the increasingly
visible French, who built a fort at Senudebu in 1845. When
Saada died in late 1851, the Bulebane branch, confident of its
alliances, refused to relinquish the leadership to Kussan,
igniting a devastating civil war. Al-Hajj Umar Tal (q.v.) took
advantage of the power vacuum and exerted control over the
area in the early 1850s.

Louis Faidherbe (q.v.) allied with Bokar Saada Sy (q.v.), a
descendant of the Bulebane house and opposed to Umar Tal,
appointing him almamy of Bundu in 1858. In the 1860s and
1870s, Bokar Saada, with full French support and primarily
through raiding, expanded the sphere of influence and extended the borders of Bundu by annexing parts of the upper

Gambia, the Ferlo and Bambuk. With Bokar Saada's death in December 1885, the Sy lineage was overthrown by the Soninke cleric Mamadu Lamine Drame (q.v.), who was eventually killed by the French in December 1887. The Sissibe lineage was restored with the appointment of Usman Gassi Sy, who ruled until his death in 1891, and then the installation of Malik Ture Sy, a nephew of Bokar Saada.

By the turn of the century, the almamy was little more than a figurehead. When Malik Ture died in 1905, the French formally abolished the almamate of Bundu and split it into two parts: Bundu septentrional, centered on northern Bundu near the Senegal River valley, and Bundu meridional, to the south and focused on the Dakar–Bamako railroad (q.v.). The partition corresponded to the shift in French interest from the Senegal River to the railroad and the groundnut basin. Like other areas in eastern Senegal during and after the First World War, Bundu became a labor reserve for the groundnut basin in Senegal and the Gambia. At independence, the area was incorporated into the region of Sénégal-Oriental.

BUR. The Wolof word for king, it was taken as a title by the *Bur-ba* Jolof (q.v.), the *Bur* of Sin (q.v.) and the *Bur* of Salum (q.v.). Other Wolof kings took titles particular to their kingdoms. The Wolof called the governor at the European trading post of Saint-Louis *Bur Gej* (lit. King of the Sea).

- C -

CAM, DILE (fl. 1827–30). Military leader of a jihad (q.v.) that overtook Walo (q.v.) in 1829, following the inspiration of the Kajor cleric Njaga Isa Jop (q.v.). Cam was of blacksmith (caste, q.v.) origin, which was unusual but not unknown at the time, and which clearly indicates that the movement was part of the reformist egalitarian tradition. According to oral tradition, Cam was among Njaga Isa's disciples in Kajor when he was possessed by a spirit urging him to lead a holy war. He marched easily and triumphantly through neighboring Walo, which was in the middle of a civil war. The Walo king fled to Saint-Louis (q.v.) and received aid from the French, who did not want a reformist Islamic movement in control of the mainland kingdom adjacent to their trading station. Dile was defeated by a coalition of Walo and French forces. French reports claim that Cam was shot in battle, but a participant described how he was forced to eat pork and drink alcohol, both forbidden to Muslims, before being hanged. The tree is still pointed out by residents.

CAPE VERDE (or CAP VERT). The peninsula jutting into the Atlantic Ocean and the site of Dakar (q.v.). Portuguese (q.v.) sailors arrived at islands directly offshore in 1444 and named them *Cabo Verde* since they were the first green land sighted after sailing down the African coast. The islands are now the independent nation of Cape Verde Islands, and the peninsula, called Cap Vert, is the smallest but most densely populated region (see ADMINISTRATION) of Senegal.

When the Portuguese arrived, the peninsula was part of Kajor (q.v.), then a vassal of the Jolof Empire (q.v.), and inhabited by Lebu (q.v.) fishermen and farmers. The Lebu prevented European settlement on the peninsula, restricting the Europeans to the offshore island of Gorée (q.v.) and to Rufisque at the base of the peninsula, which served as the primary port of trade with Kajor. In the 1790s, a group of exiles who had attempted to overthrow the monarchy of Kajor established a clerical oligarchy on the peninsula. For the next century, they managed to maintain a tiny theocratic republic, whose political energies were devoted to keeping independence from Kajor.

During Louis Faidherbe's (q.v.) governorship in 1857, a small French military post was established at the village of Ndaxaru (Dakar) on the peninsula, and jetties were built to shelter ships taking on charcoal and water. Gorée, however, remained the main French base in the area for another 40 years. In 1897 the port at Dakar began to be developed, and the decision to make it the terminus for the Dakar–Bamako railroad assured its future growth, particularly at the expense of Saint-Louis (q.v.). In 1902, Dakar was made the headquarters for the governor-generalship of French West Africa (q.v.), though Saint-Louis remained the capital of the colony of Senegal.

As the peninsula grew into the administrative, commercial and communications hub of French West Africa, some Lebu were able to convert their traditional land rights into profitable urban real estate, but most were simply displaced. The population of the Cap Vert region grew from an estimated 2,000 in 1878, to about 37,000 in 1923, and to almost 1 million by the 1976 census. By 1991, the region contained approximately 1,500,000 inhabitants. (See DAKAR.)

CARPOT, FRANÇOIS. *Métis* (q.v.) lawyer from Saint-Louis (q.v.) who served as Deputy of Senegal to the French Chambre from 1902–1914, establishing the deputyship as an important office in local politics. Bordeaux commercial interests had dominated the office from its creation in 1871 until Carpot's time, and he was succeeded by the first African deputy, Blaise Diagne (q.v.). Thus he also represents a brief transitional *métis* leadership in the movement toward popular African electoral politics in Senegal. Although of aristocratic family and French education, Carpot attempted to represent the interests of all Senegalese, not merely the elite of Saint-Louis. The most notable example was his intercession with the French government to bring the Murid leader Amadu Bamba Mbake (q.v.) home from exile.

CASAMANCE. The southernmost area of Senegal, lying along the Casamance River between the Gambia and Guinea-Bissau and extending eastward from the Atlantic Ocean to Senegal-Oriental. Ziguinchor (q.v.) is the largest city. In the mid-1980s, the Casamance was divided into two administrative regions: Ziguinchor (or lower Casamance) and Kolda (or upper Casamance).

The name Casamance originates in a Portuguese corruption of Kasa Mansa (King of Kasa), the principal Portuguese trading partner in the area in the fifteenth century. The original inhabitants of the area were apparently the Banun (q.v.), a branch of which founded the early kingdom of Kasa (q.v.). Successive waves of migrants from the Mali Empire began moving into the upper Casamance in the thirteenth and fourteenth centuries, founding the empire of Kabu (q.v.). In the late seventeenth and eighteenth centuries, the Jola (q.v.) from the west, Balant from the south and Mande from the east began to dominate the area. The central authority of the Kabu Empire disintegrated, and small constituent states gained autonomy. Many of these small groups retained their traditional religion and political structures.

In the fifteeenth and sixteenth centuries, Fulbe migrants from Futa Toro and Bundu (both q.v.) gradually settled on the plains of the upper Casamance. By the nineteenth century, the Fulbe accounted for over half the population of the upper Casamance. Between 1867 and 1872, under the leadership of Alfa Molo Balde (q.v.), they overthrew their Mandinka overlords and established the *Almamate* of Fuladu (q.v.). The Casamance was the last area of Senegal to be conquered by Europeans, with the main invasions occurring in 1903. Pockets of resistance remained through the First World War. During the colonial and early independence periods, it was a distant and neglected province of the colony and then the Republic of Senegal. The lower Casamance was generally inhabited by non-Muslims belonging to distinct linguistic and ethnic groups not found elsewhere in Senegal.

Several movements for the independence of Casamance from Senegal developed in the late 1960s and 1970s. The war of independence in neighboring Guinea-Bissau and the large number of refugees also caused some tensions in the region.

A few separatist groups emerged in the early 1980s, and there were serious clashes between security forces and separatists in Ziguinchor in 1982 and 1983 when at least 25 were killed. There was renewed violence in 1987. In December 1990, there was another serious uprising among the Jola (q.v.), in Ziguinchor. The revolt was quickly and forcefully crushed by the Diouf government. The leaders were imprisoned in Dakar, but released under a general amnesty in mid-1991, after pledging their full support for Abdou Diouf and the central government. Because regional parties are banned, the separatists have overwhelmingly voted for the opposition Parti Démocratique Sénégalais (q.v., PDS).

With the completion of the trans-Gambia highway linking Ziguinchor and Dakar, the politics and culture of the Casamance are being more closely integrated to the rest of the country. The 1990 uprising directed the government's attention to the region's problems. Migrants flood north to the groundnut basin, and trade and transport are growing rapidly. The Sahelian drought (q.v.) of the 1970s, which crippled the economy of the peanut basin, encouraged development planners to see the relatively rain-reliable Casamance as a major hope for the future. In addition, tourism on Cap Skirring was also developed. Recently, however, efforts to attract tourists have focused on the Petite Côte (q.v.) just south of Dakar.

CASTE. Most Senegambian ethnic groups had a caste system, based primarily on specialization or occupation. The most rigid and elaborate systems existed among groups like the Wolof, Fulbe, Mandinka, Soninke and Moors (each q.v.) with relatively complex economies. The Serer, Jola and Tanda (each q.v.) groups exhibited little evidence of a caste system. All groups in stratified societies were segregated according to vocation and married within their group, but usually only artisans and griots (q.v.) were referred to as castes. Families of griots (praise singers and musicians), blacksmiths, leatherworkers, weavers and carvers were historically attached to individual noble families. They provided goods and services to the nobles, their suites and dependent peasants. Many caste families owned slaves (q.v.).

Indigenous traditions link the taint of inferiority attributed to casted groups with their handling of dangerous and unclean materials like fire, metal, carcasses, wood and, in the case of griots, words. Despite an inferior position in society, casted groups supposedly possessed special physical and spiritual powers that earned them a certain respect. Blacksmiths usually served as the village circumciser and frequently served as the spokespeople for important religious and political figures. Caste status was inherited through the father, and only men worked with certain materials. Designated family names were associated with specific castes, and people maintained their caste status even if they did not practice a craft. Casted women worked in pottery and cotton spinning, and usually served as midwives.

Islam, the dominant religion, offered no systematic rationale for separate castes comparable to that of India's Hindu religion. Occasional Muslim clerics (q.v.) even declared the caste system contrary to Islam and tried to abolish it, but to little avail. It was not until modernization and independence began to offer alternate educational and vocational options that the caste system began to disintegrate in certain parts of the country, most notably the cities. Since independence, it has become illegal to refer to a person's caste or slave origin, or to discriminate against casted groups in employment. Endogamy, however, is still generally observed, and persons of caste origins are likely to meet obstacles in certain careers. Casted persons cannot become clerics or imams (q.v.) and in certain rural areas, they cannot be elected village chiefs or occupy administrative posts. People who continue to practice the inherited crafts live much like their ancestors. Yet, they are generally accepted as Muslims today, rarely give the deferential kneeling salutation and need not live in segregated neighborhoods, nor be buried separately.

CAYOR. See KAJOR

CEDO. (sometimes CEDDO) Wolof term for crown slaves (q.v.) who policied precolonial Wolof kingdoms as appointed titleholders, tax collectors and warriors. The word was also sometimes used in reference to the aristocracy that employed the slaves, and recently this has become the accepted usage. The term was occasionally used for someone who was irreligious and not worthy of being called a Muslim. Negative connotations continue to predominate in modern Wolof usage, although Ousmane Sembene (q.v.), in the film *Ceddo,* has attempted to restore some of the original aura of grandeur associated with the *cedo* way of life.

CFA FRANC. See FRANC, CFA.

CHEIKH. See SHAIXU, SHEXU.

CITOYEN. Coveted legal status of Africans born in the four urban *communes* (q.v.) of colonial Senegal. From 1848 onward, Africans resident in Saint-Louis and Gorée (both q.v.) voted in municipal elections with *métis* (q.v.) and local French residents. African residents of the communes insisted that they were full French citizens and sought to enlist voluntarily into the regular French army, but it was only in 1917 that the Blaise Diagne laws (q.v.) granted their point. Full French citizenship also permitted appeals to French law courts or local Muslim tribunals instead of the arbitrary *indigénat* (q.v.); provided freedom of travel; and guaranteed privileges in the civil and military service not available to rural people. These special privileges were one of the bitter symbols of the inequalities and arbitrariness of colonial rule. In 1946, to appease the *sujets* (q.v.), the statures of *sujet* and *citoyen* were both eliminated in favor of the single status of "citizen of the French Union."

CLAN. An anthropological term for an extended kin group tracing descent from a common ancestor. In Senegal, however, the wide range of sizes and structures in lineage groups makes the term too ambiguous. It is now usually used as a political term to describe factions in Senegal's ruling elite and refers to a political leader or coalition of leaders and all of their followers and dependents. Social scientists label this type of group a patron–client network. Traditionally, every head of family had a patron, either secular or clerical, whom he visited regularly for guidance and aid and to show respect. He might also depend on the patron for access to land and a wife, in which case he also owed the patron substantial services.

President Senghor (q.v.) apparently first began calling political networks and coalitions "clans," and the press and western political scientists continued the usage. Both secular and clerical clans include those branches of the patron's extended family, families of caste (q.v.) and slave (q.v.) origin with historic links to his family and sometimes even the employees of those who support him. Trade unions, cultural associations and vocational organizations some-times join or form their own clans for political purposes. Within the clan network, adherents help one another get jobs, promotions and political favors and in coping with the cumbersome Senegalese bureaucracy. At election time, clan members are expected to vote as a bloc according to the instructions of the patron.

CLERIC. Islamic teacher and leader, called *marabout* in French, *Serin* in Wolof and *Cerno* or *Torodo* (pl. *Torodbé*) in Pulaar. Among the Wolof, Futanke, Mandinka and some Serer (all q.v.) societies, clerics were a distinct endogamous social estate within the category of freeborn persons. Some were assigned their own lands, on which they enjoyed considerable political autonomy and often exemption from taxes and military service. Some were active in political life and held titles, though only titles designated exclusively for religious leaders. Most clerics were of noble birth, though some peasants rose to the rank. Casted and slave persons (both q.v.) could not aspire to the rank of cleric.

There were frequent power struggles between nobles and clerics. Clerical leaders successfully created regimes or took over exisiting states under Koli Tenegela Ba (q.v.) and *Almamy* Abdul Qadir Kan (q.v.) in Futa Toro, Jal Jop on Cape Verde (q.v.), Malik Sy of Bundu (q.v.) and throughout Senegambia in the 1850s through 1880s. In each case, the ruling clergy tended to become a gradually secularized hereditary nobility, distinct from their former clerical colleagues. There were also several unsuccessful clerical uprisings, including the Tubenan of 1673–77 (q.v.), various attempts by *Almamy* Abdul Qadir Kan to extend his geographic scope in the 1790s, the Njaga Isa Jop/Dile Cam (each q.v.) affair in 1828–30, and the revolt of 1859 in Kajor. The revolutions of the latter nineteenth century offered an alternative and dynamic leadership in the wake of French and British military pressure, but all eventually succumbed.

During the colonial conquest, the French and British destroyed the traditional nobilities of the Senegambia, leaving clerics the obvious political heirs. The new colonial rulers sought their cooperation in restoring and maintaining order. The nobility were effectively eliminated from the social structure, being incorporated into the freeborn estate, so that the highest status today is generally cleric. Since independence, the political power of the clerics is subordinate to that of a secular state, but it is a potent electoral and local force that may yet renew the quest for supremacy.

CODE DE LA FAMILLE . (Family Code). Set of laws passed in 1964 to regulate marriage, divorce and inheritance according to modern, mainly French-inspired precepts. It operates alongside, and sometimes openly in conflict with, the much more widely accepted and used Muslim traditional law. It allows, for instance, a husband and wife to contract for a monogamous marriage. If there is no contract, a husband may legally take up to four wives. It also allows women to sue for divorce much more easily than under Muslim law and protects women and children from abuses of paternal authority.

The law has little application except among the urban elite well enough informed and financed to use the court procedures it requires. It is bitterly resisted by conservative traditionalists, notably the *marabouts* (q.v.), who are the interpreters and arbiters of Muslim law. The general provisions are becoming more widely known among the urban poor, who are increasingly having recourse to it. In the rural areas, which comprise most of the country, the code is virtually unknown.

COHABITATION. Political term used to describe the entry of the opposition leader, Abdoulaye Wade (q.v.), formerly of the Parti Démocratique Socialiste (q.v.), into the administration of Abdou Diouf (q.v.). In a surprise move, Diouf appointed Wade a minister of state in early 1991. The situation is analagous to the period in France in the mid-1980s when François Mitterand and Jacques Chirac shared power. It remains to be seen how effective this political action will be in solving Senegal's political and economic problems.

COLIN, JEAN. (1924–) The most important and longest lasting of the French civil servants retained by the Senegalese government since independence, Colin has had an intense and highly controversial political career. He was arguably the most important political figure in Senegal after President Abdou Diouf (q.v.) until his abrupt dismissal in 1989.

Educated at the Ecole nationale de la France d'Outre-Mer

and the Ecole des Langues Orientales, Colin came to Senegal to stay in 1957. Previously he had spent a decade in colonial administration in the Cameroons and had a brief tour with Radio-Senegal. He was appointed *Chef de Cabinet* in the first Senegalese government under the *loi cadre* (q.v.), served two terms as governor of the Cap Vert region (q.v.), two years as secretary-general of the government and from 1962 to 1964 as secretary-general at the Presidency. Named minister of finance in 1964, Colin was resented by rivals who had hoped to see the post go to a Senegalese. He held the post until 1971, when he was named minister of the interior, an equally important post. Colin also had an active career in party and electoral politics, first in Joal and then in Thiès. He was regional secretary-general of the party for Thiès and a member of the Central Political Bureau. He also served as the elected mayor of Thiès and its senior deputy to the National Assembly.

During the election disturbances in Dakar in May 1988, Colin was given extended powers under a declared state of emergency in the capital. Yet, in 1989, as part of a far-reaching administrative reform program, President Diouf dismissed Colin from his posts. The surprise move was generally well-received by the Senegalese political elite, which strongly resented Colin's influence.

COMMUNES. During the colonial period, the settlements of Dakar, Gorée, Rufisque and Saint-Louis (each q.v.) were known as the *Quatre communes,* or the Four Communes. Each commune was endowed with a council, which was elected by all its adult males, and a mayor who was the president of the council. All the indigenous inhabitants were French citizens and legally enjoyed the same civil and political rights as Frenchmen. They were called the *originaires* (q.v.).

When the 1848 Revolution broke out in France, the residents of Saint-Louis and Gorée sought and won the right to be counted as one of the *communes* of France and elect their own deputy. In 1880, the commune of Rufisque, and in 1887 the commune of Dakar were created, though there was still only one deputy, usually from Saint-Louis. The distinction between residents of the communes and rural inhabitants acquired its greatest political importance before and during the First World War. *Sujets* (q.v.) living in the rest of Senegal were subject to involuntary conscription for forced labor and military service, while citizens (q.v. *citoyens*) of the communes were exempt. In 1946, when the vote was extended to the rest of the colony, the communes lost their privileged position and very quickly declined in political importance.

COMMUNES-MIXTE (MIXED COMMUNES). Shortly after the flare-up of resentment against the privileged status of the communes during World War I, some interior cities (notably Thiès, Kaolack and Ziguinchor) won the appelation *communes-mixte*. Their residents could elect local officials, but could not vote for the deputy nor send delegates to the Colonial Council. In 1946, when the vote was extended throughout the colony, the mixed communes were abolished.

COMPAGNIE DE GALAM. With slight variations, the name of a series of joint-stock companies beginning in 1820 and ending in 1848. Previously, the French government had chartered a joint-stock company named the *Compagnie du Sénégal* (q.v.) to administer trade along the coast.

The companies of Galam were organized by the colonial government at Saint-Louis (q.v.) and the local *habitant* (q.v.) traders for the annual high-water trip up the Senegal River to Galam (q.v.). The voyages occurred between July and November and usually focused on slaves and gum arabic (both q.v.). Like their African and European trading partners, these intermediaries hoped to unite behind monopoly prices. Most of the companies began with a relatively low minimum subscription and large participation, but prominent *métis* (q.v.) and Wolof merchants tended to emerge dominant. Smaller *traitants* (q.v.) then tended to confine their work to the *escales* (q.v.) on the lower portion of the river, which was navigable year-round. The company was abolished in 1848 at the beginning of the concerted French conquest of the interior via the Senegal River.

COMPAGNIE DU SENEGAL. With slight variations, the name of a series of joint-stock companies chartered by the French government from 1673 through 1758 and 1789 to 1791 for trade on the Senegambian coast.

Usually in exchange for a commercial monopoly, the companies were required to administer forts and trading posts and ensure a regular supply of slaves to the French Caribbean islands. In local politics, their governors acted with considerable autonomy, negotiating treaties, administering capital punishment and sometimes even making war. Every few years the companies failed and were reorganized by a new group of stockholders. The repeated bankruptcies can be attributed to the expenses of administration, to wars with Dutch- and British-chartered companies and to the established practice of private profit-taking among company officers. Despite the regular failures, chartered companies remained the favored administrative structure for the slave trade among all European participants until the late eighteenth century. In theory, it sheltered the governments from the risks of war and colonial overextension, passing on costs to slave purchasers, while also assuring the operation of the mercantile triangle trade on which France's economy depended. In 1763, the French crown decided to assume direct administration of the Senegambian trading posts, effectively ending the Company era. (See COMPAGNIE DE GALAM.)

COMPAGNIE FRANÇAISE DE L'AFRIQUE DE L'OUEST (CFAO, French Company of West Africa). The major Marseilles import-export firm in colonial Senegal. Founded in

1887, it drew on two centuries of Marseille dominance on the Senegalese coast, and on a special collaborative relationship with the government during the conquest, to carve out a major share of the colonial trade.

As the company and a few similar firms spread throughout the interior during the first third of the twentieth century, they gave credit preference to French and Lebanese (q.v.) agents, eliminating the former Wolof, Jula and Moorish interior networks from all but the smallest markets. Keeping the peasants perpetually in debt with advances of seeds, tools, consumer goods and sometimes preharvest food relief, the major companies monopolized the collection and market-ing of the groundnut harvest each year. The CFAO remained entirely commercial, with a low rate of local reinvestment until World War II. After the war, it moved into light industry, including peanut oil refineries, textiles, and ce-ment, and rode a wave of commercial prosperity that peaked in 1951.

The groundnut marketing system was one of the major issues in the period of struggle for self-government, and with the coming of independence, the CFAO withdrew somewhat from colonial commerce. It founded major chains of super-markets in France and the Monoprix chain in West Africa. Peanut exports were nationalized, but the CFAO of Senegal tried to save its retail trade by taking in African partners in a new firm called AFRIDEX. This venture failed and was absorbed in 1967 by the Compagnie Sénégalaise du Sud-Est, composed entirely of Senegalese.

COMPANY OF MERCHANTS TRADING TO AFRICA. A British-chartered company, successor to the Royal African Company (q.v.), charged from 1751 through 1765 with maintaining British slave-trading forts and factories on the West African coast to facilitate the trade of private British merchants. Following the French shift to direct royal admin-istration of the Senegambian trade in 1763 (see COMPAG-

NIE DU SENEGAL), the British created a Royal Province of Senegambia and withdrew that section of the coast from the Company of Merchants. The Company continued operating in Sierra Leone and the Gold Coast until 1821.

CONFEDERATION OF THE SENEGAMBIA. An attempt during the 1980s at unity between the republics of Senegal and the Gambia that quickly failed.

On August 2, 1981, President Diouf (q.v.) agreed to an emergency request by the Gambian president, Sir Dawda Jawara, to use Senegalese troops to restore him to power, following a coup d'état during his absence abroad. The operation was successful, though reportedly at considerable cost to Gambian lives. The Senegalese troops were then asked to stay to maintain order and discourage further unrest. Jawara and Diouf worked toward setting up a confederation between the two countries, with coordinated Senegambian policies in defense, foreign affairs and economic and financial matters. An agreement to establish the Confederation of Senegambia was ratified in December 1981 by the Gambian House of Representatives and the Senegalese National Assembly. Diouf was named president of the Confederation, with Jawara designated vice president. The agreement went into effect in February 1982. A Senegambian council of ministers and the confederal assembly met for the first time in January 1983. There were initial attempts at integrating defense and security forces, but this mainly resulted in an increased Senegalese military presence in the Gambia. Proposed economic and financial integration was slow in forthcoming, with each side blaming the other for the lack of progress. It quickly became clear to Gambians that they were effectively being absorbed by Senegal, and they blocked further integration.

By the mid-1980s, it was clear to both the Senegalese and Gambian administrations that the confederation was not working as planned, and the project was gradually abandoned, to the relief of most Gambians. Diouf was increasingly occupied by domestic political and economic problems and did not force the issue. The confederation was officially abolished in September 1989. Today Senegal and the Gambia maintain cordial relations and, by necessity, retain many economic links. Despite some rhetoric, there have been no further attempts at unity or closer integration.

CONSEIL SUPERIEUR DES CHEFS RELIGIEUX (Superior Council of Religious Chiefs). Council of *marabouts* or clerics (q.v.) representing each of the major religious brotherhoods (q.v.) in Senegal. The council was founded in 1957 to ensure religious interests, principally Islamic, during the transition to independence. Saidou Nourou Tal (q.v.) organized the body, which was originally named the Council of Islamic Reorganization. It sought to defend the interests of Muslims vis-à-vis the government, promote the use of Islamic law, and review the new constitution to ensure the position of Islam.

The first officers were Tijani president Saidou Nourou Tal, Murid president Falilou Mbacke, Vice President Bassiru Mbacke, Secretary-Generals Ibrahima Niass and Cheikh Mbacke and Treasurer-General Abdul Aziz Sy (each q.v.). They represented both current heads and rival branches of the Murid brotherhood and the two Tijani branches.

President Senghor (q.v.) acceded to the demand for Muslim input, but defused the power play by consulting the clerics individually rather than collectively. The Conseil Supérieur became and has remained a prestige body whose members are regularly consulted by the government, but lack unified deliberative power. Under President Abdou Diouf (q.v.), the council is largely ceremonial and has consistently supported the president and the ruling Parti Socialiste.

CONSTITUTION OF THE FIFTH FRENCH REPUBLIC. Also called the DeGaulle Constitution, this 1958 act had two major provisions affecting French West Africa. First, it dissolved the Federation of French West Africa, dashing Léopold Senghor's (q.v.) hopes of a unified federation at independence. Second, in the wake of British moves toward independence, it offered a popular referendum to French West African voters. A *no* vote in the referendum would mean immediate independence, complete dissolution of ties and no assistance in the transition (currency and banking, civil service, government records, equipment and international and diplomatic relations). A *yes* vote would mean internal self-government within a greater French union. Senegal and all other colonies except Guinea-Conakry voted *yes*. Guinea's refusal led France to grant it immediate independence on the threatened harsh terms, but it also undermined the concept of a French Union in Africa. Within two years, Senegal and the others had won their independence in much more amicable circumstances.

CONSTITUTION OF THE FIRST SENEGALESE REPUBLIC. Adopted August 26, 1960, when Senegal withdrew from the Mali Federation (q.v.) and declared its own national independence. This constitution was modeled directly on that of the Fifth French Republic of 1958 (q.v.). It called for two heads of state, including a president, elected indirectly, and an executive prime minister responsible to the unicameral 80-member National Assembly. Léopold Senghor (q.v.) was elected president and Mamadou Dia (q.v.) was voted prime minister. Tensions quickly surfaced between supporters of the two heads of state, culminating in the constitutional crisis of 1962 (q.v.), followed by the 1963 Constitution of the Second Senegalese Republic (q.v.).

CONSTITUTION OF THE FOURTH FRENCH REPUBLIC. (October 1946) The post-World War II government of France considerably liberalized its relations with the colonies, hoping to perpetuate economic dominance and centralization by easing the more stringent aspects of colonial rule. The constitution established the French Union, with an assembly where voting membership was evenly divided between metropolitan and overseas France. African representations in the National Assembly and the Council of the Republic (upper house) were also expanded.

In French West Africa, it eliminated the legal distinction between *originaires* or *citoyens* (both q.v.) of the *communes* (q.v.) and *sujets* (q.v.) in the protectorate. Both now became "citizens of the French Union," and voting rights were granted on the basis of economic, educational and administrative restrictions rather than place of birth. The *loi cadre* of 1956 (q.v.) extended universal adult suffrage throughout the colonies. The 1946 Constitution also allowed the rest of French West Africa to elect deputies, which eliminated Senegal's historic position of leadership in colonial electoral politics.

CONSTITUTION OF THE SECOND SENEGALESE REPUBLIC. The current constitution of Senegal, adopted by national referendum on May 4, 1963, in the wake of the constitutional crisis of 1962 (q.v.). The constitution has been amended numerous times since it was first promulgated. It asserts that sovereignty resides in the people, exercised through their representatives or referenda; suffrage is universal and secret. Individual and religious freedom are also ensured.

This constitution abandoned the bicephalism of its predecessor in favor of a single president elected by universal direct suffrage every four years at the same time as the National Assembly deputies. The president was designated commander of the armed forces, and he may assume emergency powers and rule by decree when the security of the state is in grave danger. Ministers were now responsible to the president rather than the Assembly, which could no longer censure or vote no-confidence in the Cabinet. The president also had the power to initiate most legislation and to submit laws to national referendum instead of the Assembly if he chose.

In 1967 the constitution was amended to extend the terms of both president and deputies to five years, and to allow the president to dissolve the Assembly after three years, whereupon both presidential and Assembly elections were to be held. In 1970, Senghor re-created the post of prime minister and appointed Abdou Diouf (q.v.), whom he groomed as his successor. For the 1973 elections, the Assembly was enlarged from 80 to 100 deputies.

In 1976 there was much more substantial constitutional reform, legally establishing multiparty democracy within carefully defined limits. Multipartism had never been outlawed in Senegal, but the country had been ruled by a single dominant party since before independence, and for a long time after 1966 the Union Progressiste Sénégalaise (q.v.) was the only legal party. In 1974 Senghor approved the formation of the moderate, avowedly nonopposition Parti Démocratique Sénégalais (PDS, q.v.), insisting it would revitalize Senegalese politics and help attract young people. He also urged Senegal and other African socialist parties to join the Socialist International, which required them to operate in a democracy. Other parties began to emerge, so a constitutional reform was prepared to regulate this "return to democracy." The new constitutional provisions defined three valid ideological tendencies, with a subsequent law allowing only one party to be registered with each ideology: Liberal Democratic (PDS), Socialist (UPS changed to PS, q.v.) and Marxist-Leninist (PAI, q.v.). A fourth tendency, Islamic nationalist and conservative, emerged, which Senghor legalized after the February 26, 1978, elections. A fifth illegal party of intellectuals (RND, q.v.) and another faction of the PAI emerged, but Senghor refused to recognize them, despite a petition signed by 300 Senegalese in *Le Monde* of May 1, 1977.

The reform of 1976 also contained three provisions designed to allow Senghor control over his successor. It eliminated the five-year limit on the president's term, allowed him to resign in mid-term and designated the presidentially appointed prime minister the automatic successor in case of death or resignation. These measures paved the way for the appointment of Prime Minister Abdou Diouf, Senghor's handpicked successor, as president of Senegal when Senghor resigned on December 31, 1980.

Diouf further reformed the constitution by legalizing all political parties in 1983. The political opposition eventually fragmented into 14 officially recognized parties, virtually assuring the ruling PS party dominance in every election. The National Assembly was increased to 120 seats. Senegal's multiparty system has often been hailed by outside observers as an example for other African countries, which in the late 1980s and early 1990s, increasingly embraced the concept of multipartism. Further constitutional reforms in the late 1980s permitted Diouf to abolish the post of prime minister and to dismiss Jean Colin (q.v.) from the government. In 1991, Diouf appointed opposition-PDS leader Abdoulaye Wade (q.v.) as a minister of state, instituting a period of *cohabitation* (q.v.).

CONSTITUTIONAL CRISIS OF 1962. In mid-December 1962, the First Senegalese Republic (see CONSTITUTION OF THE FIRST SENEGALESE REPUBLIC) ended in a crisis of confrontation between the supporters of President Léopold Senghor (q.v.) and Prime Minister Mamadou Dia (q.v.). The crisis was one of the most important events in independent Senegalese politics. Senghor often refered to this showdown as an attempted coup d'état. During his long imprisonment (1962 to 1974), Dia consistently denied such an attempt, claiming he had only invoked his executive powers to forestall an illegal censure motion by dissident deputies.

On the actual events themselves, there is some agreement. Within the first two years of independence two factions had developed within the bicephalous government. One behind Dia was supported by younger deputies seeking social reform—first, supplanting *marabout* (q.v.) dominance of rural land tenure and social structure with government-organized land reform and cooperatives; and second, supplanting French commercial interests with State enterprises. They tended to favor the firm bureaucratic leadership that characterized Dia, assuming it necessary to overcome the influence of entrenched French and Senegalese interests. The second group, supported by *marabouts* and merchants, mobilized more against Dia and his threatened reforms than around a clear position taken by Senghor. Senghor had decided by late 1962 that bicephalous government was unworkable and prepared to introduce a constitutional reform with a strong executive president. He was co-opted by Dia's opponents within the Party, who determined on December 14 to introduce a motion of censure against the prime minister. Dia claimed the motion illegal both because of a state of emergency then in effect and because members of the ruling Party were not allowed to censure their own leader. On December 17, when all measures to forestall the censure vote had failed, Dia called on the gendarmerie to lock the National Assembly building and arrest four leaders of the censure movement. Senghor, with the support of Lamine Guèye (q.v.), then called out the army, which peaceably took charge, arresting Dia and four of his ministers. Dia was subsequently tried for treason and an attempted coup d'état, convicted and imprisoned together with Valdiodio Ndiaye, Ibrahima Sarr, Joseph Mbaye and Alioune Tall. The constitutional reform proposed by Senghor was polished and passed during the following months. (See CONSTITUTION OF THE SECOND SENEGALESE REPUBLIC.)

- D -

DAKAR. The capital city of the Republic of Senegal, and from 1902 to 1960 headquarters of the Government-General of French West Africa. Situated on a rocky plateau at the tip of the Cape Verde peninsula (q.v.), the westernmost point of Africa, it has emerged in the twentieth century as an urban metropolis and a hub for sea and air traffic linking Africa, Europe and the Americas.

Dakar is a prominent example of a colonial city in West Africa. Colonial cities, established by Europeans for their own purposes of administration and trade, played a critical role in the process of colonial political and economic domination, and in the extraction of profit by colonial business enterprise. The new colonial towns usually absorbed one or more traditional African settlements, but in-migration from rural areas ensured an African majority among the population. The strong links between rural and urban sectors have remained critical to the continued functioning of colonial cities, and Dakar is no exception. The character of these towns generally came to depend on African decisions and initiatives, within a framework set up by the European minority.

In 1857, the Commandant of Gorée (q.v.), Pinet-Laprade (q.v.), sketched a plan for a city-to-be on the site of the Cap Vert, even though France had no foothold on the peninsula. Pinet-Laprade dreamed that it might become the capital of a colonial empire, with a port and administrative headquarters for the anticipated but not-yet-realized French West Africa, and a commercial entrepôt funneling the trade of the Western Sudan to French merchants. He apparently saw no obstacle to the fact that France had not yet conquered Cap Vert, much less a West African empire.

The rocky plateau area facing Gorée was occupied by a few small, independent Muslim fishing villages. One of these villages, inhabited by the Lebu (q.v.) ethnic group, was named Ndaxaru, whose name in French would become Dakar. Because of the lack of a centralized African power and the dispersed nature of settlement on the peninsula, the French were able to construct the first rudimentary fort, port and commercial facilities without dominating the Lebu or forcing them to move. The European settlement of Dakar grew rapidly, with many people moving from Gorée Island to the mainland at Dakar, which quickly became the major commercial center in the southern Senegambian region. The new town, however, was still outranked by Saint-Louis (q.v.) to the north and at the mouth of the Senegal River (q.v.), the main trade artery into the interior of Senegambia and the Western Sudan. The French decision to build a railroad (q.v.) from the Atlantic coast to the Niger River dramatically enhanced the position of Dakar, which was located at its terminus. The railroad meant increased and more diversified trade, and necessitated the expansion of the harbor. The port was greatly enlarged, and Dakar dominated sea trade between France and West Africa. Another rail line was built linking Dakar to Saint-Louis. The Lebanese (q.v.) population increased markedly. By the early twentieth century, Dakar was the most populated city in the French colonies south of the Sahara and had the largest number of Europeans and Lebanese in West Africa.

In 1902, Dakar was designated the capital of the Government-General of French West Africa. Pinet-Laprade's dream seemed to be coming true. Government buildings, European dwellings, city institutions and a Catholic cathedral were constructed on the high plateau at the tip of the peninsula. Regulations prohibited African housing in this part of town, and the Plateau area continues to be the preferred site for Senegalese administrative buildings, international embassies and residences of government officials, diplomats and wealthy Senegalese.

Besides the original plans, which foresaw a pattern of separate European–African development, a more rigorous move in the direction of complete segregation came during the cholera epidemic that struck the city in 1914. In the ensuing panic, African housing on the plateau was burned, and the inhabitants were resettled in a newly created outlying village called the Medina (q.v.). *Cordon sanitaires* (q.v.), or sanitary corridors, were constructed to isolate European from African residential sections and to halt the spread of disease from the African quarters. Military camps and a prison also separated the different sections. After World War II, a brief period of urban growth forced the expansion of the modern sector, which jumped around the Medina. The wealthiest areas extended along the coastal *corniche* to become the University, Fann-Residence and Point-E. In the 1950s, middle-class dwellings were also constructed in this location, mainly by joint government-private enterprises.

With the end of colonial rule and the dismantling of French West Africa, Dakar suddenly lost much of its economic and administrative significance. Abidjan, in the Ivory Coast, with its superior harbor facilities and more productive hinterland, rapidly surpassed Dakar in population and economic importance. Abidjan also became the preferred site for the West African headquarters of international organizations and firms. Yet, *bidonvilles* (q.v.), or shantytowns, continued to grow around Dakar's periphery, at an average rate of approximately 10 percent per year, or about 50,000 new arrivals annually. The Senegalese government has periodically cited health and aesthetic reasons to justify the forcible removal of slums and their residents from the Plateau area. The shantytowns are now so large and extend so far from the city proper that transportation, sanitation, crime and unemployment are reaching crisis proportions. Health care (q.v.) is sorely inadequate. Dakar also faces a critical housing shortage for middle-level salaried workers. The government has started several subsidized developments, but the projects have stalled for lack of finances and changing national priorities.

Dakar today is a study in striking, if disturbing, contrasts. The Plateau area and the coastal strip contain numerous spacious villas and well-kept gardens owned by prosperous Senegalese or expatriates. Usually, the gardens and villas are maintained by Senegalese domestics who commute from the shantytowns where they live in wooden shacks without indoor plumbing or electricity. The four-star hotels, built for the growing tourism industry, are located on the spacious Place de l'Indépendance downtown and have their own generators, owing to frequent citywide power failures. Dakar's main boulevard, the Avenue Pompidou, is lined with Parisian-style boutiques, bookstores and outdoor cafés. The Avenue and most city streets are also filled with street vendors, mostly immigrants from rural areas who have been unable to find salaried work. There are also several major markets, including Sandaga, Kermal and Soumbedioune.

Dakar is administered by the appointed governor of the region of Cap Vert (under the Ministry of the Interior) and two *prefets,* with the advice of the elected Municipal Council. There is also a mayor of Dakar.

DAKAR MATIN. From 1961 through 1970 the leading daily newspaper of Senegal. A successor to the colonial *Paris-Dakar, Dakar-Matin* was initiated the year after independence by Daniel de Bergevin, a friend of President Senghor (q.v.). Its tenor was consistently moderate and pro-establishment, in support of Senghor's administration and its ties with France. In 1970, it was replaced by *Le Soleil* (q.v.).

DAMEL. Title of the king of Kajor (q.v.), apparently both before and after the state won its independence from the Jolof Empire (q.v.) around 1550. Oral traditions claim that the *Laman* of Palen Dedd was vassal of the *Bur-ba* Jolof (q.v.) for the Kajor area under the empire, but a fifteenth-century Portuguese source already refers to *Bu-domel,* which can be identified as an early form of the title *Damel.* Most Damels, following the pattern of their founder Amari Ngone Sobel Fal (q.v.), tried to rule as *Damel-Ten,* dual monarch of Kajor and Bawol (q.v.). The Damel belonged to one of the three branches of the Fal patrilineage descended from the first independent sovereign, Dece FuNjugu Penda Fal. In the sixteenth and seventeenth centuries membership in any of seven royal matrilineages was sufficient, but the powerful ruler Lat Sukabe established the dominance of his Gej matrilineage in Kajor throughout the eighteenth and nineteenth centuries.

DARA. In Wolof, a group of disciples, or *talibes* (q.v.), attached to a Muslim *marabout* (q.v.), sometimes translated as a Quranic, or Koranic, school and sometimes as a cooperative work group, reflecting its two most prominent aspects. Children in rural areas are generally given to a marabout as disciples sometime between the ages of four and twelve and remain in his household entirely subject to his authority until they are released or sent to Francophone schools, any time from age seven to thirty-five. The discipleship is seen as a socialization process, teaching the child endurance, discipline, humility, work and religious learning. One well-studied form of *dara* is the Murid (q.v.) frontier pioneers, who in groups averaging eight to ten disciples, are sent to clear an area of land, dig their own wells and bring land into agricultural production. They average eight or more years at the task, and their main reward is the discipline learned. If their family is too poor to help them obtain land and a wife, however, they may turn to the marabout for a share of what they have cleared and for help with the dowry. At the opposite extreme is the urban dara. In return for a cash payment, marabouts take children Sundays and Wednesdays, when French schools are not in session, and teach them to recite the Quran. Those who live with the marabout or who do not attend school are often sent to beg in the streets.

DENANKE. The ruling dynasty of Futa Toro (q.v.) from the time of legendary founder Koly Tengela Ba (q.v.), about 1490, until the clerical revolution of 1776. Their patronymic was Ba, and their royal title *Satigi.* Because the dynasty was overthrown by Muslim clerics, it is often assumed to have been pagan, but contemporary evidence indicates that the rulers were Muslim and possibly even of clerical origin. While wielding power, they adapted a militaristic, secular life-style and came to look down upon nonruling clerics. The clerics, in turn, came to regard the rulers as corrupt warmongers and not true Muslims. In the eighteenth century, when the Denanke proved incapable of holding together the kingdom and protecting it from Brakna Moor (q.v.) raids, the clerics mobilized a holy war and overthrew them.

DEPARTEMENT. Basic middle-level administrative unit of Senegal. Each region is divided into several departments, which in turn are divided into arrondissements. It is administered by an appointed prefet. (See ADMINISTRATION.)

DIA, AMADOU CISSE. (1915–). First president of the National Assembly. Educated locally as one of the first African physicians, Dia served as head of the Health Department's regional office in Sine-Saloum from his graduation in 1940 until 1959. He had entered politics as a delegate to the Colonial General Council and founding member of Senghor's Bloc Démocratique Sénégalais (q.v.) in 1946–1947. A leading member of the Assembly of the Mali Federation (q.v.) of 1959–1960, he was subsequently in rapid succession Senegal's minister of commerce and industry, minister of health and social affairs, minister for foreign aid and technical cooperation and minister of the armed forces. From 1965 through 1970, he served as minister of the interior, and in 1968, he was elected President of the National Assembly. He retired from politics in the early 1980s. He also authored a play, *The Last Days of Lat Dior,* which was performed at the

First World Festival of Negro Arts in Dakar in 1966 and has remained popular.

DIA, MAMADOU. (1910–). Former prime minister of Senegal and coleader, with Senghor (q.v.), of the pre-independence struggles. Born in Khombole in 1911, Dia was trained at the Ecole William Ponty, emerging as a teacher, journalist and economist. After World War II, he joined Senghor in founding the Bloc Démocratique Sénégalais (q.v.) and participated in its sweeping electoral victories. While Senghor was elected deputy to the French National Assembly, Dia served as senator in the French Council of the Republic (1948–56). In the movement toward self-government inaugurated by the *loi cadre* (q.v.) in 1956, Dia and Senghor moved into a pattern of joint leadership. In 1957 Dia became vice president, then president of Senegal. In 1959, when Senegal briefly united with Mali in the Mali Federation (q.v.), he served as president of the federation. When the Mali Federation broke up in 1960, he became prime minister of Senegal, with Senghor as president. Dia took charge of the daily running of the government while BDS secretary-general, then president of the republic. Senghor focused on the struggle for West African unity, foreign affairs and broader constitutional questions.

Dia won a reputation as a vigorous administrator, autocratic and impatient for reform pushing hard for a national system of farmers' cooperatives, land-tenure reform, and nationalization rather than private Senegalization of important commercial sectors. During 1961 an anti-Dia coalition emerged, comprised largely of threatened interest groups (marabouts, Senegalese and French businessmen and wealthy deputies). Senghor began to work toward constitutional change that would have downgraded Dia's position, but a group of dissident deputies forced the constitutional crisis of December 1962 (q.v.), which resulted in a much more radical resolution of the tension. Accused of an attempted coup d'état, Dia was tried and sentenced to life imprisonment but served only to 1974. During his imprisonment, there were repeated rumors that he was offered release in return for a confession and political retirement, but he never agreed.

In 1974, Dia and his ministerial colleagues Valdiodio Ndiaye and Ibrahima Sarr were released unrepentant from prison, and the following year their civil rights were restored. Dia founded the International African Force for Development and began publishing books on topics ranging from Islam to economic development (see Bibliography). In the democratization movement that began around 1974, Dia was vocal through the journal *Ande Sopi* (Wolof for "Unite for Change"), but was not formally affiliated with a party. In the 1983 elections that returned Abdou Diouf (q.v.) to office, he formed his own party but received only 2 percent of the vote. He did not run again in 1988, and has effectively retired from public life.

DIAGNE, BLAISE. (1872–1934). First African Deputy to the French National Assembly, serving from 1914 to 1934, Diagne also helped to Africanize the local Senegalese political scene during that era. Yet, he later came to terms with conservative interests.

An *originaire* (q.v.) of Gorée (q.v.), Diagne came under the patronage of the wealthy métis merchant Adolphe Crespin, who sent him to a Catholic grammar school and provided for him to attend secondary school in France. Diagne became homesick and returned to Senegal, where he completed his education in Saint-Louis in 1890, a rare achievement in the period of the colonial conquest. Before entering politics in 1914, Diagne spent 22 years at various posts overseas in the French customs service. French assimilation (q.v.) theories had taught him that as an educated African he would be accepted as an equal, but he was passed over for promotion because of his color. Disgruntled, his civil-service career became a long series of virulent attacks on the daily experience of racism. Diagne regularly spoke out and took legal action in defense of himself, his nonwhite co-workers and conquered peoples throughout the French colonial empire, making himself persona non grata among his white superiors in six colonies.

At the urging of Galandou Diouf (q.v.), Diagne returned to Senegal to challenge the métis incumbent Deputy François Carpot (q.v.). African voters of the *communes* (q.v.), threatened with the withdrawal of the assimilationist ideal, mobilized behind Diagne in a bitter election campaign. Amadu Bamba Mbake (q.v.), whose Murid (q.v.) movement dominated the interior, contributed substantial campaign funds. Although Diagne's election was contested in Senegal, he went and was seated in France without incident, becoming the first black African to achieve a high post in the government of a European colonial nation.

Six weeks afterward World War I broke out. Diagne seized upon military service as the key to full citizenship for originaires. While *sujets* (q.v.) residing outside the city limits were subject to involuntary conscription into colonial units, Diagne and residents of the communes insisted that urban residents should fight as voluntary enlistees in regular units at the side of their French cocitizens. Very few originaires served at all until Diagne pushed through the Law of October 19, 1915. When they did begin to serve, their privileged conditions antagonized their countrymen from the protectorate areas. In 1918, France's manpower needs for the war became desperate, and Diagne agreed to become commissioner for recruitment of African troops, with the rank of governor-general, in exchange for a French pledge to improve social services in Senegal. Diagne conducted a sweepingly successful, but much criticized recruitment campaign across French West Africa, drawing more than 100,000 enlistments, while simultaneously insisting on veterans benefits and other privileges to be won by fighting for France.

After the war, Diagne commanded the West African political scene, founding the first Western-style political party, the Republican Socialist Party of Senegal, and seeing his candidates elected to the Colonial Council. For the first time, Senegalese politics were dominated by black Africans.

From 1923 until his death in 1934, Diagne entered a period of better relations with the Bordeaux merchants and the colonial administration. While it may have permitted him to aid his constituents more readily, this rapprochement alienated many of his former supporters who labelled him a conservative. His most outspoken rival was Lamine Guèye (q.v.). Galandou Diouf ran against him in 1928, but the colonial government supposedly rigged the election to give Diagne his seat. In 1930, at Geneva he defended France's hated forced labor policy, and the next year he was made undersecretary of state for the colonies. He again defeated Galandou Diouf in the 1932 elections. During the early Depression, he greatly aided Senegalese farmers by negotiating the first subsidies for their peanut crops, but by 1934, the year of his death, he rarely visited Senegal, having become virtually a Frenchman.

DIOP. (See also JOP.) Modern French-educated figures whose names are spelled Diop as a matter of record are so listed. Their homonyms (and often ancestors) are listed under the phonetic JOP.

DIOP, CHEIKH ANTA. (1923–1986) African historian of international renown, and opposition politician. His major contribution to history was the thesis that ancient Egypt was Black African in origin and was in turn the cultural ancestor of much that is great in Semitic and Western, as well as African, history. His historical work, while generally discredited, has been influential. After his death, the University of Dakar (q.v.) was renamed the Université Cheikh Anta Diop, and his name was added to IFAN as well.

Born in Diourbel, Diop received his baccalaureate in Senegal and then went to Paris to study. From 1946 to 1960 he engaged in student politics and research in France. His political orientation was Pan-Africanist and anticolonial. These remained his themes, even as his homeland passed from formal colonized status to a neo-colonial situation, and most of his political colleagues lost interest in Pan-Africanism. He was among the founders of the student branch of the Rassemblement Démocratique Africain (q.v.), serving as secretary-general from 1950 to 1953. He also published in their journal, *Voie de l'Afrique Noire*. He helped organize the first post-war Pan-African students' political congress, held in Paris July 4–8, 1951. His doctoral thesis on the Egyptian origin of African civilization was initially rejected by the University, but won international recognition when published by Présence Africaine in 1955 under the title *Nations nègres et culture*. He was subsequently awarded the Doctorat d'État.

After independence, Diop returned to Senegal, continuing his career in research and politics. His second major work, *L'Afrique noire précoloniale,* appeared in 1960, and in 1961 he was given a research appointment at IFAN in Dakar (see EDUCATION). He founded an opposition political party, the Bloc des Masses Sénégalaises (q.v.). It folded in 1963, when most of his colleagues were asked to join the government, but Diop remained hostile. He then founded the Front National du Sénégal, which was banned in 1965, along with other opposition parties. After 1973, when Senghor began to allow a legal opposition, Diop founded the Rassemblement National Démocratique (q.v.) and began publishing a journal, *Taxaw* (Wolof for "Stand Up"). The RND was denied legal status, on narrow constitutional grounds, but functioned openly as an interest group. When President Abdou Diouf legalized all political parties in 1983, the party operated openly and won one seat in the National Assembly. Cheikh Anta continued his research from the radio-carbon laboratory that he founded at IFAN. He died in February 1986. His major publications are listed in the Bibliography.

DIOUF, ABDOU. (1935–). President of Senegal since January 1981; prime minister of Senegal from 1970 to 1980. A native of Louga, Diouf was educated at the University of Dakar and received a law degree from the University of Paris. Upon his return to Senegal, he held increasingly important government positions and became known as President Leopold Senghor's (q.v.) protégé. In 1964, Diouf was named secretary-general to the presidency. In 1970, when Senghor decided to reintroduce the office of prime minister—previously abolished during the constitutional crisis of 1962 (q.v.)—he chose the little-known Diouf, then only thirty-eight years old, above many senior civil service leaders and established politicians. The new prime minister was viewed by many as the embodiment of Senghor's attempt to establish a technocratically oriented administration with a low-profile subordinate in the new office. Diouf extended his rule into all facets of government through many changes in the Cabinet. He was praised as an extraordinarily able and efficient administrator.

On December 31, 1980, Senghor, approaching his seventy-fifth year, stepped down from the presidency in favor of Diouf, who immediately lifted many of his predecessor's restrictions on political opposition parties. He also restructured his administration in ways that were generally credited with making it less corrupt and more efficient. Diouf was quickly perceived as a considerably more adept technocrat and administrator than Senghor. Some reform-minded opposition leaders claim Diouf's reforms have not gone far enough, while others suggest that Diouf has had to struggle against his party's old guard and entrenched interests.

Under Diouf's presidency, the formerly strong opposition party, the PDS (q.v.), saw its support steadily eroded and some of its members arrested on suspicion of having received money from Libya. Diouf launched an anticorruption campaign, and his prime minister, Habib Thaim, dropped two influential ministers in a reshuffle in July 1981—Adrien Senghor, the ex-president's nephew, and Louis Alexandrenne, the minister of planning.

In August 1981, Diouf responded to a plea from Gambian president Sir Dauda Jawara for assistance against an attempted coup d'état. Senegal's intervention restored Jawara, and by the end of the year, the two countries agreed to form the Confederation of Senegambia (q.v.), which stressed military cooperation and coordination in foreign affairs and economic and financial matters. The promises of confederation were not realized, however, and the project was abandoned in September 1989.

In 1983, Diouf was elected president in his own right with 82 percent of the vote, partially because the opposition parties were badly fragmented. The ruling PS won 111 out of 120 seats in the National Assembly. There was also a heavy abstention rate. Diouf then took steps to replace the old-line politicians with younger men, which created some tension in the government and the party. He also strengthened the office of president and abolished the office of prime minister. In 1985, Diouf was elected head of the Organization of African Unity. A deteriorating economy, a growing separatist movement in the Casamance (q.v.) and the failure of the Senegambian confederation posed many problems for Diouf. Diouf and the PS faced serious opposition from Abdoulaye Wade (q.v.) in the April 1988 elections. Diouf won easily with 73 percent of the popular vote, and his PS party won 103 out of 120 seats. There was evidence of some vote rigging, however, which sparked disturbances in Dakar. Diouf declared a state of emergency to quell the unrest. Since the 1988 election, Diouf has steadily lost some public support. The latest elections were held in early 1993.

In 1989, Diouf abolished the post of prime minister and dismissed Jean Colin (q.v.), a longtime government minister and influential political figure of French nationality. In 1991, Diouf re-created the post of prime minister. He also invited opposition leader Abdoulaye Wade to join the government as a minister of state.

Diouf has retained close ties with France, both politically and culturally. The relationship between Senegal and France was strengthened by the election of François Mitterand and the Socialist Party in France in 1981. In the disputes among African countries over Western Sahara and Chad in 1982 and 1983, Diouf sided with the conservative states, supporting the Moroccan position in the former case and opposing Libya in the latter. The Libyan leader, Muammar al-Gaddafi, visited Dakar in November 1985, but major political differences remain between the two countries. Senegal has also monitored events closely in neighboring Guinea since the death of Sekou Toure. Relations with Mauritania broke down completely after clashes between Senegalese and Mauritanians in April 1989. (See MOORS.) In neighboring Mali, the overthrow of longtime military ruler Moussa Traore in 1990 was welcomed by the Senegalese government, but they did not play an active role in the revolt.

DIOUF, GALANDOU. (1875–1941) In 1909, Diouf was elected to represent the commune of Rufisque in the General Council at Saint-Louis (q.v.), making him the first African elected to office since the conquest. Born in Saint-Louis and raised as a Muslim, Diouf attended Catholic secondary school before embarking on a career as a teacher and minor bureaucrat. He became a defender of African equality and opponent of discrimination. He maintained enough moderation to rise to the position of chief accountant for the merchant firm Buhan and Teisseire in Rufisque, where he won the respect of both Muslim Africans and the Bordeaux merchant community. In the famous first election of 1909, these two interests combined to put him in office, and throughout his career he was faithful to both. A strong believer in the corrective power of the press, he collaborated on *La Démocratie* and later founded his own paper, *Le Sénégal.* Despite his early prominence, Diouf was rapidly surpassed by Blaise Diagne (q.v.), whose career was partially launched by Diouf. The rivalry between the two was open in the late twenties, when Diouf ran unsuccessfully against his protégé Diagne for deputy. Their competition was mirrored in a succession struggle among their Murid (q.v.) backers, when Diouf was allied with the unsuccessful Shaix Anta Mbake, while Diouf supported the successful *Xalifa-Général* Mamadu Mustafa Mbake (q.v.). After Diagne's death in 1934, Diouf succeeded him as deputy, but had an undistinguished Depression-era tenure in Paris.

DRAME, AL-HAJJ MAMADU LAMINE. Also called Mamadu Lamine or Demba Dibassi Drame. (c. 1835–87). Soninke cleric in the upper Senegal valley who led one of the briefest but most important reform movements in the late nineteenth century during the period of French conquest and African resistance. He has variously been portrayed as a Muslim reformer, an anti-imperialist resistance hero and, most frequently, a Soninke ''nationalist'' against the French and their main allies in the upper Senegal, the Fulbe.

Mamadu Lamine was born about 1835 into a family of Soninke marabouts (q.v.) at Gunjuru, an important center of Islamic learning in Khasso (western Mali). According to traditions, he joined the jihad of al-Hajj Umar Tal (q.v.) in the 1850s, and then travelled to Mecca where he spent several years and gained enormous prestige from his hajj (q.v.). In the late 1870s, he began his return to the upper Senegal, visiting the Islamic states of Masina and, probably in 1880, Segu, the capital of Amadu Sheku Tal (q.v.), son and successor of al-Hajj Umar Tal (q.v.). Relations between Amadu and Lamine quickly turned hostile, and Lamine was imprisoned until 1885. Upon his release, he returned to Khasso and preached religious reform and attacks on non-

Muslim states in the upper Senegal. Because of his antago-
nism toward Amadu Sheku, an enemy of the French, some
colonial officials initially regarded Lamine favorably, and he
moved freely about the region.

Lamine's first strategic move was in Bundu (q.v.) in late
1885, when he sought permission from Bokar Saada Sy
(q.v.), a French ally, to travel to Gamon in the south. He was
rebuffed by the *almamy,* who died shortly thereafter in
December 1885. Bokar Saada's successor did not have the
support of the Sy family, and by early 1886, Lamine
effectively controlled all of Bundu, with support from Fulbe,
Mandinka and Soninke inhabitants. He soon exerted control
over most of the upper Senegal valley, excluding the French
forts at Bakel (q.v.), Medine and Kayes. In April 1886, the
French under Henri Frey, who had been occupied with
Samori Turé in the south, attacked Lamine. The Soninke
leader drove them back, cut the telegraph line and besieged
the fort at Bakel. When reinforcements arrived, he was
driven south into the southern Bundu province of Diakha.
His capital at Diana became an important commercial center,
and caravans travelling to both the Gambia and Senegal
River valleys included Lamine's headquarters.

The tide turned in late 1886, when Joseph Gallieni replaced Frey and mobilized his considerably enlarged forces
in the fight against Lamine. Gallieni marched through
Bundu, destroying many settlements, including Diana. Lamine fled first to Nettebulu and then to Tubactua in the upper
Gambian state of Wuli (q.v.). He shifted his base of operations to the upper Gambia, but his forces were demoralized
by recent defeats and deserted the movement. In December
1887, a French force led by Gallieni pursued and killed
Lamine in the upper Gambia area.

After Lamine's death, the Fulbe Sy lineage was restored in
Bundu under French hegemony. The colonial administration
turned its attention in the upper Senegal to reestablishing
control, maintaining order and preventing future rebellions.

The entire region was placed formally under French protectorate, and the military and bureaucracy were expanded. Today Soninke oral traditions focus on the glories of Mamadu Lamine and his revolt against the Fulbe and the French.

DROUGHT. A frequent scourge, either localized or generalized in the Senegambia, owing to the highly irregular arrival of the rain-bearing intertropical front from the south. The severe Sahel-wide drought of 1968 through 1973, renewed in 1976 through 1978, intensified research into its causes, consequences and possible mitigation. A less severe drought occurred in 1983 through 1985, and the rainy season of 1991 was also erratic throughout most of the country. The search for a cyclical pattern in the twentieth century has proven fruitless, although a long-term trend toward desiccation is perceived by some scientists. The last major drought prior to independence in Senegal was in 1911 through 1914, and earlier ones are recorded in 1864–1871, 1846–1853, 1747–1758, 1680, 1639–1642 and 1536.

The major consequences of the droughts of the 1970s and 1980s were widespread malnutrition, despite international emergency food aid, the decimation of herds, especially cattle, and migration of both people and herds toward better-watered areas or cities. Long-term social and political consequences are still being debated. At the national level, groundnut revenues, which in 1966 constituted about 70 percent of Senegal's total exports by value, fell from 26,600 million CFA to 15,275 million CFA, or 36 percent of exports in 1976. These figures have declined throughout the 1980s. Development strategies inspired by the drought experience include crop diversification, attention to ecology, numerous rural development programs concerned with health, nutrition and water supply and, finally, a determination to seek food self-sufficiency through dam construction for irrigation on the Senegal, Gambia and Casamance Rivers. (See OMVS.)

DUMBUYA, *FODE* KABA. (baptized Ibrahima, and usually called Fodé Kaba) (c. 1818–1901) Jaxanke (q.v.) cleric who conquered and Islamized parts of the lower Casamance beginning about 1870 and culminating in 1901 when French forces annihilated his *tata* (q.v.), or headquarters, at Medina-Fodé Kaba (formerly Bapikum).

Born into a clerical family, Ibrahima (later Fodé Kaba) emigrated with his father Fodé Bakari to Kerewan, near the present Gambia–Casamance border. They built a power base on their religious following, with Bakari serving as spiritual leader while Fodé Kaba took military command. The marabouts armed themselves early and well, trading directly with British and French private traders and collecting arms and munitions from African Jula traders travelling through their territory. About 1870, the Dumbuyas broke with their local overlord, killing him and his prominent Fulbe marabout Abdul Xudoso, a missionary sent by the almamy of Futa Jalon. The marabout's death enraged the almamy, who invited another local ally, *Alfa* Molo Balde (q.v.), to avenge it. That was the beginning of the Dumbuya–Balde feud, which dominated the Casamance into the early twentieth century.

The vendetta became a focus of larger historical forces: ethnic, sectarian and territorial political rivalries all operating in the shadow of encroaching French and British imperialism. The old Mande Kabu empire was deteriorating, with the active encouragement of its expansive Fulbe neighbor, Futa Jalon. Fodé Kaba based his own expansion on Mande and Jaxanke recruits, and allied himself with Kabu and with the Tijaniyya movement headed by Ma Ba's (q.v.) brother, Mamur Ndari. His rivals *Alfa* and later Musa Molo (q.v.) of Fuladu spearheaded local Fulbe nationalism and allied with Qadiri clerical chiefs in Futa Jalon. British and French authorities, jockeying for position along still undefined borders, offered protection alternately for several decades to whichever African ruler the other was pursuing.

Fodé Kaba's father was killed by Alfa Molo at the beginning of the struggles in 1870 in vengeance for the death of Abdul Xudoso. Informed of his father's death while at the court of Mamur Ndari in Rip, Fodé Kaba was given 72 of the latter's best cavalry to help him avenge it. As they crossed the Gambia, messengers came from Alfa Molo proposing peace—all but one were killed on the spot as Fodé Kaba's answer. Throughout the Seventies his forces tried, with little success, to dislodge the Baldes of Fuladu. In 1876, they trapped them briefly at Kerevan, but Musa Molo was able to escape.

By the later 1870s, when it was clear that Fuladu offered little prospect of collapse, Fodé Kaba turned his holy war south and west against the animist Balant, Banun and Jola. Recruiting Mandinka Muslim warriors in Pakao and Buje, by 1890 he had established a significant territorial base, embracing Foni and Kiang. He built two tatas, the main headquarters at Medina-Fodé Kaba (formerly Bapikum, Foni) and another at Dator in Kiang. Those who resisted or refused to pay him allegiance were enslaved, and revenues from the sale of slaves were invested in armaments. Conflict with the Jola was chronic and Fodé Kaba, like his expansive rivals in Fuladu and Futa Jalon, built his power primarily on slave raiding and trading.

British officials began plotting Fodé Kaba's capture in the 1880s, but the French negotiated two treaties of protection with him in 1891 and 1893. In the first, the French recognized his sovereignty over Kiang and Foni, and in the second, they took over Foni, paying him in exchange 5,000 francs annually in revenues extracted from Foni.

In 1900, the fragile modus vivendi collapsed, after a British travelling commissioner and seven men were killed by villagers loyal to Fodé Kaba. The commissioner had been trying to impose an appointed chief on the unwilling village and arrest its own chief. Subsequently, the villagers took refuge with Fodé Kaba, who refused both French and British demands to turn them over. In March 1901, French forces joined with the old enemy Musa Molo Balde to invade from the south while British troops came down from the north. The eighty-three-year-old Fodé Kaba was trapped in his fort at Medina, where he is said by his family to have perished and been buried. His body was never recovered after a thorough French search, however. The other fort at Dator was also destroyed. Musa Molo's troops took the booty and prisoners, including eldest son and heir Ibrahima, who was given slave labor to do at Hamdallahi. In 1903, when Musa Molo in turn fled from French forces into the British Gambia, Ibrahima was transferred to Podor in Futa Toro. Finally, in 1912, he was allowed to return to the Casamance and eventually made a canton chief in Inor.

- E -

ECOLE DES OTAGES (School for Hostages). Important early colonial school established in 1857 at Saint-Louis (q.v.) by Governor Louis Faidherbe (q.v.). The institution was modeled on African prototypes where the sons of provincial chiefs served political and military apprenticeships at the king's court as quasi-hostages. Faidherbe and later colonial governors required rulers whom they defeated to enroll their sons in the school. Upon graduation from a curriculum in colonial administration, the chiefs' sons returned to their homelands as French-appointed administrators. The school also trained the sons of clerics for diplomatic and interpreting roles. During Faidherbe's second term as governor (1863–65), the name was changed to Ecole des Fils de Chefs (School for the Sons of Chiefs). In the early twentieth century, it became a teachers' training school, and in 1918 was renamed the École Normale William Ponty (q.v.). Since independence in 1960, it has been called the École Normale Superieure.

ECOLE NORMALE SUPERIEURE. Training school for secondary-school teachers in Dakar. (See also ECOLE NORMALE WILLIAM PONTY.)

ECOLE NORMALE WILLIAM PONTY. As the first institution of higher education in French West Africa, the school trained the colonial elite as teachers, interpreters, clerks and lower-level civil servants. It was created in 1918 out of the old School for the Sons of Chiefs in Saint-Louis, partly because the colonial government needed low-cost, skilled manpower, and partly as a reward to the colonies for providing massive numbers of troops in World War I. It was moved to Gorée (q.v.), then in 1930 to Sebikotane, and finally back to Dakar, where following independence in 1960, it was named the Ecole Normale Superieure.

ECONOMIC COMMUNITY OF WEST AFRICA (Communauté Economique de l'Afrique de l'Ouest, CEAO). A regional organization of Francophone West African nations initiated in 1971, with President Senghor (q.v.) as the prime proponent, and inaugurated in 1973 under his presidency. Abdou Diouf (q.v.) continues to play an active role in its affairs. It aims to improve regional economic and political cooperation and the individual states' bargaining position vis-à-vis France. From its inception, it has been one formula for relating to Europe, while a rival formula is embodied in the counterpart Economic Community of West African States (ECOWAS, q.v.). The latter wields considerably more influence both regionally and internationally.

ECONOMIC COMMUNITY OF WEST AFRICAN STATES (ECOWAS; Communauté Economique des Etats de l'Afrique de l'Ouest, CEDEAO). A regional organization of all major Anglophone, Francophone and Lusophone West African states formed by treaty in 1975. By grouping countries of several former colonial masters, it aims both to break down local linguistic and historical barriers to cooperation as well as to provide a more united base for negotiations with the European Economic Community. Senegal reluctantly signed the treaty, because Senghor preferred the CEAO (q.v.), which he initiated, and because Senghor feared Nigerian (Anglophone) dominance. Abdou Diouf also prefers the CEAO and is suspicious of Nigerian and Anglophone dominance of ECOWAS.

ECONOMY. *Precolonial.* Agriculture, pastoralism, trade and craft manufacture dominated the economies of most of the societies and states in the Senegambian region. The trans-Atlantic slave trade figured prominently in the economies of coastal regions. (See listings for individual states.)

Colonial. During the early years of colonial rule, the French encouraged groundnut (q.v.) production and throughout most of the colonial period, the colony of Senegal had a monocrop economy based on the groundnut. Africans also continued to cultivate food crops, practice herding and crafts and engage in local, regional and long-distance trade. The Great Depression of the 1930s hit Senegal's monocrop economy particularly hard.

Independence. More than 30 years after Senegal achieved independence, its resource-poor economy remains fragile and dependent upon groundnuts and international donors for continued viability. Independent Senegal's overall economic performance has been disappointing, even though its economy is one of the more developed in West Africa. Between 1965 and 1990, the average annual GNP growth rate was negative (approximately -0.6 percent). The country's major resources are agriculture, fishing, mining and manufacturing (each q.v.). Livestock husbandry includes cattle, sheep, goats and poultry. The country's economic fortunes are still tied to variations in the volume and value of groundnut exports. Though declining in importance during the last five years or so, the groundnut industry remains at the heart of the economy. Output has fluctuated between more than 1 million metric tons in good years to less than 500,000 tons in drought years.

GNP is only $650, and unemployment and underemployment remain extremely high. Urban unemployment in 1990 was estimated at 25 to 30 percent. Senegal also has a large outstanding international debt, which totalled a projected $200 million in fiscal year 1991. Shortfalls in food production, owing partly to population growth and partly to drought, have necessitated substantial food imports and occasionally food aid.

EDUCATION. Although Western education was introduced during the first half of the nineteenth century, it was not until the last half of the century that an organized education system was established. The real basis for western education was laid by Governor Louis Faidherbe (q.v.) in the late 1850s. The education system of Senegal and French West Africa was designed to train people to assist in the running of the colonies and to inculcate Africans with French culture. The structures and content of education followed ever more closely the system of metropolitan France.

Independent Senegal inherited the core of the educational system of colonial French West Africa and has increased enrollment without altering its basic structure or orientation. The system is highly centralized geographically and administratively. Planning, personnel, enrollment and curriculum decisions are made in Dakar for the entire country. The Ministry of National Education is responsible for elementary and secondary schools, and the Ministry of Higher Education governs the university and professional and technical schools.

French is the language of instruction at all levels, and the basic goal is to produce an elite of graduates comparable to those in France. The ideal has been modified to allow some "Africanization" of the curriculum content in primary schools and to a lesser extent in secondary and post-secondary. In the colonial period, the system graduated clerks, interpreters, teachers, lower-level civil servants and chiefs. Since 1960, the system has produced mostly bureaucrats and teachers, with only a sprinkling of other professionals. Efforts to develop a technical education providing the skills necessary for Senegal's economic development have been frustrated by resistance among students, parents, politicians and French advisors.

Public facilities are free and provide for elementary, secondary and higher levels of education. Education is compulsory at the primary-school level, but there are not enough places to accommodate all children. In the rural areas, most children never attend school. Each of the three levels is divided into alternate short and long cycles, the completion of which usually entitles students to hold certain certificates. Students are required to pass qualifying examinations to pass to the next level.

Overall enrollment in Senegalese schools has more than quadrupled since independence, from 143,000 to approximately 765,000 in 1989, with female enrollment growing by 56 percent. In 1989, 56 percent of the primary-age cohort attends school, up from 46 percent in 1980. Secondary-school enrollment has increased from 11 to 13 percent of the twelve- to seventeen-year-old cohort, while university enrollment has nearly doubled. The University Cheikh Anta Diop in Dakar had 14,500 students registered in 1989. Between 75 percent and 80 percent of adults were thought to be illiterate in 1988. (See also MEDICAL EDUCATION, ECOLE NORMALE WILLIAM PONTY, UNIVERSITY OF DAKAR/CHEIKH ANTA DIOP.)

ELECTIONS. Presidential and general elections have been held every five years since 1963. The 1963 elections were necessitated by the Constitutional Crisis of 1962 (q.v.). During Senghor's term of office (until 1980), the president and his party, the Parti Socialiste (q.v.), won overwhelming majorities in every election. There were high absentee rates as well, however. In 1963, Senghor and his party were unopposed, winning 94.2 percent of the vote. Senghor ran unopposed again in February 1968, but two months later there were serious student and national strikes called by labor unions. In 1978, Senghor allowed the opposition party, the Parti Démocratie Sénégalais (q.v.), led by Abdoulaye Wade (q.v.), to run candidates in both presidential and general elections. Senghor was reelected with 81.7 percent, against Wade's 17.7 percent. The PS took 82 seats in the National Assembly, while the PDS and the PAI (q.v.) opposition won 18 seats.

Abdou Diouf took over the presidency when Senghor resigned on December 31, 1980. Diouf served out the remainder of Senghor's term and then announced elections for April 1983 as scheduled. By election time, 14 parties were officially recognized, but only Wade's PDS posed any challenge. Diouf was elected president in his own right with 82 percent of the vote, partially because of the fragmented opposition. The PS won 111 seats; the PDS won 8 seats, and the RND (q.v.) won 1 seat.

The most recent elections in Senegal were held in February 1988. Diouf won 73.5 percent, with Wade taking 25.8 percent in the presidential vote. In the general election, out of 120 seats, the PS won 103 seats, and the PDS won 17 seats. While some observers believed that the election had been plagued with fewer irregularities than in the past, opposition protests against alleged fraud and ballot-box stuffing sparked serious rioting in Dakar. Wade and other opposition leaders were arrested, tried, convicted but then granted amnesty and freed.

The last election was held in early 1993. The PS retained power, and Diouf will most likely run again and win in 1998. At present, there is no limit on the number of presidential terms.

ELIMAN. Wolof and Pulaar adaptation of the Arabic title *al-Imam,* designating the one who leads the Muslim congregation in prayer. By extension, it also means the head of a mosque, of a particular clerical community or of a polity ruled by clerics. (See also ALMAMY; BUNDU; CAPE VERDE.)

ESCALE. The French term for port of call. In the Senegal River (q.v.) trade, it designated annual fairs organized and administered by African states at fixed points along the river during the gum arabic (q.v.) and grain trade months from February through May. The major points were the Escale du Desert in Walo (q.v.) and the Escales du Coq and Terrier Rouge in Futa Toro (q.v.) near Podor. A "floating post" (*escale flottant*), based on a barge moored to the riverbank, operated in the upper river region. At the beginning of each fair, prices and other terms of trade were fixed by negotiation between representatives of buyers and sellers. They were enforced by brokers and market authorities assigned by local rulers. The French resented their dependency on this structure and sought repeatedly to establish forts along the river so they could trade year-round and administer the market themselves. They occasionally had an isolated fort in the upper river region during the slave trade (see, e.g., BAKEL), but it was only with the beginning of the conquest period in the mid-nineteenth century that they succeeded in establishing a chain of forts along the Senegal River.

EVOLUE. An anachronistic term used to designate someone who has supposedly evolved to the French level of civilization, as determined by the French. Drawing on the language of social Darwinism that was popular among many Europeans during the colonial period, the term was used to refer to an African who had been educated in French and/or adopted French customs. An *évolué* could change his legal status from *sujet* (q.v.) to *citoyen* (q.v., French citizen) by requesting classification as an *assimilé* (q.v.).

- F -

FACTOR, FACTORY. Throughout the era of the slave trade (q.v.), European companies maintained small local trading posts on the coast or on the upper Senegal River as liaisons with their larger trading networks. In contrast to the *escales* (q.v.), these factories were permanent posts, but without the fortifications and military presence characterized by European forts. The trading post was called a factory, and the agent stationed there was named a factor. In the colonial period, the term was extended to all small trading posts manned by Europeans, Lebanese (q.v.) and Moors (q.v.) in the interior and linked to the major European import-export houses.

FAIDHERBE, LOUIS LEON CESAR. (1818–89). The most famous and arguably the most influential governor of colonial Senegal, serving from 1854–1861 and again from 1863–1865. He is credited with initiating the French West African empire and, to a large extent, determining its administrative structure.

A career military officer who had participated in the French conquest of the Algerian interior, Faidherbe was posted to Senegal in 1852 as a captain of the engineers. Powerful local Bordeaux merchants, recognizing his aggressiveness and strategic brilliance, requested in 1854 that he be assigned to replace the existing governor. Both Faidherbe and the merchants hoped to establish French hegemony over the entire Senegal River (q.v.), overland to the Niger River and down the coast to Sierra Leone. The merchants wanted to trade when and where they pleased, with neither African control nor British competition, and without customs obligations, river tolls and the market administration system of their African trading partners (see ESCALE). Faidherbe predicted this could be done the same way the Algerian interior was being occupied, by a series of fortified posts linked by telegraph lines and mobile reinforcements. Initial wars would be necessary in most instances, but he expected minimal resistance.

During his first term as governor, Faidherbe implemented the first stages of his plan by waging war against every major power along the Senegal River and down the coast, and by constructing a telegraph and numerous small forts and blockhouses. The initial wars, however, caused fierce local resistance (q.v.), sparking a period of almost 50 years before the conquest was complete. His most formidable foe in Senegal was al-Hajj Umar Tal (q.v.), whom Faidherbe defeated at Medine (Khasso) and drove into the Western Sudan interior (modern-day Mali). Faidherbe quickly exerted French control over most of the upper Senegal region, appointing loyal African allies like Bokar Saada Sy (q.v.) in Bundu (q.v.). Faidherbe's strategic brilliance, daring and administrative energy earned him the rank of brigadier general by his second term. He also established a territorial administration throughout the colony of Senegal, with officials assigned to specific regions and charged with supervising local chiefs. He divided the colony into three *arrondissements:* Saint-Louis (or Lower Senegal), Gorée (including all French possessions south to Sierra Leone) and Bakel (or Upper Senegal). The *arrondissements* were divided into *cercles.*

In addition to his military and administrative service in Senegal, Faidherbe wrote extensively about French "pacification" in Senegambia, though he focused on the jihad of al-Hajj Umar in the 1850s. His version of the French conquest of Senegal was, until recently, accepted as standard. He also wrote about other topics, including Senegambian languages, Islam and local and ethnic history, but with considerably less skill and enthusiasm than his own exploits. Although never healthy after his tropical service, he lived to serve with distinction in the Franco-Prussian War.

Among the many colonial institutions and practices that

trace their origins to Faidherbe are the Ecole Normale William Ponty (q.v.); the Tirailleurs Sénégalais (q.v.); the Muslim Tribunal of Saint-Louis; government sponsorship of loyal clerics' pilgrimages to Mecca; and the publication of the *Moniteur du Sénégal* (q.v.).

FAL, AMAR. (or HAMMAD) (c.1660–17??) Founder of the famous Islamic school at Pir Sanoxor (q.v.) in Kajor (q.v.), c. 1690–1700. Born about 1660 in Kajor of a nonruling branch of a royal patrilineage, Fal was taken to Futa Toro (q.v.) at an early age by his father, possibly in the 1670s during the Tubenan (q.v.) religious reform movement. He was raised in Futa Toro and married the daughters of two prominent *torodo* (q.v.) clerics. He moved back to Kajor to the outlying clerically dominated province of Njambur, but the king considered him too dangerous to be allowed to stay there. Instead, he was invited to be *Qadi,* head of the clerical community of the kingdom and advisor to the crown. After some years the Wolof clergy had him ousted, complaining that he spoke Pulaar, the dominant language of Futa Toro, rather than his native Wolof. He returned to Futa Toro, and only after several years did his sons return to reclaim the estate at Pir that the king had given him.

Demba Hady Fal, his successor, is remembered in traditions as highly educated and radical, like his father and grandfather. During the eighteenth century, he trained a generation of Wolof and Futanke clerics at Pir in Islamic law. The founder of the *almamate* of Futa Toro, Abdul Qadir Kan (q.v.), studied with him. Another of his pupils was Matar Ndumbe Jop (q.v.), founder of the Islamic school at Koki (q.v.), which also became a center for the spread of theology and law.

FAL, AMARY NGONE SOBEL. (c.1530-c.1600) Founder of independent Kajor (q.v.) and Bawol (q.v.), c. 1550. Amary's father, Njugu Penda Fal, was *Damel* of Kajor, and his maternal uncle Noxor Njai was *Ten* of Bawol in the first half of the sixteenth century, when both kingdoms were still tributary to the Jolof Empire (q.v.). There are several different traditions concerning the struggle for independence. The events on which they agree are that Amary persuaded his father and uncle to refuse the tribute they owed Jolof and then led their united forces in defeating the *Bur-ba Jolof* Lel Fuli Fak at Danky, c. 1550. After the victory, the electors of both kingdoms chose Amary Ngone as Damel of Kajor and *Ten* of Bawol. Jolof never recovered its empire, and other provinces followed Amary Ngone's lead, leaving it an isolated remnant of a kingdom.

The causes of this independence movement are obscure and can only be inferred. Some oral traditions describe it as a simple independence of spirit in Amary Ngone Sobel. Written sources suggest Portuguese (q.v.) trade, particularly in horses, may have been an important factor on which Amary capitalized. Until the previous century, Kajor and Bawol had been at the outer periphery of a continental commercial and political network centered on Tekrur (q.v.) to the north and the Ghana, Mali, and Songhai empires in the interior. All the empires had based their military superiority on cavalry, while Kajor and Bawol were still affected by tsetse fly and lacked access to fresh supplies of horses. For a century before the wars of independence, Portuguese had been trading at several ports along the coasts of Kajor and Bawol, especially importing horses and iron.

During a reign lasting most of the last half of the sixteenth century, Amary Ngone consolidated his rule, built a new capital at Mbul and became a trusted trading partner of the Portuguese. Kajor offered them beeswax, amber, slaves, musk, gum arabic, hides, ivory and cotton cloth. Imports included horses, wines, iron, jewelry, cloth and some slaves from elsewhere on the coast. Amary Ngone left the throne of Kajor to his son Massamba Tako and that of Bawol to the latter's son (by Amary Ngone's own sister) Mamlik Coro. In an attempt to reunite the two crowns—a goal that was to become the plague of the Fal dynasties—Mamlik attacked and killed his father. He was, however, immediately chased out of Kajor by his paternal uncles and the nobles, so that the succession remained divided.

FAL, LAT SUKABE NGONE JEY. (ruled 1697–1719). One of the most powerful and famous joint *Damel-Ten* of Kajor and Bawol (both q.v.). The son of an obscure matrilineage (Gej) and a hitherto nonreigning branch of the royal patrilineage (Fal, Ker Ce Yasin), he came to power when the kingdom had been in a state of crisis for more than 30 years in the wake of the Tubenan (q.v.) religious reform movement.

After wresting the throne of Bawol from his two elder brothers, Lat Sukabe conquered Kajor, to which he had no hereditary claim. Traditions remember him as the first damel to use firearms extensively (though they were known along the coast long before then), which may help explain his success. Once in power, he proved to be an astute politician, solidifying not only his own rule, but establishing his Gej matrilineage in Kajor for the next two centuries. He greatly expanded the crown-slave army, appointed loyal vassals and engineered a set of marriages to ensure continuity. He also temporarily solved the problem of relations between clerics (q.v.) and the state, giving them important offices and privileges instead of fighting them as his predecessors had. He built his capital at Maka on the border between Kajor and Bawol, but it was rarely used by his successors. At his death, he left the throne of Kajor to the son of a wife from Kajor (Isaa Tend) and that of Bawol to the sons of a wife from Bawol (Kumba Jareng Njay). The struggle to reunite the two thrones immediately resumed.

FAL, SHAIX IBRA. (1858–1930). Chief disciple of the Murid (q.v.) founder Amadu Bamba Mbake (q.v.) and founder of a distinctive strain within Muridism. In his origins, personal ethos and legacy he represents a direct link between the *cedo* (q.v.) of the precolonial Wolof kingdoms and the Murids.

Born in a crown-slave family two years before the first French invasion of his native Kajor (q.v.), he grew up in a society where *cedo* were being eliminated by the French and rejected by their own people. Positions of religious, political and military leadership were passing into the hands of clerics. Fal performed his obeisance to Amadu Bamba in traditional crown-slave fashion, disrobing and falling forward to the ground. He was accepted and given authority, but apparently not obliged to abstain from alcohol as other Muslims did. He became the rallying point for the many courtiers who joined Amadu Bamba, to the shock and dismay of many contemporary *marabouts*. He and his branch kept the *cedo* traditions, wearing colorful rags and tatters, wide leather belts, long tresses, carrying a huge wooden club and drinking regularly from the familiar flask of spirits, all of which was abhorrent to clerics.

Of the three major teachings of Amadu Bamba—piety, obedience and hard work—Fal made a fetish of the latter two and totally rejected piety. Those who were recruited into his branch, known as the *Bay Fal,* worked the *Xalifa*'s farms, did heavy road and railroad construction, formed his bodyguard, kept order, or at least terrorized the crowd at religious gatherings, and neither studied, fasted, nor prayed. Although formed around a crown-slave nucleus, the Bay Fal were joined by volunteers from caste (q.v.) and slave (q.v.) backgrounds, and possibly some freeborn. The organization has continued since Shaix Ibra's death in 1930, under a Xalifa, his oldest son, who in turn depends on the Xalifa-General of the Murids. Under the Xalifa are the sub-branches, each headed by a *shaix* descended from Shaix Ibra.

FARABANNA. A famous refuge slave haven in Bambuk (q.v.), the village had a reputation in the nineteenth century for being entirely populated by runaway slaves from Bundu (q.v.) and Khasso (western Mali). After a series of wars in the 1820s with neighboring Bambuk communities, Bundu and Khasso, the chief of Farabanna promised freedom to any slave who sought refuge in the severely depopulated settlement. By the mid-nineteenth century, between 3,000 and 4,000 people of diverse ethnicity resided in the village. The runaways had to work in mining and agriculture for the village chief for five years before obtaining their freedom.

Al-Hajj Umar Tal (q.v.) briefly established his capital at Farabanna in 1854. Besides its strategic location above the confluence of the Senegal and Faleme Rivers, the settlement had been an unwelcome symbol of resistance to the rulers of nearby polities whom Umar wished to court. In order to secure their allegiance, Umar returned some of the refugee slaves in Farabanna to their former masters. After Umar moved his capital in 1855, local rulers constantly tried to reclaim their slaves, initially through force and then, with the establishment of French control, by diplomatic means. In the 1860s and 1870s, Bokar Saada Sy (q.v.) reinstituted the policy of raiding the settlement and the surrounding area for "runaway slaves." French officials generally ignored his raids. Farabanna functioned as a "safety valve" for slaves in the area and threatened an important source of wealth for the ruling families of Bundu and Khasso.

FELOUP. See JOLA.

FERLO. The dry, sparsely inhabited wasteland covering much of the northern half of the interior of Senegal, immediately south of the fertile riverbanks and east of the groundnut basin. The annual rainfall is so scanty and the thin, sandy soil so porous that water can be obtained during the dry season only from wells located along the few shallow depressions that cross the flat landscape. Several deep well pumping stations have been built in recent years. Fulbe, Moor and

Wolof herders and farmers have found parts of it to be suitable pasture and farmland only in the rainy season.

FESTIVAL OF NEGRO ARTS. Pan-African cultural fair that was held in Dakar in 1966. The first conference was held at the Sorbonne in Paris in 1956, and the second took place in Rome in 1959. The third festival, held in Africa for the first time, was a practical and symbolic triumph. Bringing together black artists and performers from around the world, but especially from the many newly independent African countries, the festival celebrated the flowering of an African cultural renaissance. During a period of three weeks, more than 10,000 visitors from 37 nations attended the festival. Artists, connoisseurs and politicians alike were inspired by the diverse geographic origins of the participants and the artistic richness of their contributions. The festival was a tremendous personal triumph for President Senghor (q.v.) and a national triumph for Senegal. The universally acclaimed success of the event led to its institutionalization. It was decided to hold similar festivals in African capitals every five years, and subsequent gatherings have been held in Algiers and Lagos. Yet, administrative disputes and economic problems have delayed recent stagings of the festival.

FISHING. Numerous ethnic groups have engaged in fishing along the coast and rivers since precolonial times. The fishing sector is one of the premier hard currency earners for independent Senegal. Fishing became important in the late 1970s, accounting for between a fifth and a quarter of export earnings. In 1988, the total catch was about 400,000 metric tons. Government estimates for 1988 show that Senegal earned about $210 million from its exports of fish and fish products, about 28 percent of merchandise export earnings. The government earns additional revenue from foreign vessels fishing in Senegalese waters. Joint-venture companies have been set up with European fishing concerns, but there have been several long-standing disputes about the proportion of catches landed in Senegalese waters. The issue was settled in 1986 with aid from the European Community. A new fishing code was introduced in mid-1987, and an additional two-year agreement with EC nations took effect in February 1988. The agreement was renewed for another two years in 1990.

FLEUVE (RIVER). The northernmost administrative region of Senegal, which takes its name from the Senegal River (q.v.). More generally, the term also refers to both the Mauritanian and Senegalese banks of the river from its mouth on the Atlantic coast to about Matam in the upper river area. This larger area is considered the Futanke (q.v.) homeland, although Wolof dominate the delta area, and Mande groups, especially the Soninke, predominate in the upper river region.

The ancient empire of Tekrur (q.v.) developed beside the river beginning in the fourth century and flourished in the tenth and eleventh centuries. It was succeeded by the Jolof Empire (q.v.) and then beginning about 1490 by the independent kingdoms of Futa Toro (q.v.) in the middle valley, and Gajaaga (q.v.) in the upper valley.

Portuguese (q.v.) explorers and traders arrived at the river mouth in 1444, and Dutch, English and French followed in the seventeenth century. In the seventeenth through the nineteenth centuries, the river became the main artery of French commercial penetration into the Senegambia, in competition with the British to the south on the Gambia River. Slaves and gold from the upper Senegambia-Niger area could be exported by either route or north across the Sahara Desert. Polities along the river attracted wealth and population because of this commerce, but also experienced severe internal conflict, primarily through centuries of exposure to the slave trade (q.v.). In 1776 *marabouts* (q.v.) established a state in Futa Toro, vowing to provide citizens greater protection from enslavement. They were able to prohibit the export of their own citizens and collect tolls on other slave cargos. Yet, while unable to create a stable political system, they made Futa Toro the main source of clerical leadership in Senegambia.

The last great cleric from Futa Toro, *al-Hajj* Umar Tal (q.v.) inspired a host of disciples and imitators throughout Senegambia and across the Western Sudan. One of the effects of his campaigns was to begin out-migration, which has had a disastrous effect on the fortunes of the region. Recruitment for his and his son's campaigns began in the 1850s and continued until the defeat of 1890, draining thousands annually from Futa Toro to their upper-Senegal-Niger base.

During the conquest, the French used the river as their main artery into the interior. With colonial rule, the exodus continued because the river region had lost its central economic importance to the peanut basin and the coast, served by railroads. Futanke emigrants were the first to respond to the completion of the Dakar-Bamako railroad in 1923 by moving to terminal towns. A head tax, payable in cash only, obliged men to seek wage-earning employment. Their homeland along the river lost its men, while women, children and the elderly sank into a stagnant system of subsistence farming.

Since independence, the government of Senegal has tried to reverse this trend, but with little success. Construction of dams on the upper river has been supervised by the OMVS (q.v.) to permit year-round irrigation in the river valley and to make the river navigable as far as Kayes, Mali. The region's future depends greatly on this project.

FODE KABA. See DUMBUYA, FODE KABA.

FRANC, CFA. The basic currency of the states of former French West Africa, except Guinea and Mauritania, which have established independent currencies. Mali had its own currency until 1983, when it joined the CFA group. The CFA is issued by the Banque Centrale des Etats de l'Afrique de l'Ouest (CFAO, q.v.), which in 1974 moved its headquarters from Paris to Dakar. From its origins in 1946 until 1962, the initials CFA referred to "Colonies Françaises d'Afrique," and since then to the "Communauté Financière d'Afrique," created by most of the former French colonies. The BCEAO franc, which is tied to the French franc, is freely convertible as follows: at parity with the Central African CFA franc; 5 CFA = 1 Mauritanian Ouguiya.

FRENCH WEST AFRICA. (Afrique Occidentale Française, AOF). Following the military conquest of the 1880s and 1890s, the French territories of Senegal, Guinea, the Sudan and Ivory Coast were united under a single command in 1895. In 1899, Dahomey was added, and in 1902 the AOF was declared a federation, with a government-general headquartered at Dakar (q.v.). Between 1919 and 1922, the Sahelian territories from Mauritania to Niger were added to the federation, making its total land area more than 4.5 million square kilometers, nine times the size of France.

In 1902, when the government-general was given general budgetary discretion and, in particular, control over customs receipts, Senegal kept its fiscal autonomy but lost most of its revenues. Senegalese colonial politics during the early part of the century revolved around this problem, and around the misfortune of having the governor at Saint-Louis (q.v.) and the governor-general at Dakar. In the post-World War II period of African electoral politics, the main issue in AOF politics became whether France would grant self-government at independence to a united AOF or to individual colonies. The 1956 *loi cadre* (q.v.) resolved the question in favor of disintegration.

FULA. Mande (q.v.) term for the Fulbe (q.v.) This term has also been adopted into Gambian English, and sometimes in Senegal Oriental and upper Casamance into French usage.

FULADU. Late nineteenth-century *almamate* built by *Alfa* Molo Balde (q.v.), reportedly with the blessing of al-Hajj Umar Tal (q.v.) and the help of the *Alfa* of Labe in Futa Jalon (modern-day Guinea), to which *Alfa* Molo remained tributary. Between 1867 and 1872, *Alfa* Molo and his Fulbe Firdu followers subdued three small Mandinka states, Kantora, Tomani and Jimara, situated on the south bank of the Gambia River. In subsequent years his son and general, Musa Molo, extended the realm and organized the territorial administration. When *Alfa* Molo died in 1881, succession legally passed to the *Alfa*'s brother Bakari, but Musa also sought power. By 1893, after a decade of struggle, Musa was able to reconquer the kingdom and end the tribute to Futa Jalon. Caught between Muslim reformers and European conquerors, Musa Molo instituted a totalitarian regime unequaled in Senegambian history. He ruled by decree, assassinated potential rivals and taxed heavily. During the 1890s, he kept the kingdom allied with the French, playing off British and Portuguese competitors, for the French were not yet ready to conquer and administer. In 1903, as the French penetrated the Casamance and built a post at Musa's capital, Hamdallahi, Musa moved to the British portion of his kingdom, where he ruled until his exile in 1919.

FULBE (sing. PULO). Term for the predominantly pastoral people known as the Peul among French ethnologists. It is the Fulbe's own designation for themselves, whereas Peul comes from the Wolof.

The Fulbe, one of the most sizable populations and easily the largest pastoral group in West Africa, are dispersed throughout the Sahel and savanna zones from southern Mauritania to Chad and Cameroon. Arbitrary distinctions between Muslim and non-Muslim and between nomadic and sedentary Fulbe have caused variations in terminology and some confusion among researchers. All Fulbe speak Fulfulde, and those in the upper Senegal valley call themselves

Haalpulaar'en (speakers of Pulaar, the local dialect of Fulfulde). English observers in northern Nigeria used the Hausa term, Fulani, while ethnographers in the Gambia and Sierra Leone borrowed the Mande word, Fula. Consequently, people with an essentially similar language, identity and social structure appear in the ethnographic and historic literature under a variety of names. Fulbe are found throughout Senegal, especially in northern and eastern regions.

Nineteenth-century French ethnographers divided *Haalpulaar'en* into Toucouleurs (or Tukolors) originally from Futa Toro, and Peuls (or Peuhls) consisting of Fulbe from other areas. By the mid-nineteenth century, Toucouleur had become the standard designation in the French literature for Fulbe considered "Muslim fanatics," openly hostile to European commercial and military activity and in favor of the establishment and maintenance of an Islamic state. In the 1850s, al-Hajj Umar Tal (q.v.) of Futa Toro, given his tense relations with the French and his call to jihad (q.v.), reinforced this stereotypical image. The Toucouleur were contrasted with the seemingly more docile and cooperative Peuls of the upper river region and the upper Casamance.

Several theories have been advanced concerning Fulbe origins. Oral traditions consistently point to an eastern origin, perhaps in the Middle East, which is a common theme in West African Muslim traditions. Earlier European ethnographers made wild speculations linking the Fulbe to the lost tribes of Israel, to Egyptians and to Berbers. They may have been descended from a pastoral group inhabiting the Western Sahara in the Chadian wet phase 5,000 to 10,000 years ago and to have moved into the Mauritanian Adrar as the Sahara dried up. Later they may have gradually filtered down into the Senegal River Valley and the Sahel zone along the Senegal and Niger rivers. Whatever their mythical origins, the Fulbe language, Fulfulde, belongs to the West Atlantic subgroup along with Wolof and Serer (both q.v.).

Fulbe myths of origin reflect the division of the social

structure into freeborn, artisan (see CASTE) and servile levels. While the Fulbe shared this tripartite hierarchy with neighboring savanna groups, further distinctions existed within each status. The freeborn consisted of nobles and relatives of rulers and the remainder of the "pure" Fulbe. Artisans belonged to specialized, hereditary, endogamous, occupational groups, including ironworkers, silver- and goldsmiths, woodworkers, leatherworkers and entertainers, including griots (q.v.). Slaves (q.v.) consisted of non-Fulbe acquired through capture or purchase, and those "born in the house," meaning second- or later-generation slaves.

Many of the clerical (q.v.) reform movements and attempted revolutions of the fifteenth through nineteenth centuries were led by Fulbe leaders. Both Futa Toro (q.v.) and Bundu (q.v.) were dominated by the Fulbe before French rule. The Fulbe have a reputation for being experts at cattle raising. Their numbers in Senegal have been augmented in recent years by a massive influx of Fulbe from Futa Jalon (q.v.) in Guinea.

FUTA JALON. Precolonial kingdom located in the highlands of modern-day Guinea-Conakry, where the Senegal, Niger and Gambia rivers all have their origins. Historically, its Fulbe population and rulers were closely related to Futa Toro, Bundu, Fuladu (all q.v.) and the Fulbe inhabitants of upper Casamance (q.v.).

FUTA TORO. Country stretching along the middle valley of the Senegal River. Futa is the general name that the Fulbe (q.v.) gave to the areas where they lived, while Toro is the region with the oldest identity in the middle valley and lies in the western portion around the towns of Podor and Njum. Today the north bank lies in Mauritania, the south bank in Senegal. The distance between the southernmost Senegalese tier and the northernmost Mauritanian tier was rarely more than 15 miles, whereas the length of the region, from Dagana in the lower valley to Dembankane in the upper valley, is approximately 250 miles.

Futa Toro's predecessor was ancient Tekrur (q.v.), situated on both banks of the river and contemporary with the Ghana Empire. The dominant ethnic group was Fulbe, with minority populations of Wolof, Berber and Soninke. In the period from about 1490 until 1776, Futa Toro was ruled by the Denanke (q.v.) dynasty founded by Koly Tengela Ba (q.v.), whose royal title was *Satigi* (q.v.). Its rulers and a significant portion of its people were Muslims. The first recorded Futanke conversion was that of the ruler War Jabi (q.v.) in the early eleventh century. From the sixteenth to the eighteenth centuries, Futa was often the subject of raids by Moroccan forces eager to expand the influence of their state and acquire the wealth in gold and slaves from the Western Sudan. From Futa Toro and its environs, a clerical diaspora helped spread Islam throughout West Africa.

In 1776 the clerics of Futa Toro, resenting the exactions of the secular rulers, united to overthrow Denanke rule and establish a clerical oligarchy, headed by an *almamy* (q.v.). The first and most famous to hold that title was Abdul Qadir Kan (q.v.), though the early inspiration for the revolution came from Sulaiman Bal (q.v.). In the process of reform, the Islamic clerical community constituted themselves as a new class, the *torodbe* (q.v.), and added that status to the social structure. The new regime endured for more than 100 years, but its ability to control the middle valley was spent by the early 1800s.

The Futanke, or residents of Futa Toro, engaged in agricultural and pastoral activities as well as in trade. The middle valley enjoyed an economic advantage over its highland neighbors because it produced a second crop of grain and cotton on the floodplain of the river when the annual flood receded. The additional harvest made Futa a "breadbasket" for surrounding regions, and it drew immigrants from other areas. Although lacking exploitable mineral deposits, it also lay across the main commercial artery of the region, the Senegal River (q.v.). Salt was carried upstream and gum arabic (q.v.), gold and slaves (q.v.) passed downstream once the Europeans arrived on the coast in 1444. A second north–south trade axis linked Futa Toro to the westernmost of the trans-Saharan trade routes, along which slaves and grain were exchanged for horses, salt and manufactured goods from North Africa and the Middle East. The Futanke managed to control European access to the upper river and used this control to their advantage.

During the nineteenth century, the almamate survived in its basic institutions, but it never recovered the strength and zeal of the earlier period. By the 1850s, Futa was threatened by two external forces. The French began to dominate the region, especially under Governor Louis Faidherbe (q.v.). The second threat came from a native son, Umar Tal (q.v.), who launched a jihad (q.v.) against the predominantly non-Muslim Mandinka and Bambara to the east. To achieve this goal, he recruited heavily in his homeland of Futa Toro. The power of the *almamy* was reduced, and a regional chief named Abdul Bokar Kan (q.v.) emerged as the dominant figure in the middle valley between 1860 and 1890. By the late 1880s, however, the French had conquered virtually all of Futa as part of their subordination of Senegal and conquest of the Western and Central Sudan. The middle valley became a staging area for expansion into the interior. In addition, with a shift to the peanut basin and rail traffic, the region became a border instead of a commercial center. By the 1920s and the completion of the Dakar-Bamako railroad, the region had been reduced to its marginal status within the colony of Senegal.

After independence, the government made a brief, concerted effort to revitalize the Futa region, but with little success. The droughts of the 1970s and 1980s as well as the increasing desertification of the area have further depleted Futa's already low productivity. The region has become a virtual labor reserve, with people moving to Dakar and other cities to seek work. Many villages in Futa are inhabited almost entirely by women, children and the elderly. It remains to be seen whether the recent investments in dams, irrigation and other projects will be able to restore the economic importance of the entire river valley, including Futa Toro.

FUTANKE (pl. FUTANKOBE). A Fulbe (q.v.) native of Futa Toro (q.v.).

- G -

GAJAAGA. Kingdom on the upper Senegal River, centered on the Bakel (q.v.) area and dominated by the Soninke (q.v.). The polity, which once controlled both Gidimaka (q.v.) and Bundu (q.v.), stretched for 80 kilometers along the Senegal River. The Faleme River divided the province into upper and lower portions named Kamera (q.v.) and Goy (q.v.), which frequently quarreled and operated independently. The French called the entire area Galam (q.v.).

Traditions agree that Gajaaga was founded by Soninke from ancient Ghana, but date that event anywhere from the eighth through the fourteenth century. Situated at the upper limit of navigability of the Senegal River, Gajaaga became the crossroads for overland routes linking the Senegal River traffic to the Niger River empires. Residents participated actively in commerce, most notably in gold from Bambuk (q.v.) directly to the south, in gum arabic (q.v.) with the Idawaish Moors (q.v.) to the north and in the trans-Atlantic slave trade (q.v.). Frequent local and regional conflicts provided a steady flow of captives for export. The residents also practiced wetlands cultivation along the Senegal River, and the Soninke of Gajaaga controlled most of southwestern Gidimaka (q.v.). The king, or *tunka,* belonged to the Bathily (or Bacily) family that originated from the village of Tuba. A dozen villages on the Senegal, dominated by Muslim cleric lineages, traditionally maintained some autonomy from the secular government. These "maraboutic" settlements were larger than other villages in the province and contained considerably more slaves. In c. 1690, the *tunka* gave the Futanke cleric Malik Sy (q.v.) most of the area of Bundu (q.v.). In addition, a group of Wolof refugees settled at the site of Bakel (q.v.) and negotiated a similar autonomy; their presence was a principal factor in the French decision to construct a fortified post there in 1820.

By the early 1830s, different branches of the Bathily lineage claimed the central office of *tunka*. As a result, the eldest male from a preordained list of six towns became ruler. This system quickly broke down, in large part because of competition for increased profits from the rapidly expanding "legitimate" commerce, mainly in gum arabic. The French took advantage of the power vacuum and officially split the area into its two traditional parts. This included upper Gajaaga, or Kamera, south of the Faleme River with its capital at Maxana, and lower Gajaaga, or Goy (also spelled Goye or Goi), on the northern side of the river, which retained the traditional capital of Tuabo. Goy included Bakel, the region's major trading center by 1850. Gajaaga was also affected by the jihad of al-Hajj Umar Tal (q.v.) in the 1850s and the revolt of Mamadu Lamine (q.v.) in the late 1880s. The Bathily lineage ruled under French hegemony, but by 1890, the area was firmly under colonial rule. (See also GIDIMAKA; GALAM.)

GALAM. Precolonial French term for the upper Senegal River region, centered on Gajaaga (q.v.) where, from July to October, when the river was in flood, they could trade in gold, slaves (q.v.) and gum arabic (q.v.). Sometimes the name referred to the entire commercial region around the European trading posts at Fort Saint Joseph, and later Bakel (q.v.), Maxana and Medine (Khasso), including the king-doms of Gajaaga (q.v.), Bambuk (q.v.), Bundu (q.v.) and Khasso (modern-day western Mali). More often, it meant only Gajaaga. (See also COMPAGNIE DE GALAM.)

GIDIMAKA (or GUIDIMAHKA). Kingdom along the upper Senegal River, ruled by the Gajaaga (q.v.) Soninke and now divided between southeastern Mauritania and northwestern Mali. The Soninke lived and farmed only in the compara-tively secure and well-watered southwestern portion of the province bordering the Senegal River. Primarily engaged in the gum arabic (q.v.) trade and specialized exchange with the Moors (q.v.), the Gidimaka Soninke did not benefit from the gold and slave traffic centered on the left bank of the Senegal. No effective central power existed, although theo-retically a *tunka* from the Kamara family ruled with a council of notables representing the most important lineages. Moor-ish incursions, particularly in the north, frequently disrupted trade and production, and Gajaaga residents cultivated exten-sive areas of Gidimaka. When the French arrived on the upper Senegal in the mid-nineteenth century, the province consisted of dispersed, independent settlements, which of-fered no sustained resistance.

GOREE. A small island off the coast of Dakar (q.v.) that served as an entrepôt for successive European slave-trading companies from the latter fifteenth through early nineteenth centuries. The Portuguese explorer Dinis Diaz found the island unin-habited in 1444, and a later expedition built a stone church, cemetery and unfortified trading post. From Gorée and the Cape Verde islands, Portuguese colonists and *métis* (q.v.), called *tangomaos,* established a local trading network to supply the Atlantic trade. Slaves, ambergris, beeswax, hides, grain, fuel and fresh water were gathered from points south of the Cap Vert peninsula (q.v.) to the Bissao rivers, stored on Gorée and sold to European ships.

In the latter half of the sixteenth century, French, Dutch and English competition began to drive the Portuguese shippers, but not the *tangomaos,* out of this trade. In 1617 the Dutch received the right to build there from a ruler on Cap Vert named Biram, and shortly thereafter built Fort Orange on the island's hill and Fort Nassau commanding the harbor. They named the island Gorée, while in earlier sources it is called Palma or Beseguiche. During the European wars of the slave trade era, Gorée changed hands several times. The Portuguese forced the Dutch out from 1629 until 1645, and the English captured it from them briefly during the war of 1664–1667. In 1677, the French Admiral Estrées drove the Dutch out permanently, razing their forts to the ground. The French held Gorée most of the time thereafter and constructed their own forts of Saint-Michel and Saint-François on the former Dutch sites. There were interludes of British occupation, but most of the time the British tapped the mainland trade from Fort James on an island in the Gambia River.

Gradually an Afro-French community grew up, comprising free sailors called *laptots* (q.v.), slaves and *métis* descended from passing soldiers and traders. *Métis* women, called *signarés* (q.v.), developed extensive mainland commercial networks to which European men gained access by marrying them "à la mode du pays." The regular garrison of precolonial Gorée ranged from 10 to 100 men, and the total population was still only 300 free Africans and a few Europeans in 1758. In the 1780s it reached a brief apogee with 1,840 inhabitants, 200 slaves awaiting shipment and a flurry of permanent housing constructed. The slave house on the island today is typical of that era, with spacious merchants' quarters upstairs and chilly dark slave dungeons below.

In the mid-nineteenth century the island had a fairly active "legitimate" commerce, the slave trade having been outlawed but not entirely suppressed, and the population reached its all-time peak of about 4,000. Between 1857 and 1902 French headquarters were gradually moved to the mainland at Dakar (q.v.), which led Gorée into a period of decay. In 1939 construction began on an esplanade linking Gorée to the mainland. Traces can still be seen, but the project was abandoned in 1940. In September of that year the British and Free French bombarded the island trying to take French West Africa, but the Vichy regime prevailed. In 1944 the entire island was decreed a historic site, which halted all new building there for 30 years and saw the population drop to about 700. In 1977–1978, Mme. Senghor initiated construction of a school for daughters of Members of the Order of Lions, and elaborate tourist development is planned. It is currently reached from the mainland by a 20-minute ferry ride, and is very popular with tourists. In 1984, the entire island was declared an international historic site by UNESCO.

GOY (or GOYE). A province of Gajaaga (q.v.) on the right bank of the upper Senegal River near Bakel (q.v.), which periodically was an independent kingdom. Goy, situated west of the Faleme with its capital always at Tuabo, was also called Lower Gajaaga. The French annexed Goy in 1850 and administered it from their post at Bakel, which was located in the province.

GRIOT. French term for a caste (q.v.) whose traditional profession included everything to do with communications: oral history, genealogies and social rankings, messages of social or diplomatic import, talking drumming, war drums, royal and dancing drums, music, storytelling and buffoonery. Griot families were attached to particular noble families, receiving protection and often generous remuneration in exchange for their services. Every major ethnic group in Senegal had a griot caste. Until recently, they were considered tainted, frequently obliged to live in segregated sections of villages and (like the bards of medieval Europe) denied underground burial among some groups. Today such discrimination is illegal and the worst aspects of it suppressed. Many of the most popular Senegalese entertainers today are descended from griot families.

GROUNDNUTS (or PEANUTS). The principal agricultural export crop of Senegal and an important food crop. In the mid-1980s, the country ranked among the top 10 world producers of groundnuts. Production in 1989–1990 reached 844,000 metric tons. For many years, groundnuts were the country's principal export commodity and hard-exchange earner. Groundnuts generated about 25 percent of GDP and furnished 70 to 80 percent of exports. By the mid-1970s, owing to several factors, groundnut production was in decline. Although the groundnut sector's contribution to foreign exchange earnings has dropped below those of fishing (q.v.) and phosphates (see MINING), the sector continues to play an important role in both the domestic and export economy.

Groundnuts were introduced by the French in 1840, and production rose significantly, especially in the central and coastal regions. Climatic and soil conditions were ideally suited to groundnuts, which rapidly replaced all other exports from the region. Western coastal areas were especially productive, but soon cultivation spread throughout most areas under French influence. Groundnuts played a significant role in many important developments during the colonial period, including railroad construction (q.v.), the shift in French interest from the river valley to the coast and central regions and the expansion of the Murid brotherhood (q.v.). Since independence, the government has tried to reduce the emphasis on groundnuts and to diversify the economy, but the crop still dominates the agricultural sector of several areas of the country. Annual production varies widely, primarily dependent on rainfall but also on farmers' decisions about what to cultivate each year.

GUEYE, LAMINE. (1891–1968). Lawyer and politician who founded the first Senegalese socialist party in 1937, which was also Francophone Africa's first modern political party.

Born in the French Sudan (Mali) of a Senegalese family of Saint-Louis (q.v.) origin, Guèye studied law in France during World War I, becoming French Africa's first black lawyer. He returned to Senegal in 1922 as a supporter of Blaise Diagne (q.v.). Guèye served as mayor of Saint-Louis from 1925 to 1926, but was defeated by Diagne in the 1928 elections for deputy. Guèye took up a magistrateship in Réunion in 1931. With Diagne's death in 1934, Guèye returned to run for deputy but was defeated by Galandou Diouf (q.v.). In 1935, he reorganized the *Parti Socialiste Sénégalais* (PSS, q.v.) along modern lines to attract the young Senegalese elite, but it failed its first test in 1936 when Galandou Diouf again defeated Guèye. After the election, the SFIO (q.v.) absorbed the PSS.

The fall of France in 1940 temporarily halted local politics. In 1946, however, with the support of the SFIO, Guèye and his protégé Léopold Senghor (q.v.) easily captured the deputyships from the urban *communes* (q.v.) and Protectorate respectively. In 1946 Guèye was also elected mayor of Dakar. In the Chamber of Deputies he sponsored legislation to win African bureaucrats the same pay as their European counterparts in Africa. He continued to draw on the support of urban and traditional elites and largely ignored the rest of Senegal. Because of this policy, Senghor broke with him in 1948 to found his own party (see BDS). In 1951, Guèye was resoundingly defeated by his former protégé.

After a decade of trying to regain leadership, Guèye ceded to the younger generation and rural dominance by merging his PSAS (q.v.) in 1958 with Senghor's BPS (q.v.) to form the new UPS (q.v.). The two men were also united in their opposition to other African leaders who favored autonomy for each French African territory rather than a form of federation. Guèye remained active in politics as an important counselor within the ruling party, and presided as President of the National Assembly until his death in 1968.

GUM ARABIC. A resin secreted by gum trees growing in the Senegal River and used in Europe primarily to fix textile dyes and in certain pharmaceutical products.

Gum arabic, also known as *gum acacia* or *gum Senegal,* is a natural exudate of the *acacia senegal* tree, which flourishes in the arid Sahel desert-side. Requiring from 300 to 500 millimeters of precipitation, the amount of gum exuded by a tree depends on rainfall levels and the intensity of the *harmattan,* the hot dry Saharan winds. Though several harvests a year are possible, most gathering occurs in March, April and May when the *harmattan* reaches its greatest strength. A single tree yields 800 grams in an average year. Senegalese use the gum for medicinal purposes and in textile production. Beating gum arabic into indigo-dyed cloth fixes the color and produces a highly desirable glossy surface, while its bonding qualities strengthen the fabric.

During the precolonial and colonial periods, it was sold by Moors (q.v.), who dominated the mainland trade. When both Britain and France outlawed the slave trade in the early nineteenth century, gum arabic became the major "legitimate" trade good from the Senegal River region. Peanuts soon replaced gum arabic, however, and a drastic fall in the price in the late 1890s virtually wiped out the long-distance trade in gum arabic.

- H -

HAALPULAAR'EN. (or HAL PULAAR). Literally, "those who speak Pulaar," the Senegambian dialect of Fulfulde, which is spoken throughout West Africa. They also call themselves Fulbe (q.v.). In Wolof, French and common Senegalese usage, the Haalpulaar'en of Futa Toro are called Toucouleur or Tukolor, derived from Tekrur (q.v.), the name of the ancient state in the middle Senegal valley contemporary with the Ghana Empire. The Fulbe are known by a wide range of names derived from their local African neighbors' languages and adapted into French, English and Arabic. Among the more common variations are Peuhle, Peul, Pulo Futa, Fula, Fulani, Fellata.

HABITANT. Precolonial term for a permanent resident of the coastal trading posts, mainly Saint-Louis or Gorée (both q.v.). Usually the term implied a *métis* (q.v.), but Europeans who assimilated to local culture and wealthy Africans might also be included. *Habitants* dominated the politics of Saint-Louis and Gorée from the seventeenth through nineteenth centuries, as well as diplomatic and commercial relations with mainland kingdoms. European governors and merchants, though theoretically their superiors, were transitory and depended entirely on habitant knowledge, contacts and cooperation. The habitants evolved a mayor and council of freemen long before the French officially recognized this institution in 1821. At the end of the nineteenth century, with the colonial conquest and the implementation of colonial rule, the habitants tried to profit from their historic role as intermediaries (e.g., see CARPOT), but found themselves the excluded middle in a racially polarized system. (See also TRAITANT.)

HAJJ. The pilgrimage to Mecca, Arabia, which is one of the five pillars of Islam, and obligatory for Muslims who can afford the trip. Senegambians were among the first West Africans to accomplish this journey, beginning at least by the eleventh century. During the early period, pilgrims travelled several years, on foot or by camel caravan, receiving hospitality and stopping en route to study law and trade. Four major routes crossed the Sahara, departing from Tekrur (later Futa Toro, q.v.), Timbuktu, Hausa-Bornu and the Nile Valley, and converging on the intellectual and commercial metropolis of Cairo. The West African section of the city became known as the Tekruri quarter, and West Africans, regardless of their ethnic origin, as Tekruri. Several important religious reformers of Senegambia, including al-Hajj Umar Tal (q.v.) and Mamadu Lamine Drame (q.v.), gained enormous prestige by their pilgrimages to Mecca.

During the colonial period, the government encouraged the *hajj* by organizing charter boats, and later flights, and paying the fare for favored loyal Muslims. Governor Faidherbe (q.v.), who initially proposed banning the pilgrimage, was the first colonial governor to encourage the practice of sponsoring loyal Muslims. In 1861, he sponsored the marabout Bu al-Mogdad Seck (q.v.) on the hajj. In the early 1900s, when the French became worried about a resurgence in the Islamic world, several officials in Senegal proposed banning the hajj, but to no avail.

Today's charter flights, which ferry several thousand Senegalese pilgrims annually to Mecca, have transformed the tradition. Many still stay to study, but most stay only one to three weeks. Returned pilgrims are addressed as *al-Hajj* (male) or *al-Hajja* (female) (Fr., *El Hadji* and *El Hadja*). In Senegal this title may occasionally be given as a name, in which case it obviously does not imply completion of the pilgrimage.

Many Murids (q.v.) decline to make the pilgrimage to Mecca, arguing that founder Amadu Bamba Mbacke (q.v.) taught that Wolof should substitute a *magal* (q.v.), an internal pilgrimage to their central mosque at Touba. This is vigorously disputed by some Murids and most non-Murids.

HEALTH CARE. Before independence, health care was overwhelmingly centralized in Dakar and primarily limited to the European and African elite population. Both urban and rural Senegalese relied mainly on traditional healers. In addition to health care facilities, colonial medical authorities created *cordon sanitaires* (q.v.) to separate European and African populations, ostensibly for health reasons.

After independence, the Ministry of Health was given responsibility for all aspects of health. Under the Ministry of Health, each of the 10 administrative regions (see ADMINISTRATION) of Senegal is headed by a general medical officer and has its own hospital complex and pharmacy. There is also a nationwide Public Health Service, Maternity and Child Welfare Service and School Medical Service. Each prefecture has a dispensary, usually staffed by a doctor and a midwife, comprising separate outpatient and inpatient facilities, a maternity ward and a hygiene unit. Each sub-prefecture has an aid post staffed by a male nurse. Under the Ministry of National Education is a health and sanitation office responsible for school hygiene and vaccination programs.

Health care continues to be centralized in Senegal, even in comparison with the same tendency in other African countries. Markedly better and more care is available in Dakar than elsewhere in the country. There are three major hospitals, including Principal, the former French army hospital, le Dantec and Fann. Also in the capital are a psychiatric center, a blood-transfusion center and numerous private clinics in addition to standard nationwide institutions. In the late 1980s, there was one doctor for every 5,000 people in Dakar, while in the rest of the country the ratio ranged from one per 25,000 in the Fleuve Region to one per 85,000 in the Diourbel Region.

In principle, health care is free and universal. In practice, it is a major expense in most Senegalese households. Public dispensaries and hospitals, supposed to be stocked by the government, have never had adequate supplies. Patients are issued prescriptions to be filled in commercial, predominantly French-owned pharmacies, where medications, when available and after import duties, cost about twice their retail price in France. Some outdated medicines are routinely sold in pharmacies. Food, bedside care and bedding are customarily supplied by relatives of hospital patients.

In the health sector, standard indicators of health status have shown some improvement in the 1980s. According to World Bank data, life expectancy increased from forty in the early 1970s to forty-eight in 1987, while infant mortality declined from a rate of 147 per thousand live births in 1980 to 131 in 1987. The fall in infant mortality apparently occurred mainly in the rural areas. In the mid-1980s, the government launched a series of vaccination campaigns that reduced morbidity rates for major diseases, including measles, whooping cough and tetanus. Childhood malnutrition levels for Senegal are average for Africa, with roughly 30 percent of children under five showing some signs of malnourishment. (See also MEDICAL EDUCATION and VETERINARY MEDICINE.)

HIVERNAGE. French for rainy season. It usually begins in the Casamance (q.v.) in late May and in northern Senegal by late June or early July, ending from north to south between mid-September and the end of October.

- I -

INDEPENDENCE. Senegal was granted independence from France in 1960, like most other Francophone African colonies. None of the country's most prominent political leaders at the time, Léopold Senghor (q.v.), Mamadou Dia (q.v.) or Lamine Guèye (q.v.), initially sought independence in the late 1950s.

In the period from 1945 to 1960, when Anglophone colonies around the world were actively seeking self-government, Francophone West African politics focused on securing reforms, equal rights and Africanization within the context of greater cooperation with France. The most sought after reforms, including the abolition of forced labor, the *indigénat* (q.v.), the status of the *sujet* (q.v.) and the name "colony" for overseas territories of the French Empire, were accomplished by the First Constituent Assembly of 1945–1946. France also abandoned the policy of making the colonies pay for their own colonial administration and began contributing substantial aid for both government costs and development projects. In the 1950s, few Francophone African leaders advocated immediate independence, seeking instead to extract benefits from France. Independence was also contrary to the assimilationist (q.v.) ideals of the French imperial tradition, and their hesitation also reflected the increasing dependence of the overseas territories on French aid and trade. Only the Marxist PAI (q.v.) and the overseas student FEANF sought independence, and only in 1956. Until the late 1950s, various models of the French Union were debated, the central question being whether French West Africa should remain unified, affiliated with France as a federation or as individual territories. As a subtheme in the common struggle for greater rights, a two-sided struggle emerged, between Senegal's Senghor and Ivory Coast's Felix Houphouet-Boigny, over the form unity should take, and implicitly over the eventual leadership of an autonomous AOF. In 1946 Senghor declined to join Houphouet-Boigny's Pan-Francophone African party, the Rassemblement Democratique Africain (q.v.). Several years later, Houphouet-Boigny took the relatively wealthy Ivory Coast out of the French West African federation, the capital of which had been Dakar. France had opposed both attempts at unity, perceiving them as weakening its bargaining power.

The events that ultimately led to independence began with the Algerian war of independence and the fall of the Fourth French Republic. When Charles de Gaulle came to power in 1957 and conceded Algerian independence, he sought simultaneously a formula for the French Union that would ensure indefinitely the links between the remaining overseas territories and France. His proposal was embodied in the Constitution of the Fifth French Republic (q.v.), which was offered to African voters in a referendum. The Senegalese people, following the lead of Senghor and Dia, voted overwhelmingly in favor of the plan, as did all other West African territories except Guinea, led by Sekou Toure. Guinea's *no* vote gained it a brutally abrupt and total independence, but it also proved the wedge that drove apart the remaining colonial network. Francophone West African leaders had consistently asked to reserve the right to independence eventually, even if they did not seek it right away. France's harsh and vindictive treatment of Guinea offended the other colonies. Senegal's relations with France deteriorated over Senghor's attempt to build a Mali Federation (q.v.) out of the remnants of part of the French West African federation. Finally, on April 4, 1960, France signed an accord granting independence to the Mali Federation, comprising Senegal and Sudan (Mali). Independence was officially granted on June 20, but when the federation broke up two months later, Senegal declared its separate independence. At that time it chose to celebrate Independence Day on April 4 (the day the accord with France had been signed), rather than either June or August, when its independence had actually been acquired.

Formal political independence has brought less change in the political and economic links between Senegal and France than perhaps any other country in Africa. Although there have been some moves toward diversification, France remains the dominant source of aid and trade. Local politics and cultural links remain strong. Some military links have also been maintained. Senghor's assertion of the primacy of black African culture in *négritude* (q.v.) is countered by his concept of the "civilisation de l'universelle" in which French culture is prominent. French remains the official language of Senegal, and France has by far the largest embassy and cultural center of any other country in Dakar.

INDIGENAT. Body of law that applied to *sujets* (q.v.) in the protectorate during French colonial rule. The laws, alongside customary law, were administered by native tribunals consisting of French-appointed chiefs and *qadis* (q.v.).

The system was used to enforce colonial tax collection, forced labor drafts and military conscription. There were widespread complaints in Senegal that the justice so administered was neither customary nor just, and the system came to symbolize arbitrary colonial rule. Residents of the four *communes* (q.v.) were exempt from the *indigénat*, making it all the more bitter to people in the rural areas. The system was finally abolished by the French Constituent Assembly laws of December 22, 1945, and February 20, 1946.

INDUSTRY. In 1990, the industrial sector accounted for about 27 percent of GDP, with manufacturing accounting for about 17 percent. Senegal's annual level of industrial output is largely determined by agricultural performance. Most major manufacturing is located in and around Dakar.

Food processing is the largest activity, comprising 43 percent of industrial production. Groundnut extraction is the single most-important agro-industry. Senegal's textile industry is one of the most important in Francophone West Africa, with four cotton ginning mills and spinning, weaving, dyeing and printing plants. It accounts for about one-tenth of industrial output. Other major industrial production includes phosphate mining (see MINING), chemicals and oil, metal and mechanical industries, construction materials and paper industries.

The Dakar Industrial Free Zone, a government-owned and operated free trade zone, was established by the government in 1974 to encourage foreign and domestic investors to set up labor-intensive export-oriented industrial companies to help reduce Senegal's chronic trade deficit and create jobs. A liberalization program was launched in 1986, involving tax incentives, relaxation of tariffs and price controls and a schedule for privatization of state enterprises. In 1991, there were nine companies operating in the free trade zone, far below the number anticipated by the government.

Senegal also has a very active light industry or craft sector. This sector, generally based on the household, includes hand-made textiles, gold, silver and iron smithing, pottery-making, woodworking, basketry, leatherworking and other traditional crafts. Craft manufacture occurs at all levels in the country, including Dakar, the major towns and most notably in the rural areas. Because craft manufacture does not figure in official government statistics, it is impossible to speculate on its contribution to the national economy and overall production.

- J -

JAMBUR. Wolof term for all freeborn persons, or people of neither slave nor caste ancestry. There were three distinct endogamous estates within the freeborn category: the military aristocracy (see CEDO), the *marabouts* (q.v. and see CLERICS) and the peasants (see BADOLO).

JARA (DIARA). Ancient Malinke-Soninke kingdom, founded by the Naxate clan in the area east of Tekrur (q.v.) after the collapse of the Ghana Empire in the twelfth century. It was a vassal first of the Sosso and then the Malinke empires. In the fourteenth century, a new dynasty, the Jawara, gained control and asserted Jara's independence from the Malian Empire. Lying across the northernmost trade route linking the Senegal and Niger Rivers, it was of some economic importance. A period of civil wars beginning in the late sixteenth century ended with the conquest of Jara by neighboring Kaarta in 1754.

JAW, YORO. (c.1847–1919) Author of the *Cahiers de Yoro Dyao,* the most complete early collection of oral tradition on the Wolof states. As the young son of a prominent noble of Walo (q.v.), Jaw was taken hostage during the conquest of Walo in 1855 and became one of the first students in the Ecole des ôtages (q.v.). After a few years in Saint-Louis (q.v.), where he learned French, lost his ties with his family and adopted the French cause, he was appointed chief of one of the cantons in his newly annexed homeland. Later he collected and submitted to the French a wide range of information on the history, customs and social and political structure of the Wolof of Walo and Kajor (both q.v.). In the early twentieth century, his notebooks were edited and published by French colonial scholars Henri Gaden and R. Rousseau (see Bibliography). The originals have since disappeared.

JAXANKE. (also Jakhanke and Diakhanke). A network of Mande-speaking Muslim scholars, itinerant merchants and farmers. Their indigenous traditions suggest that they are descended from a group of Soninke (q.v.) from Ja on the Niger River who migrated after the decline of Ghana/ Wagadu. In the late fifteenth century, they settled in two trading towns on the Bafing River, Jaxaba and Bambuxu Jaxa, under the leadership of *al-Hajj* Salim Suware. The group were missionary clerics and merchants who traded gold, slaves and cloth on the routes between the upper Niger, Senegal and Gambia rivers. They established specialized commercial and religious settlements throughout the region, especially in Bundu (q.v.). These settlements remained relatively autonomous from the states where they were located. They may be considered a branch of the Jula merchant-clerics of Soninke-Mande origin, who dispersed and settled along old trade routes throughout the central-western Sudan.

Linguistically part of the Mandinka (q.v.), the Jaxanke's similar origins, profession and allegiance to Islam and mercantile orientation linked them closely together, even over long distances. Not all historians accept indigenous traditions describing themselves as exclusively religious communities seeking to preserve their identity and piety with minimal commercial involvement. Though lacking any formal, centralized political authority, the Jaxanke trading diaspora functioned effectively and continuously throughout numerous local and regional upheavals. The Jaxanke of Bundu in particular maintained close ties with the Gajaaga Soninke (q.v.) and likewise benefitted from the flow of gold and slaves from the southern forest zone through Bundu to the Senegal River. The Jaxanke theoretically rejected political and military involvement, remaining neutral in disputes, which permitted them to continue uninterruptedly their mercantile activities. They share the common Mande, tripartite social structure. In the early 1800s, the Jaxanke networks on the Gambia and Senegal rivers maintained close ties. This system, however, deteriorated in the late 1840s and early 1850s because of the civil wars in Bundu and Gajaaga, French expansion in the upper Senegal valley and the Umarian jihad (q.v.). Today the Jaxanke inhabit several large villages in eastern Senegal and occupy quarters in other villages.

JIHAD. Holy war in the name of Islam. In Muslim theology, jihad is an obligation of every Muslim, although it is not one of the five pillars of Islam. Before taking up the sword, however, every Muslim is exhorted to wage jihad first on his own heart and then to wage jihad of the tongue, persuading his neighbor to follow the true path of Islam. He should resort to violence only if persuasion fails. As an Arabic loan word, jihad is found in all of the Senegambian languages and was a frequent occurrence in Senegambian history.

The first jihads in the area were those of the eleventh-century Almoravids (q.v.), which introduced Islam quite widely among the nobility and began the development of an indigenous Muslim clergy, especially among the Berber and the Futanke (q.v.). From then on jihad became a recurring theme in the spread and purification of Islam in the Senegambia. Although the legal conditions necessary to declare jihad are very carefully defined in Muslim law (q.v.), there is little evidence that clergy in the region were well enough versed to debate the legalities of their religious wars. Any war led by Muslims against non-Muslims or against so-called lax Muslim rulers was likely to take on the character of jihad. The most notable of these were the Almoravid movement, the Tubenan of 1673–1678 (q.v.), the Torodo revolution in Futa Toro in the 1770s (q.v.) and the numerous mid-nineteenth-century movements, frequently combining the overthrow of the traditional nobility with resistance to European penetration. The most important, long-lasting and successful was that of *al-Hajj* Umar Tal (q.v.). (See also MA BA; SHAIXU AMADU BA; ALFA MOLO BALDE; MAMADU LAMINE DRAME.)

JOKING RELATIONSHIP. An institutionalized relationship permitting certain pairs of individuals within an extended family, patronymics, caste groups, ethnic groups and precolonial nations to exchange rather blunt or even insulting comments when they meet, even if they have not known one another previously. Comments frequently focus on eating habits, cleanliness and intelligence. The relationship also entails mutual hospitality and aid. For example, cross-cousins, Jops and Njays, Serer and Fulbe, share their historic connection, which allows them to tease one another without anger. In practical terms, it mitigates underlying conflicts in symbiotic relationships, as among the pastoral Fulbe and the sedentary Serer.

JOLA (or Fr. Diola). Ethnic group dominating the area around the mouth of the Casamance River in southwestern Senegal. The Jola should not be confused with the Jula trading network. The Jola ethnic group consists of the following subgroups: Feloup (or Flup) around Usuy (Oussouye); Jamat (Ayamat) near Efok and Yutu; Jolo-Haer based at Kabrus; Jola of Jembering; Jola of Point Saint-Georges (Banjar and Hecquard); the Brin-Seleki group; and the Bayot in the Ziguinchor area. They constituted about 10 percent of the total population in Senegal in 1990. Until the nineteenth century, the Jola maintained a traditional set of religious beliefs and were grouped into semiautonomous segmentary lineage-based units, not a centralized kingdom. Most Jola were farmers, especially rice cultivation, and traders. They maintained their traditional religious beliefs as their neighbors to the north and the east increasingly adopted Islam. During and since the colonial period, their traditional culture and beliefs have been eroded by Islam, Christianity and Western education. Recently, there has been an increasing tendency of youth to migrate, at least seasonally, to urban centers (Ziguinchor, Banjul, Kaolack and Dakar). The Jola were in the forefront of recent Casamance separatist movements. (See CASAMANCE.)

JOLOF, EMPIRE AND KINGDOM. Jolof was founded sometime between the late twelfth and mid-fourteenth century, and by the mid-fifteenth century covered most of the area of present-day northern and western Senegal, from the Senegal River (q.v.) to the Gambia River, and inland about half the breadth of Senegal. The polity was always dominated by the Wolof (q.v.) people, whose language became the national language of Senegal. In addition, some Fulbe (q.v.) herders and Moor (q.v.) merchants also lived within the area. Oral traditions attribute the founding of Jolof to Njajan Njay (q.v.), legendary source of justice, authority and the Njay ruling dynasty. Some versions claim he was the son of Abu Darday, a Muslim cleric connected with the Almoravid (q.v.) movement. In the version recorded by Yoro Jaw (q.v.), after Abu Darday's death, Njajan's mother was tricked into marrying a slave, who begat the Mboj dynasty of Walo (q.v.). Njajan was so shamed by the marriage that he fled to an island retreat. When he emerged from the water one day among a group of quarreling fishermen, he settled their dispute. Seeing in him a source of order and justice, they eventually succeeded in making him king. The early history of the kingdom is obscured in legend, and the various dates in the oral traditions (late twelfth to mid-fourteenth century) cannot be correlated with other oral traditions or Arabic or European sources to provide a satisfactory chronology. For example, Malinke oral traditions indicate that a general of Sunjata Keita (c.1235–1260) named Tirimaxan Traore led a military expedition through the area, conquering Jolof, imposing tribute and then later settling in the south and himself founding the empire of Kabu (q.v.). Yet Wolof traditions are silent on this subject. It is not known whether this Malinke conquest occurred before, during or after the consolidation of the Jolof Empire by Njajan Njay.

What is known is that the Portuguese (q.v.) found the empire flourishing in the mid-fifteenth century, and over the next century both witnessed and participated in its decline. Mid-fifteenth-century Jolof was a black Muslim country, with a sparse population and a mixed farming-herding economy based on millet, cattle, slaves, horses and cloth. Its capital was traditionally Warxox, although some individual *Bur-yi* administered from other villages. Until the European arrival, its main trading partners were the Moors (q.v.), involved in the trans-Saharan trade, and the Malian Empire, situated near the Niger River to the east.

The Portuguese arrival on the coast in 1444 inaugurated an era of maritime long-distance trade. Jolof's control of mainland trade patterns gradually lost relevance, and the empire disintegrated. The first blow was the establishment of the Denanke (q.v.) dynasty along the fertile Senegal River basin by Koly Tengela Ba (q.v.) in 1490. Then Kajor, Bawol, Walo and Sin (each q.v.) fought for their independence in the mid-sixteenth century, completely cutting Jolof off from the coast. Finally Salum, Niani and Wuli (each q.v.) were established by the early seventeenth century, imposing independent territory between Jolof and the Gambia River. From then on Jolof was an isolated remnant of a kingdom, protected from destruction by its position as founding father, but unable to re-create its glory.

In 1673 Jolof, along with its neighbors, was conquered by Muslim reformers under the leadership of Nasir al-Din (q.v.). While the movement was short-lived in neighboring kingdoms, the kings of Jolof who adhered to it were not overthrown. They created instead an enduring merger of the roles of *Bur* and *marabout* (q.v.). The Burs of Jolof were strong enough to conquer Kajor (q.v.) twice (c.1690 and 1758–59) and invade several other times during the succeeding two centuries, often with a pro-clerical and anti-European motivation, in addition to the ambitions of re-creating the empire.

In the era of the trans-Atlantic slave trade, however, it was Kajor that consistently dominated Jolof, rather than vice versa. When the slave trade began to decline in the nineteenth century, Kajor's historic advantage became overt hegemony. Nobles whose real power base was in Kajor dominated Jolof from the 1850s until the French conquest in 1890, in the persons of Tanor *Silmaxa* Jeng and Albury Njay (q.v.).

JOP, LAT JOR NGONE LATIR. (1842–86). Better known as simply Lat Jor or Lat Dior, this leader of the anti-French resistance in Kajor (q.v.) has become a national hero for all Senegalese. His military and diplomatic encounters with the French and with his contemporaries have been immortalized in drama, film, novels, creative arts and regular radio broadcasts. The focus is usually Lat Jor's campaign against the French construction of a railroad through Kajor, linking Saint-Louis and Dakar (both q.v.) in 1879–1883.

Lat Jor first became a candidate for *Damel* of Kajor in 1860, while still a minor. He had been appointed *Ber Get,* or successor, shortly before and had already proved himself a dynamic young military leader. His patrilineage was a disadvantage, however, since all previous Damels had been Fals, and he was a Jop. He was also not yet circumcised. His mother's surviving sister, *Linger* Debu Suka, sought support for his candidacy from the French Governor Louis Faidherbe (q.v.), and from within Kajor and Jolof (q.v.). The majority of the freemen, however, turned to a more mature candidate, *Ten* Makodu Kodu Juf Fal, father of the deceased Damel.

Lat Jor retreated with his troops and followers to Sagata and called for young men throughout the kingdom to join him in a circumcision ceremony. Those who rallied became his elite fighting force in a military career that lasted 26 years. In the spring of 1861 Faidherbe invaded Kajor several times and eventually forced out Makodu, installing Majojo Jigen Kodu Fal in his place, with a French resident supervisor. Within a year, Lat Jor had defeated the puppet and forced the new French governor Jauréguiberry to recognize him as Damel. Then he began campaigning for the throne of Bawol as well.

Faidherbe returned to the governorship in 1863, forced Lat Jor into exile and reinstated Majojo. By 1865, however, even Faidherbe admitted that Majojo could not govern the country, so he ousted him and proclaimed the annexation of Kajor, although there was no effective occupation. Lat Jor, meanwhile, had joined forces with the Tijani marabout resistance leader Ma Ba (q.v.), who had established himself in Rip and Salum. Seeking to overcome the traditional vocational segregation and suspicion between clergy and royalty, Lat Jor was initiated into the Tijaniyya (q.v.). From then on, throughout the region, the resistance to European imperialism was led by Lat Jor and others like him who had found a new basis of unity and legitimacy in the combined roles of warrior and religious leader. Lat Jor and Ma Ba drove back a major French invasion at the battle of Patebajan (Pathebadiane) near Kaolack in November 1865. In July

1867, however, the two were defeated when they tried to invade Sin. Ma Ba was killed, and Lat Jor secretly fled back to Kajor.

By 1869, Lat Jor had established enough support to reassert his claim to the Kajor throne, but the French recognized him only as canton chief of Get (*Ber Get*). He allied with a new Tijani prophet, Shaixu Amadu Ba (q.v.), and together they drove back French invaders at Mekhe in 1869. Shaixu Amadu Ba soon split with Lat Jor, however, and conquered Jolof and the Njambur province of Kajor in 1871. Lat Jor found himself on the defensive. That year, when the French agreed to recognize him as Damel, he accepted, hoping for their aid. In 1874, Shaixu Amadu and his ally Abdul Bokar Kan (q.v.) of Futa Toro invaded Kajor, defeating Lat Jor and his Jolof ally Albury Njay (q.v.). In 1875, the latter two then turned to the French, and the three allies together defeated and killed Shaixu Amadu. Lat Jor regained the throne of Kajor, and he and the French helped Albury install himself on the throne of Jolof.

Four years later Lat Jor and Albury found themselves allied again on the last major issue facing them: the French plan to build a railroad (q.v.) through the center of Kajor to link Saint-Louis and Dakar. For its French sponsors, the railroad was a means of dominating the still-independent Kajor, first militarily and then commercially. In 1879, Lat Jor allowed his *qadi* (q.v.) to sign a treaty with the French, authorizing the construction of a ''trade route'' through Kajor on which the French would organize the rapid movement of goods via big cars drawn by steam engines. No soldiers, French or Ajor, were to be allowed near it. In turn the French promised military aid to Lat Jor and the Gej family descendants should Kajor be invaded. Lat Jor later wrote that the French had also promised him the restitution of annexed territories surrounding Cape Verde (q.v.) and Saint-Louis, and support for his claim to the throne of Bawol. When Governor Brière de l'Isle departed Senegal in 1881 without the promised military aid, Lat Jor immediately renounced the railroad treaty and vowed to leave Kajor barren and depopulated before he would allow the French to have it for their railroad.

When the French invaded and began building the railway in 1883, Lat Jor led a mass exodus of Ajor into Bawol, Salum, Jolof and Walo. Then he sent Samba Laobe at the head of his army to attack. After more than a month of continuous skirmishing, Samba Laobe retreated and offered public submission to the French at Saint-Louis. Hoping Samba Laobe would attract some of the farmers back into Kajor, the French let him return there, and a few months later installed him as Damel. Lat Jor's forces dwindled in exile in Rip, and he finally joined Albury Njay in Jolof with only a few hundred followers left from his original suite of 4,000. For two years they raided and harassed French posts and affiliated villages. Finally, in 1885, famine in Jolof forced Albury to make a separate peace with the French and chase Lat Jor from his kingdom. On July 6, 1885 the new railroad was inaugurated.

Within a year the chain of events began that led to the end of the reign of the Damels. Following a family quarrel that had led Samba Laobe to invade Jolof and Albury to threaten a return invasion, the French intervened as arbiters. They imposed an indemnity on Samba Laobe, which he refused to pay. Since they were under orders not to undertake a military expedition, a small force was sent to settle the matter amicably. He reportedly was insolent, they charged, he fled on horseback and the French officer pursued and killed him.

Lat Jor, with the support of a merchant group in Saint-Louis, hoped to see himself restored to the throne. From the fort that he had built at Jaje (Diadie) in eastern Kajor, he began collecting his followers. Instead, the French divided Kajor into five provinces among Lat Jor's former crown-slaves, and served Lat Jor with an expulsion order. On October 26, 1886, the French force sent to supervise his departure from Bawol engaged him in his final combat, the battle of Dekele on the Bawol-Kajor border. According to the French account, Lat Jor attacked them by surprise at dawn and had them nearly encircled. But they managed a rapid-fire rally in which Lat Jor, two of his sons and 78 of his warriors were killed on the spot. Lat Jor was mourned even in Saint-Louis, and the governor was accused of having plotted his murder. Although the archives are inconclusive, it would have been an extraordinary breach of military discipline for two French field commanders to "accidentally" kill two kings in the same month without orders to do so. Following the deaths, Kajor was pacified.

JOP, MATAR NDUMBE. (1701–1783) Renowned *marabout* and founder of the Islamic university at Koki (q.v.) in Njambur, one of the largest and most influential centers of Islamic study in the Senegambia region.

Matar was born into a family recently initiated into the clerical calling, his grandfather having decided late in life to abandon the high post of *Gankal* in the Kajor administration and become a marabout. Matar studied in Futa Toro (q.v.) under Massabma Cam, son of Ibrahima, where his fellow disciples included Malamin Sar and Maharam Mbake (great-grandfather of Amadu Bamba Mbake [q.v.]). Matar went on to Mauritania to learn Arabic grammar and then returned to Pir Sanoxor (q.v.), in Kajor, to continue jurisprudence (*fiqh*) and diction (*luga*). Matar Ndumbe was given an estate in Njambur on the northwestern frontier of Kajor by *Damel* Maisa Tenda Wej. He named his new town Koki, after the family home in Koki, Mbakol. It rapidly became a major intellectual and political center for clerics from Futa Toro and all of the Wolof countries, training such luminaries as *Almamy* Abdul Qadir Kan (q.v.) of Futa Toro and Saxewar Fatma Jop, grandfather of Lat Jor Jop (q.v.).

During the violent years from 1776 on, lives first brought together in scholarship came together again in war. Abdul

Qadir established clerical rule in Futa Toro and encouraged neighboring countries to follow his lead. Among his supporters in Kajor was his master's classmate Malamin Sar, who was assassinated by the Damel's men, setting off a clerical uprising there. The marabouts were decimated in battle, and the remnant fled to found a small, independent republic on the Cap Vert (q.v.) peninsula. Abdul Qadir was called into the fray by the then *Serin Koki* (Matar's son), but suffered a disastrous defeat at Bunxoye (c.1790) and was taken captive. Finally, Maharam Mbake emerged as peacemaker, persuading the Damel to release Abdul Qadir unharmed. The contacts established in this generation between marabouts of Futa Toro, Njambur, Pir and Cap Vert continued among their descendants until, and even after, the French conquest a century later.

JOP, NJAGA ISA. (fl.1827–40). A nineteenth-century descendant of Matar Ndumbe Jop (q.v.), Njaga Isa held the title of *Serin Koki* in the 1820s, attracting numerous disciples, both from the Wolof countries and from Futa Toro (q.v.). In 1827 *Damel* Birima Fatma Cub, perhaps seeking to bring him into his fold, gave Njaga Isa one of his sisters in marriage. Shortly thereafter, however, the Damel demanded public expressions of obedience and submission from the *Serin* and met with defiance. The Damel marched on Koki, forcing the weaker clerical forces into exile in Walo (q.v.).

Walo proved fertile ground for prophetic teaching, having been the scene of turbulence and political decline for half a century. Dile Cam (q.v.), one of Njaga Isa's followers, took command of the disciples, conquered Walo in a rapid sweep and began attacking French posts and farms in the area. In 1830 Governor Brou joined the exiled Walo-Walo nobility in defeating and hanging Dile. Njaga Isa fled into exile with his clerical brethren on Cape Verde (q.v.), and both the Damel and the French tried unsuccessfully to have him extradited. By 1839 he had been reconciled with the Damel and returned to

Koki as a simple marabout. Sometime afterward, however, the Damel asked for his daughter's hand in marriage; he declined, and a new quarrel broke out. The Damel took the girl by force, and the weaker Njaga Isa could only avenge himself with a few raids before retreating into exile in Futa Toro. He remained in Njum, Futa Toro, until his death in 1840.

JOP, SIDIA NDATE YALA (also known as Léon Diop). (c.1842–1870+) Leader of Walo (q.v.) during and immediately after the French conquest of the country. A contemporary and cousin of Lat Jor Jop (q.v.), Sidia was the son of the famous *Linger* Ndate Yala by Maroso Tase Jop. He received his military training from 1854 to 1860, while the royal party of Walo was taking refuge in Kajor from French invaders. Sidia and Lat Jor were among a group of young Walo-Walo and Ajor who conducted guerrilla-style harassment of French and cooperators in Walo from their camp across the border in Niomre, Kajor (q.v.). Governor Faidherbe (q.v.) tried to dislodge them through diplomacy for three years, and finally in 1858 invaded and burned the town. The refugees stood by in a nearby town and then resumed the struggle with the help of an incensed population. Kajor was considered neutral territory and Niomre sacred. The twin offenses by the French fueled guerrilla resistance for another two years.

Sidia was finally lured back to Walo in 1860 when Faidherbe created the canton of Nder and offered to make him chief. He was then among the first to be enrolled in the Ecole des ôtages (q.v.) and in 1861, continued his studies at the Lycée d'Alger. But upon returning to his conquered land, Sidia was offended to find his crown-slaves instead of noblemen as canton chiefs under the French. In November 1869, he led a party of like-minded nobles in a revolt and joined forces with Lat Jor to fight the French. Although Lat Jor in 1871 won French recognition of himself as *Damel*, Sidia was not so fortunate. Captured under obscure circumstances, he was deported to Gabon.

Sidia was a contemporary of the other great Senegalese resistance fighters, but he had the unique experience of coming from the frontline country for French penetration. His schooling gave him a deeper insight into the French, and his return found him one of the most determined advocates of a united Wolof-Futanke front against the French.

- K -

KABU. Malinke empire, located between the middle Gambia River, the Rio Grande and the hills of Futa Jalon (Guinea-Conakry). An offshoot and longtime dependency of the great Mali Empire of the Western Sudan, it originated from a thirteenth-century military expedition led by Tiramaxan Traoré, general to the founding emperor of Mali, Sunjata Keita. Although Tiramaxan reportedly reached the Atlantic Ocean, it is unclear whether he established Malian overlordship over Jolof (q.v.), or whether the Jolof Empire had been consolidated by then. His descendants settled and imposed their dynasty, called the Nanco, over a loose confederacy of provinces known collectively as the Kabu Empire. The capital was located at Kansala, in what is now Guinea-Bissau, and its provinces included Firdu, Pata, Kamako, Jimara, Patim Kibo, Patim Kanjaye, Kantora, Pakane Mambura, Kudura, Nampaio and Pacana. It grew in population and strength alongside its patron, Mali, and was fed by successive waves of migrants from the homeland from the thirteenth century on. Even after Mali was conquered by Songhai in 1492, Kabu continued to expand, reaching its apogee in the sixteenth century. The arrival of Portuguese (q.v.) traders on the coast in the mid-fifteenth century gave Kabu's markets on the Gambia and Rio Grande rivers added value, and it became a major exporter of slaves.

Beginning in the middle of the seventeenth century, Kabu entered a period of decline in which its provinces tended to assert their independence, and local ethnic rivalries broke out in many of them among Fulbe minorities and Malinke rulers. Fulbe pastoralists and farmers had been filtering into the area for several centuries, from nearby Futa Jalon, Khasso and Bundu (q.v.). The rise of a militant Islamic state in neighboring Futa Jalon from 1725 contributed to Kabu's decline. The new rulers of Futa Jalon, the *Alfa* of Labe in particular, supported local Fulbe groups against their Malinke masters and attempted to establish Jalonke hegemony in the area. Ultimately, in the latter nineteenth century, the local Fulbe under the leadership of *Alfa* Molo Balde (q.v.), supported by Futa Jalon, succeeded in overthrowing local Malinke dynasties and carving the new state of Fuladu (q.v.) out of the ruins of Kabu.

KAJOR. The most powerful of the Wolof successor states to the Jolof Empire (q.v.), Kajor stretched along the coast from the mouth of the Senegal River to Barni, near Rufisque, and inland an average of 70 kilometers (50 miles). The capital was at Mbul near modern Mekhe, but the administrative capital moved as the king chose. The ruler was called the *Damel* (q.v.).

Amary Ngone Sobel Fal (q.v.) led Kajor and neighboring Bawol (q.v.) to their independence in the mid-1500s. Little is known of the kingdom during its prior period of vassalage to Jolof, except that it existed and was visited by Portuguese (q.v.) in the fifteenth century. Amary Ngone Sobel and his descendants made Kajor the most powerful kingdom on the coast during the era of the Atlantic slave trade. Its exports included slaves, hides, cloth, beeswax and ivory in the early period, but by the eighteenth century focused on slaves and millet (sustenance also largely for the slave trade). The European and Moorish demand for slaves, and offer of luxuries and arms in trade, corrupted the feudal structure of this and other Wolof states. An increasingly arbitrary and militaristic nobility dominated the countryside with the support of their crown-slave *cedo* (q.v.). They offered protection to loyal subjects, but pillaged and enslaved the supporters of their rivals and found ready pretexts to raid non-Muslim Serer (q.v.) in their southern provinces or make war on neighboring kings.

In 1673 the Muslim prophet Nasir-al-Din (q.v.), supported by dissident local clerics and an ousted *Linger* (Queen Mother), overthrew the *Damel* and attempted to install one who would agree to be their disciple, introduce clerical mores and curtail the abuses of the slave trade (q.v.). The movement collapsed within a few years, but left Kajor unstable for two more decades. Then Lat Sukabe Fal (q.v.) (r.1697–1719) inaugurated a period of reorganization, bringing the still-bitter clerics into the political structure, establishing dominance for his formerly commoner matrilineage (the Gej) and developing the family slaves into a formidable military bureaucracy. This system prevailed in Kajor until the end, although internal rivalries and clerical dissention frequently challenged it.

The last of the Gej monarchs, Lat Jor Jop (q.v.), held the French at bay for a quarter century, from 1860 to 1886. The final campaign of conquest in 1880–1886 involved building a strategic railway through the center of the country. The line, linking Dakar and Saint-Louis, was inaugurated in 1885, and the last two *Damels* were killed in October 1886. Geography and the railroad made Kajor the nucleus of the French colony of Senegal, as the colonial system of groundnut exportation focused on the lands accessible by the railroad.

KAMARA, SHAIX MUSA. (also Cheikh Moussa Kamara). (1864–1945). Scholar whose works in Arabic are among the most complete indigenous accounts of the Senegal River valley and provide important sources for Senegalese history. Kamara was born and resided in eastern Futa Toro and made several trips to the upper Senegal valley. A friend of French administrator-scholars Maurice Delafosse and Henri Gaden,

Kamara did most of his writings after 1920, perhaps at their encouragement. His output includes works on history, anthropology, theology and law.

Kamara's main historic works are on Futa Toro and the upper Senegal valley. He read existing histories in Arabic and conducted numerous interviews and, in the early 1920s, wrote down several versions and commented on contradictions and discrepancies in the testimonies. In his work on the life of *al-Hajj* Umar Tal (q.v.), Kamara emphasized the religious aspects of the jihad, but provided little attention to social and economic consequences. The original documents are on deposit in the Islamic Department of the Institut Fondamental Cheikh Anta Diop (q.v.) (formerly IFAN) and comprise the *Fonds Cheikh Moussa Kamara.* The *Fonds* contain 18 cahiers, or notebooks, most of which have not been translated into a European language, although a few excerpts have been translated into French. (See Samb and N'Diaye in the Bibliography.)

KAMERA. Province of Gajaaga (q.v.) in the upper Senegal valley. Kamera stretched along the upper Senegal River between the Faleme River and Khasso, with its capital at Maxana. It frequently clashed with Goy (q.v.), the lower province of Gajaaga. Kamera was dominated by Soninke (q.v.) belonging to the Bathily lineage, but also had Fulbe and Mande residents.

KAN, ABDUL BOKAR. (c.1831–1891). Futanke who dominated the politics of Futa Toro (q.v.) from the late 1850s through his death in 1891. Although a cleric by birth, a grandson of Ali Dundu Kan (see KAN, ABDUL QADIR), his leadership was in the style of the military aristocracies of the region, not the clergy. Like his contemporaries Lat Jor Jop (q.v.) in Kajor and Albury Njay (q.v.) in Jolof, he tread a delicate path, defending his patrimony from both French invaders and clerical reformers.

When Abdul Bokar first came into political prominence in the 1850s, Governor Louis Faidherbe (q.v.) was trying to dominate the river valley from Saint-Louis, while *al-Hajj* Umar Tal (q.v.) was mobilizing enormous forces to the east on the upper river. Abdul Bokar, who ruled the easternmost province of Futa Toro, resisted Umar's mobilization because it set off a massive exodus that threatened to depopulate Futa. He was also able to survive French invasions in 1862 and 1863.

In the late 1860s, however, Abdul Bokar found himself allied with the French against clerical reformers based in Futa itself, including Cerno Brahim in the east and Shaixu Amadu Ba (q.v.) in the west. Abdul Bokar defeated Cerno Brahim once in 1867, and finally sacked his town and killed him in 1869. His relations with Shaixu Amadu were more complex. Initially hostile to Amadu's movement, which took over neighboring Jolof in 1869 and 1870, he joined forces with him in 1874 to invade and conquer Kajor. In 1875, however, the French sent reinforcements to Lat Jor and Albury Njay, who retook Kajor, killing Shaixu Amadu.

Between 1879 and 1885, Abdul Bokar resisted the French construction of a telegraph line into the Sudan. Like its contemporary, the railroad through Kajor, the telegraph line was intended to both justify and facilitate the conquest of the territory through which it passed. When Governor Brière de l'Isle (q.v.) negotiated a treaty with the Almamy of Futa Toro, Abdul Bokar had the Almamy deposed. The French nevertheless built one segment of the line upriver and one on the lower river, before they were finally forced to a show-down over the Salde-Bakel section, which Abdul Bokar controlled. In 1881, Abdul Bokar skirmished with the army sent to build the line but then held back while they pillaged and finally retreated. Like many Sudanic battles, this ambiguous campaign was interpreted by both sides as a victory. The generous treaty terms offered to Abdul heightened the confusion. The published version of the Gababe accords, as they were called, allowed the line to be constructed in return for a French guarantee of autonomy. An accompanying private convention offered Abdul Bokar substantial protection money. The Futanke believed the treaty also authorized the reunification of Futa Toro, restoring the lost provinces of Law, Pete and Eastern Futa. But yellow fever struck Saint-Louis that year, killing 600, including the governor and most of the forces that might have tested the accords. The construction was put off until 1885, by which time Abdul Bokar was weaker and had to acquiesce. In return he received a generous sum of French money, political concessions and French support of his authority.

By the mid-1880s, however, French military penetration of the Senegambia had a strong momentum. Kajor was annexed in 1886, and the revolt of Mamadu Lamine Drame (q.v.) in the upper river was crushed in 1887–1888. Finally, Louis Archinard, in campaigns lasting from 1888 through 1891, decimated and occupied the state *al-Hajj* Umar had created at Segu on the upper Niger River. When the French chased Albury Njay from Jolof in 1890, Abdul Bokar gave him asylum, becoming a target himself. The two allies fled north into Mauritanian exile, where Abdul Bokar was killed by his host in 1891. Albury fled on to Nioro in Mali, and eventually crossed the Sudan. Although Abdul Bokar had never been Almamy of Futa Toro, he had dominated the attempt to retain its independence. In the period of his exile and death, it was partitioned and occupied.

KAN, ABDUL QADIR. (c.1725–1806) Founder of the Almamate of Futa Toro (q.v.) and ruler (*Almamy*) from about 1776 until his death in 1806. Abdul Qadir was born into one of the most highly educated and devout noble Fulbe families of Futa Toro. His grandfather had made the pilgrimage to Mecca in the late seventeenth century, when that was still extremely rare; his father had studied at the famous *zwaya* at Ja (Dia) on the upper Niger River, and then taught in Jolof and Salum.

Abdul Qadir was born in his father's village of Pafa Warneu, in Salum. He was educated at Pir Sanoxor, Kajor (q.v.), and in Mauritania. He settled and taught in eastern Futa Toro, where he turned fifty before entering public life. According to tradition, he was not a member of the reform movement launched by Sulaiman Bal (q.v.), which had ousted the Denanke (q.v.) by the early 1770s. When Bal and his followers were killed in battle about 1775, a Denanke who promised to adhere to Islam was briefly restored to the throne. But a new clerical faction arose backing Abdul Qadir and forced the Denanke into exile.

Although he initially hesitated to assume power, Abdul Qadir proved the most forceful Almamy in Futa's history. He defeated the Brakna Moors (see MOORS), whose chronic raiding had helped provoke the revolution, and consolidated clerical rule at home. He replaced the territorial administration with clerical appointees, reserving the top posts for his most trusted supporters. These gradually became hereditary fiefs and the elite heirs the grand electors. The principle was established that the Almamy should be chosen for his learning and piety, not by heredity. The title of Almamy itself implied a religious rather than secular political leader. Abdul Qadir sometimes also styled himself *amir al-muslimin* (commander of the Muslims) or *amir al muᶜminin* (commander of the faithful), both titles that linked his rule with the early Caliphs of Islam.

Success at home inspired Abdul Qadir to invite neighboring peoples to join him. His first formal diplomatic invitation to the rulers of Walo, Kajor, Bawol and Jolof were favorably received. When a new ruler, Amary Ngone Ndela, succeeded in 1790 to the thrones of Kajor and Bawol, however, he refused to renew his predecessor's allegiance, and Abdul Qadir called for a jihad (q.v.). In alliance with Jolof, he marched on Kajor in 1796–1797 at the head of the largest army yet known in the Senegambia.

Calculating the odds, the Damel of Kajor scorched the

earth and poisoned the wells in his own eastern provinces to save the kingdom. The Almamy's forces had to cross the *ferlo* (q.v.) wasteland for several days and arrived to find neither food nor water. Parched and starving, they surrendered unceremoniously and were sold as slaves. The Damel spared Abdul Qadir and kept him at court in style. Then, when Abdul Qadir had been temporarily replaced as Almamy, the Damel released him and sent him home laden with rich gifts.

Abdul Qadir was reinstated as Almamy but never regained mastery of either the internal or external affairs of his regime. All the neighboring states found his meddling in their internal affairs presumptuous. In 1806 the eastern neighbors, Bundu (q.v.) and Karta, allied with dissidents led by Ali Dundu to invade Futa Toro and eventually overthrow the Almamy. He is said to have died on his prayer mat, in the midst of a losing battle, shot by the Almamy of Bundu, whose brother he had earlier killed. His reign was the longest in Futa's history. After his rule, the state he created degenerated into an oligarchy dominated by a new hereditary clerical nobility.

Abdul Qadir's movement left no writings to posterity, which must be seen as a commentary on the generally low level of Islamic learning in the area. Although he had impeccable educational credentials and had studied at the best schools in the region, he is remembered primarily as a military leader and founder of a new regime.

KASA. Kingdom dominating the lower Casamance (q.v.) when the Portuguese (q.v.) first arrived in the mid-fifteenth century. It declined in the eighteenth century under pressure from Jola (q.v.) neighbors on the west and the Mande empire of Kabu (q.v.) on the east. The population was primarily Banun and Kasanke, although the title of the king, *Mansa,* is of Mande origin. Portuguese accounts from the fifteenth and sixteenth centuries, the only major sources for the kingdom, suggest that it was tributary to Kabu, which in turn was a tribute state to the Mali Empire centered in the Western Sudan. The capital of Kasa was at Brikama, and the chief port of trade with the Portuguese was Ziguinchor (q.v.).

KOKI. Village southeast of Louga in the former Njambur province of Kajor (q.v.), which was one of the most important clerical centers in Senegambia in the eighteenth and nineteenth centuries. Matar Ndumbe Jop (q.v.) brought the settlement to prominence in the early eighteenth century, and it quickly became a center of clerical teaching and political agitation for both Wolof and Futanke leaders. (See JOP, NJAGA ISA; KAN, ABDUL QADIR; BA, HAME; and BA, SHAIXU AMADU.)

KOLY TENGELA. See BA, KOLY TENGELA.

KONAGI. (sometimes Coniagui). Ethnic group akin to the Bassari (q.v.) who currently occupy a small area of eastern Senegal and the Yunkunkun area of Guinea-Conakry. Oral traditions suggest that they were once sparsely settled throughout eastern Senegal but were forced out and enslaved by their more powerful Mande and Fulbe neighbors. The Konagi, primarily farmers and hunters, were also predominantly non-Muslim with an egalitarian social organization. Today they comprise a tiny minority population in Senegal.

- L -

LAC DE GUIERS. The only large lake in Senegal, located on the south bank of the Senegal River (q.v.), with an outlet at Richard Toll. It fills with fresh water during the rainy season, mainly from the Senegal River flood. The lake used to become brackish during the dry season, when ocean water mounted above its outlet to the river, but today it is dammed off in the dry season to make a large reservoir. The fresh water is used for irrigation and urban water supply. Historically, it was also known as Lac Paniéfoule.

LAM, LAMAN. Wolof and Pulaar title for a provincial chief, usually connoting the original chief, founder or "owner of the land." In many areas, local *laman* were superseded by more powerful chiefs but retained their titles. They also reserved the right to collect token customs from those who wanted to cut wood, draw water, land on their shores or cultivate the land.

LAMINE, MAMADOU. See DRAME, MAMADU LAMINE.

LANGUAGES. The major indigenous languages of Senegal are Wolof, Serer, Pulaar (the local dialect of Fulfulde), Diola, Mandinka and Soninke (each q.v.). There are a number of others, corresponding roughly to the number of minor ethnic groups. All Senegalese languages belong to the Niger-Congo linguistic family. About 80 percent of Senegalese speak Wolof, and it is the national language. Although people continue primarily to speak Diola in Casamance, Serer in Thiès and Sin-Saloum and Pulaar in the Senegal River region, an increasing number of people speak Wolof as a second language.

French, which is the official language, fills a need for administrative and technical communications inside the country and for inter-African and international relations. About 15 percent of the population are literate in French, while a far greater number speak and understand it because it continues to be the language of education (q.v.). About 2 percent of the population has some knowledge of Arabic.

LAPTOT. Early French term for a boatman, either slave or freeborn, working the French boats that made the annual high-water journey up the Senegal River (q.v.) or gathered trade goods from posts along the coast. Slave sailors were rented from their owners for a fixed price, but they were allowed to trade on their own during the trip to supplement their income. Freeborn *laptots* also supplemented their wages with trade profits, hoping to become a *traitant* (q.v.) or, if very lucky and prosperous, a boat owner. Most laptots lived in Saint-Louis or Gorée (both q.v.), although some were from neighboring African villages, such as Ganjol, or other European trading posts as far away as Sierra Leone.

LAT DIOR. See JOP, LAT JOR NGONE LATIR.

LAW ON THE NATIONAL DOMAIN. This important law was passed on June 17, 1964, establishing the Senegalese government as the ultimate proprietor of all nondeeded land in Senegal. This law was part of a package of socialist reforms advocated by former Prime Minister Mamadou Dia (q.v.) immediately after independence. The reforms were ultimately instituted by President Senghor (q.v.) after Dia had been imprisoned (see CONSTITUTIONAL CRISIS OF 1962).

Property deeds were rare in Senegal, except on the Cap Vert peninsula (q.v.) and in other urban areas. Under the new law, owners with permanent buildings on their land were given six months to establish deeds for their plots. All land was divided into four categories: 1) urban areas, 2) reserves (including national forests and parks), 3) farmland (*zone des terroirs*) and 4) pioneer zones. The law permitted the government to declare some of the less intensively occupied lands "pioneer zones" and cede them to groups or organizations willing to develop them. The second major innovation was to undermine the numerous traditional local systems of land tenure. Land-tenure decisions were to depend on whether an individual personally cultivated or otherwise developed the land. The law abolished crop shares and land rents that former slaves and other landless persons paid to local nobility.

Other reforms included the establishment of farmers' cooperatives and rural councils to replace traditional kin and patron-client networks. The cooperatives became the basic units where farmers obtained seeds, tools, credit and marketing facilities for their crops. The law is still unequally enforced, generally diminishing in impact in proportion to the distance from Dakar.

Inadvertently, the law stimulated urban real estate speculation, which had frequently been a problem in Dakar. By fixing the ground rules in independent Senegal, the law set off a new wave of speculation and extended the tendency to regional capitals and small towns.

LEBANESE. An ethnic minority in Senegal that occupied the commercial role of "middleman" within the colonial system throughout both British and French West Africa. Migrants from Lebanon and Syria (both are called Lebanese locally) began arriving in the 1890s, and the flow grew rapidly in the period between the two world wars when Lebanon itself was under French domination. They lived in many of the towns and small market centers, speaking the local language in addition to Arabic. The Lebanese in Senegal maintain close ties with relatives in other West African countries and in the Middle East.

When European commercial firms expanded into the interior in the early twentieth century, they frequently gave employment or credit preference to Lebanese traders over Wolof and Fulbe competitors. Since independence, Lebanese entrepreneurs have been forced out of groundnut marketing by nationalization and have moved their investments into real estate, transport, wholesale commerce and light industry. They also remain predominant as middle-level merchants. At independence, the 1960 census showed 15,000 Lebanese in Senegal and 30,000 French; today the French population has declined to about 20,000 and the Lebanese population is estimated to exceed that number substantially. Rapid natural growth has been swelled by new refugees from the Lebanese civil war that began in 1975.

In the mid-1980s, the Senegalese government tried to limit the flow of money out of the country to Lebanon and Syria by strictly enforcing currency export restrictions. Yet, Lebanese prefer to export their earnings rather than invest in Senegal, causing friction between the government and the growing Lebanese community. There is also considerable ethnic tension between the Lebanese and African Senegalese, especially in Dakar. The ethnic clashes between Senegalese and Moors (q.v.) also fueled resentment toward the Lebanese, who were frequently perceived as being supportive of the Moors.

LEBU. Ethnic group originally inhabiting the Cape Verde peninsula (q.v.) and along the coast from Kayar to Mbour. Although they speak Wolof, the Lebu have a distinct sense of historic identity and today constitute a small but organized political-interest group.

The Lebu Republic of Cape Verde was not led by Lebu fishermen and farmers from the area, but by clerical refugees from Njambur, Kajor (q.v.), who fled to the peninsula after their defeat by the *Damel* Amari Ngone Ndela in 1795–1796. The clerical oligarchy, under the leadership of founding father Jal Jop, quickly assimilated and adopted a Lebu cultural identity, with strong links to Wolof. This reinforced their claims to independence from Kajor throughout the nineteenth century. The Lebu clerics of Cape Verde remained in constant communication with clerics in Kajor proper, Njambur province and Futa Toro (q.v.). The majority of Lebu converted to Islam relatively recently, and elements of their indigenous religion persisted in many aspects of their daily lives.

When the other polities of the interior were conquered and dismantled by the French in the 1890s, Cape Verde, including the rapidly expanding center of Dakar (q.v.), was simply occupied without a struggle. The French, however, could not expropriate land by right of conquest. This unique historical experience has transformed the Lebu from a tiny, neglected, peripheral people to one of the wealthiest and most powerful ethnic groups in Senegal. As Dakar grew from a small village to the capital of French West Africa and finally capital of independent Senegal, the Lebu have consolidated their political and economic power, and a few have grown wealthy on urban real estate. There is also a fairly high rate of intermarriage with Wolof.

LOI CADRE (Reorganizing Law). A French law passed on June 23, 1956, providing for basic changes in the political institutions of West Africa. Universal adult suffrage was introduced, legislative powers were added to the budgetary functions of territorial assemblies, and elected territorial councils of ministers were instituted. These reforms also moved French West Africa away from unity, a direction that was confirmed in the 1958 Fifth French Republic Constitution (q.v.), which superseded the *loi cadre* after two years.

LYCEE FAIDHERBE. Secondary school in Saint-Louis (q.v.) created in 1919 to remedy the lack of opportunity for higher education in Senegal. Blaise Diagne (q.v.) had fought for such a school in the French National Assembly, arguing that Senegalese soldiers in French armies in World War I had earned such opportunities. Along with the prestigious Ecole Normale William Ponty (q.v.), it trained the colonial elite of Senegal. Its role has declined since independence, when the capital was transferred from Saint-Louis to Dakar.

- M -

MAGAL. Pilgrimage made by disciples of Murid (q.v.) marabouts, climaxed by a night of prayer and chanting. The annual Grand Magal, which sets the pattern for lesser ones, is held by the *Xalifa-Général* in memory of the death of the founder of Muridism, Amadu Bamba Mbacke (q.v.). Followers from throughout Senegal and neighboring countries converge on Touba in western Senegal near Diourbel, site of his tomb and great mosque. They render visits of respect, gifts and obligatory contributions of substantial value, which give the event political and economic as well as religious significance. A substantial crowd of the less devout use the occasion for a night of revelry and licentiousness at nearby Mbake. A similar religious pilgrimage is made by the Tijani (q.v.) brotherhood to Medina-Gonasse in the upper Casamance. (See BA, *AL-HAJJ* MAMADU SAIDU.)

MAHDI. In Islamic theology, an apocalyptic figure who will rule the world and bring in the universal true religion immediately before the end of time. This teaching was well-known among Berber and particularly Futanke clerics in Senegal. Periodically in Senegalese history, clerics would respond to a crisis by attempting to fulfill this mystical vision. (See BA, HAME; and BA, SHAIXU AMADU.)

MALI FEDERATION. An attempt by Léopold Senghor (q.v.) and Modibo Keita to hold together the French West African colonies at independence in 1960. France refused to maintain unity by constitutional means, and advocates of unity were able to persuade only Dahomey and Upper Volta to join Senegal and the French Sudan (modern-day Mali) in a voluntary union. These four initially joined in the Mali Federation in 1959, but France and the Ivory Coast put pressure on Dahomey and Upper Volta, so that they defected within a few months. On April 4, 1960, France signed an accord granting independence to a Mali Federation composed of Senegal and the French Sudan. Houphouet-Boigny of the Ivory Coast enlisted Dahomey and Upper Volta along with Niger and Togo in the rival regional organization, the Conseil d'Entente.

Independence for the Mali Federation actually became effective on June 20, but Senegal and the French Sudan (Mali) split before the first presidential election two months later. Relations soured in July when the more radical and better disciplined Sudanese threatened the accommodationist Senegalese on a number of issues: Africanization, relations with France, command of the army and Sudanese withdrawal of support for Senghor's candidacy as president of the federation. On August 19, Mamadou Dia (q.v.) mobilized the *Gendarmerie* around key installations, and the Sudanese mobilized the Federal army. The Gendarmerie and Senegalese leaders quickly got the upper hand. The French commander of the Gendarmerie entrapped the Sudanese commander, and the rest of the leaders were exiled to Mali. Mamadou Dia then called a midnight meeting of the Senegalese territorial assembly, which voted separate independence for the Republic of Senegal. The French quickly recognized it, and within a month the Sudanese conceded the fait accompli, voting its own independence as the Republic of Mali. Mali, however, blockaded all communications with Senegal for three years, most notably the Dakar-Bamako railroad, which linked the two countries. Both nations experienced severe economic dislocation, and Senegal ultimately lost much of the vast hinterland on which its economy had thrived during the colonial period. Tensions between Senegal and Mali continued for several years, but gradually cordial relations developed, primarily out of economic necessity.

MALINKE/MANDINKA. (generally interchangeable terms). Ethnic group and language originally from the ancient Mali Empire (height: 1250–1450) centered in the Western Sudan.

Like the Soninke (q.v.) and the Jaxanke (q.v.), the Mandinka belong to the widely dispersed Mande social formation, which sent out waves of migrants from the thirteenth through the sixteenth centuries. The Mande, also referred to as the Malinke, Mandinko and Mandingue, occupied both savanna and forest zones of West Africa and dominated several precolonial states, including the empire of Mali. Centered in the upper Niger savanna, the empire expanded north toward the desert and west toward the Atlantic, eventually controlling a vast area stretching from the mouths of the Senegal and Gambia rivers to beyond the middle Niger delta. In Senegambia, settling most heavily on the banks of the Gambia River, the Malinke formed a series of small north-bank states, provided dynasties for Sin and Salum (both q.v.) and formed the loose empire of Kabu (q.v.) on the south bank. Predominantly agriculturalists, the Mande hunted extensively and engaged in iron and gold mining in mountainous areas like Bambuk (q.v.). The Mande social structure mirrored that of the Soninke and Fulbe; the Mande, however, emphasized initiations into occupational and age associations. These ceremonies continued even after the comparatively late conversion to Islam of the majority of the Mande. Numerous groups, including the Mandinka of Bambuk, did not become Muslim until the late nineteenth century.

Today, the Malinke are an important element of the population of Senegal only in Senegal Oriental (eastern Senegal) and the lower and upper Casamance. They are a majority in the Gambia.

MARABOUT. French adaptation of an Arabic term for Muslim scholar, religious leader or cleric. In Senegal, the term refers to any cleric or religious figure regardless of scholarly attainments. (See CLERIC.)

MBAKE, ABDOU LAHATTE. (c.1905–) *Xalifa-Général* of the Murid brotherhood (q.v.) since 1968, with his residence and central mosque at Touba. The seventh son of the founder Amadu Bamba Mbake (q.v.), he succeeded two of his older brothers (Mamadu Mustapha and Falilou, both q.v.) as head of the brotherhood. Following a pattern established since the end of World War II, he was a staunch supporter of President

Senghor and his successor, Abdou Diouf (both q.v.). This has been important in recent multiparty presidential elections because Murid areas traditionally have returned large, nearly unanimous votes for the Socialist Party slates.

MBAKE, AMADU BAMBA (Muslim name, Muhammad 'ibn Muhammad 'ibn Habib Allah). (1850–1927) Founder of the Murid brotherhood (q.v.) and the most prominent clerical leader in colonial Senegal.

As a young man, Amadu Bamba accompanied his *marabout* father, Momar Anta Sali, at the courts of Ma Ba and Lat Jor Jop (both q.v.). After his father died in 1880 and Lat Jor was killed in 1886, Amadu Bamba established himself at Mbake-Bawol in western Senegal. He rapidly became the focus of all those who hoped for further resistance to the French. While evidence suggests his resistance was primarily spiritual, it is also clear that he initially opposed French influence in general and that many of his followers hoped that an active struggle of resistance would begin again. In 1895 the French, deciding to end the threat, captured and deported him to Gabon in Equatorial Africa.

Most of the literature of the Murid brotherhood comes from the seven years Amadu Bamba spent in exile. He composed religious verses, which today are chanted throughout Senegal. His stature had increased so greatly by 1902, when he was allowed to return, that his exile was quickly transformed into a period of miracles and legend. Within a year after his return to Senegal, there were serious rumors that the cleric was gathering arms for a holy war against the French and their supporters, and he was again deported. This time (1903–1907) he was sent to Saix Sidiyya in Mauritania, where he was able to study and receive followers from Senegal and other countries.

Although Amadu Bamba had been a Qadiri (q.v.) member since at least 1889, and remained loyal to the Qadiri Shaix Sidiyya, it was during his Mauritanian exile that he branched off to found a new brotherhood to be called the Muridiyya (see MURID). He also developed a distinctive message, which, in addition to the religious observance of Islam, emphasized salvation through hard manual labor and un-questioning devotion to the marabout. His chief disciple, Shaix Ibra Fal (q.v.), made a fetish of obedience and hard work. As he had done in 1902, the Senegalese deputy to the French Assembly, François Carpot (q.v.), intervened to bring about Amadu Bamba's return to Senegal. The colonial administration assigned him residence in the remote village of Cheyen, Jolof, where his followers continued to flock. In 1920, he made public peace with the French, circulating a letter throughout the country advising peace and resignation to his followers. Two years later he was allowed to return to his native Bawol (q.v.). There he continued to build the brotherhood into the most powerful political force in rural Senegal. He helped to finance Blaise Diagne's (q.v.) elec-toral challenge to the colonial system, but his own style of leadership emphasized religion over politics.

One of the results of the return to Bawol was Murid cooperation for the French military recruitment drive from 1912 through the end of World War I. While urban residents, under Blaise Diagne's leadership, were using draft resistance to gain political rights, the Murid leaders in rural areas delivered ample numbers of well-disciplined recruits. This created a collaborative relationship between rural marabouts and the secular, central administration that has persisted to this day. In return, the French opened new lands to Murid colonists, facilitating the continued expansion of the brother-hood. (See TERRES NEUVES.)

Amadu Bamba's last project was the construction of a central mosque and mausoleum at Touba. He requested permission to build in 1924 and two years later received French approval. Only the foundations had been begun, however, before it was discovered that some of his followers and a French official had absconded with most of the building fund. When he died on July 19, 1927, he was buried at the unfinished site. The construction of his tomb and the mosque devolved on his successor, Mamadu Mustapha Mbake (q.v.).

MBAKE, CHEIKH. (c.1905–1978). Eldest son and claimant to the succession of the *Xalifa-Général* of the Murids, Mamadu Mustapha Mbake (q.v.). The governor of Senegal, judging Cheikh Mbake less accommodating than his uncle Falilou Mbake (q.v.), intervened to ensure the latter's election in 1945. Cheikh inherited the blueprints for the great mosque and town plan of Touba and used them to press his claim to the Xalifa-Generalship. In 1949, the governor arbitrated a compromise, creating a Murid administrative council consisting of marabouts loyal to each claimant to supervise the mosque construction. Cheikh Mbake's claim was supported by Lamine Guèye (q.v.), with whom he had a very active political alliance. When Guèye lost the 1951 election to Senghor, Cheikh Mbake's chances of succession dwindled. In 1957, when Guèye agreed to form a coalition with Senghor, Cheikh Mbake paid a courtesy visit to Falilou, a symbolic form of rapprochement. In 1959, however, he began implementing a street realignment in Touba, based on his inherited plans, which provoked another round of crisis, arbitration and compromise.

Having conceded the political struggle, Cheikh Mbake went on to become one of the most successful private entrepreneurs in Senegal. He financed the Salt Production of Kaolack (Salines de Kaolack), commercial fishing ventures, general commerce and peanut-processing enterprises. He also invested heavily in lucrative urban real estate.

MBAKE, FALILOU. (c.1885–1968) *Xalifa-Général* of the Murids from 1945 to 1968. The second son of the Murid (q.v.) founder, Amadu Bamba Mbake (q.v.), Falilou succeeded his elder brother Mamadu Mustapha Mbake (q.v.).

Falilou's candidacy received the support of the colonial governor of Senegal. His excluded rival was Cheikh Mbake (q.v.), Mamadu Mustapha's son, who continued to seek the title for more than a decade. Cheikh's strong position obliged the governor to establish a Murid administrative council in 1949, where both marabouts were represented.

Falilou was a pious ascetic Xalifa, who presided over the continued expansion of the brotherhood. In the political movements that emerged after World War II, he became an ally of Léopold Senghor (q.v.), while their respective rivals, Cheikh Mbake and Lamine Guèye (q.v.), formed an opposing alliance. The 1949 compromise permitted the continued construction of the great mosque at Touba, whose plans Cheikh Mbake had inherited. By 1957 the victory of the Senghor-Falilou alliance was evident on both fronts, and public rapprochements ended the era of competition. As Falilou aged, control of everyday affairs of the brotherhood devolved on cliques of marabouts-advisors, who have remained prominent in brotherhood affairs to the present day.

MBAKE, MAMADU MUSTAPHA. (c.1880–1945) Eldest son and successor to Amadu Bamba Mbake (q.v.), the founder of the Murids (q.v.). From 1927 to 1945, Mamadu Mustapha held the new title of *Xalifa-Général* of the Murid brotherhood. The only other claimant to the succession was the founder's brother Shaix Anta Mbake. The French refused to recognize him, however, and intervened in support of Mamadu Mustapha. The young heir quickly consolidated his authority at Touba. With the cooperation of the colonial administration, he drafted disciples to build a railroad branch to Touba to carry construction materials and then had them build the mosque. When the outbreak of World War II forced suspension of construction, the walls and pillars were nearly complete, but the project had become a source of financial and political bickering among the leading clerics. Mamadu Mustapha died in 1945 before construction resumed. The other major accomplishment of his term was continued rapid territorial expansion of the brotherhood, facilitated by vast land grants from the administration, especially in central Senegal along the Dakar-Bamako railroad. (See TERRES NEUVES.)

MBOJ, NDATE YALA. Famous *Linger* (Queen Mother) of Walo (q.v.) in the kingdom's final years, from 1847 until the French conquest in 1854 and, in an honorary sense, on into the 1860s. Immortalized in a sketch by Abbé Boilat (see Bibliography), she is one of the very few precolonial nobility depicted visually. Like her sister Njembot (q.v.), whom she succeeded in 1847, Ndate Yala was famous for her marriages and her son Sidia Jop (q.v.), as well as her own political strength. The French were first interested in her in 1841, when they favored her marriage to their candidate for *Brak,* Yerim Mbanik of the Jos matrilineage. But the son who was to help make her famous was born of her second marriage, to Maroso Tase Jop, a relative and companion of Lat Jor Jop's (q.v.) father.

From the start of her reign, Ndate Yala found herself in opposition to the French, who in 1847 were trying to free their Soninke meat suppliers from the obligation to pay tribute for the passage of their cattle through Walo (q.v.). Later she emerged as a leader of a campaign to rid the country of Moorish domination. That struggle also had a personal dimension, because the Moors were mobilized behind her dead sister's son, Ely Njembot (see MBOJ, NJEMBOT), while the "nationalist" party's logical candidate was her own son Sidia Jop.

When the French invaded, pillaged and burned the country in 1854, Ndate Yala, Maroso Tase and young Sidia took refuge in Niomre, Kajor, under the protection of the cleric of Niomre and the *Damel* of Kajor. The teenaged Lat Jor and his father joined them in harassing French troops and collaborators. Governor Faidherbe (q.v.) tried for years to persuade the *Damel* or the *Serin Niomre* to turn them over, or at least to make them leave. Finally, in 1858, Faidherbe invaded and burned Niomre and neighboring Ngik—an offense against the territorial integrity of a neutral power and the sanctity of holy towns that shocked the countryside. Sidia and Ndate Yala remained in exile there for another two years, before returning to their conquered homeland in a negotiated settlement.

MBOJ, NJEMBOT. (c.1800–46) Famous *Linger,* or Queen Mother, of the kingdom of Walo (q.v.), who dominated the political life of that state from about 1830 until her death in 1846.

She emerged on the political scene during the civil war following French withdrawal from Walo and abandonment of the agricultural colonization scheme at Richard Toll in 1829. Both the French and the Trarza Moors were seeking hegemony over Walo. Her influence was decisive in the nomination of Fara Penda as *Brak* in 1831, instead of the French-supported candidate, Xerfi Xari Daro. The Trarza *Emir* Muhammad al-Habib moved into Walo, however, filling the vacuum left by the French. Njembot and Fara Penda went into exile in Kajor.

Negotiating an already severely compromised national sovereignty, a group of the nobles proposed the hand of the most prized woman of Walo to the Emir of the Trarza. The marriage was celebrated June 18, 1833. Suddenly, the two kingdoms north and south of the mouth of the Senegal River were united in a single family, an alarming spectacle to the French commercial colony at Saint-Louis. Within a month the French forces and auxiliaries invaded, raiding, pillaging and burning crops standing in the fields to try to force the annulment of the marriage. *Linger* Njembot and her allies again sought asylum in Kajor. After two years of inconclusive warfare, Walo was barren and deserted by its inhabitants, and French trade was at a standstill. Peace negotiations resulted in a pair of treaties in 1835. By the first treaty, Muhammad al-Habib renounced all claims to the throne of Walo, for himself or his offspring (he and his wife were at that moment awaiting their firstborn). By the second treaty, the exiles in Kajor were allowed to return and resume their thrones in Walo. There were great victory celebrations in Walo, and Njembot's authority was reinforced. Five years later, when the Brak died, she was able to ensure the election of Mboj Malik through generosity to the electoral council (*Seb ak Baor*).

Njembot was never officially king, as tradition forbade a woman to reign as Brak. But her power was such that Mboj Malik was considered a front for Njembot, who was the real decision maker. She died in 1846, too soon to see her son Ely Njembot accede to the throne. Her younger sister, Mboj, Ndate Yala (q.v.), succeeded her and proved an equally notable personality.

Griots (q.v.) still celebrate Njembot's legendary marriage. In one version Njembot is the pearl of the kingdom who sacrifices herself in marriage to save Walo from the misery of the Trarza war. In another she is a woman of overwhelming ambition, who wanted to be known in history as Kumba Linger, and to leave the two kingdoms of Walo and Trarza to her son. In fact, her son Ely was crowned king of Trarza and throughout the late 1840s and early 1850s was the virtual ruler in Walo as well. His pretensions to the throne were quashed only by the French conquest and partition of the kingdom in 1854.

MBOW, AMADOU MOKHTAR. (1921-) Educator and politician who served as director-general of UNESCO between 1974 and 1987. After an early career in teaching and adult education, he was appointed minister of national education and culture in the first autonomous Senegalese cabinet in 1957. The following year, however, he was one of the group that split with Senghor to form the Parti du Regroupement

Africain (q.v.), which advocated immediate independence. In 1966 the PRA merged with Senghor's UPS (q.v.), and Mbow was once again appointed minister of youth and culture. In 1970 he took a post as assistant director for education at UNESCO and was later promoted to director-general. His directorship was marked by controversy, including charges by the United States that Mbow politicized UNESCO, mismanaged and wasted funds and was anti-Western. It was during his tenure that the United States left UNESCO. Mbow was voted out of office in 1987. He has been active in the Africanization of school curricula, participating on commissions and as an author of new texts in history and geography.

MEDICAL EDUCATION. In 1918 in Dakar, the French began training African doctors (*médecins africains*) and African pharmacists for all of French West Africa. Candidates were given a special science curriculum in the last three years of *lycée* and then four years of medical education. A total of 581 médecins africains were graduated over the next 35 years.

Until 1954 training as a full physician (a six-year postsecondary curriculum in the French system) was available only in France. The establishment in 1954 of the medical school as the nucleus of the University of Dakar (q.v.) reversed the situation. Only full physicians were educated, and paramedical education began to lag, resulting in an elitist medical orientation of questionable suitability to Senegal's socioeconomic situation. The medical school and related programs at the new Institut Universitaire Technologique are administered by the Ministry of Higher Education. Paramedical training is now conducted by the Ministry of Health and the Armed Forces. (See also HEALTH CARE.)

MEDINA (LA MEDINE). Arabic word for city or place of residence; in French colonial usage, the ''African'' or Muslim part of the city. In Senegal the best-known Medina is the large African residential section of Dakar (q.v.), which is roughly centered on the Tilène Market on Avenue Blaise Diagne.

Initially created during the 1914 plague epidemic for Africans whose homes on the Dakar Plateau were destroyed, it quickly became a permanent workers' suburb. Throughout the 1920s and 1930s, rural immigrants were encouraged to settle there, and by the outbreak of World War II, it had reached its westernmost natural limit at the marsh of Guele Tapée. It also developed a strong Islamic identity, since most residents and migrants were Muslim. It was eventually furnished with its own market and post office, but urban services remain minimal even today. Water and sewage facilities are grossly inadequate, and many of the streets are still not paved. Most housing consists of shacks made of flattened tin and scraps of lumber. Many of the dwellings consist of one room for families of seven or eight or more, with no indoor plumbing, running water or electricity. Water is secured from open, public pumps and the supply is occasionally cut off. Open sewers, which run directly through the Medina, are used for all types of waste disposal. Sanitation facilities are negligible, and there are constant outbreaks of infectious diseases. Although French and, later, Senegalese urban plans (1946, 1961 and 1971) have eliminated other slum areas, expelling poorer residents toward distant suburbs, the Medina has developed a historic, religious and political identity that has thus far preserved it.

The Medina has also become the headquarters of the political opposition to President Abdou Diouf (q.v.) and the residence of several influential *marabouts*. Serious uprisings in 1988, sparked by the controversial presidential election and increased prices for basic foodstuffs, started in Medina. In order to crush the riots, police and security forces destroyed many businesses and dwellings in the area. The structures were rapidly rebuilt, and life in the Medina returned to its normal pace.

METIS, METISSE. Someone of mixed European and African ancestry. In virtually all cases for first-generation métis, fathers were European and mothers were African. In Senegal, the term is preferred to mulatto. In precolonial and early colonial Senegal, the mixed community was a self-conscious local elite dominating the political and social life of the coastal *communes* (q.v.). Since the emergence of black politics marked by Blaise Diagne's (q.v.) election in 1914, the *métis* were overwhelmed and increasingly assimilated into the African elite. (See also HABITANT.)

MILLET. The dominant food crop in most of Senegal, millet and sorghum production, in contrast to groundnuts (q.v.), has steadily increased since independence. The output of millet and sorghum averaged 650,000 tons per year in the mid-1970s, around 100,000 tons more than at the beginning of the decade. Output for 1990 was estimated at 750,000 tons.

Millet grows in two varieties in Senegal. Bulrush millet (*petit mil* in French sources; botanically, *pennisetum*), the more widely cultivated form, requires only 500 to 600 millimeters of precipitation annually, allowing cultivation throughout most of Senegal. Sorghum (*gros mil;* botanically, *sorghum vulgare*), needs approximately 800 millimeters of rainfall, which restricts its production to more southerly areas. Farmers often interplant both varieties to increase chances for an adequate harvest.

MINING. In precolonial Senegal, mining was primarily confined to the gold deposits of Bambuk (q.v.) in the upper Senegal valley. During the colonial period, some advances were made in the mining sector, but it is only since the 1970s that Senegal has actively engaged in mining. In 1989, mining accounted for about 15 percent of the GDP.

Exports of minerals earned roughly $105 million in 1989, up over 22 percent from 1988. Calcium phosphates, mined near Thiès, are the principal Senegalese mineral, comprising

86 percent of total mineral export earnings. Salt, attapulgite and clinker phosphate rock accounted for the remainder of mineral exports. Natural gas produced offshore from Dakar (q.v.) is supplied to the Cap des Biches thermal power station.

The mining sector apparently has good potential for development. Prospecting for titanium, uranium, copper and other minerals is currently under way. A consortium of international partners is developing large-scale iron ore deposits in the Faleme River area near the border with Mali. There is also renewed oil and natural gas exploration activity under way on land and in Senegalese waters, particularly off the coast of Casamance (q.v.).

MOOR. (Fr.: *Maure;* Wolof: *Nar*). Mauritanian, or someone of Mauritanian (Arabo-Berber) descent. Mauritanian and Senegalese cultures have interacted throughout history, creating historical, political, economic, cultural and genetic links.

The Moors had linguistic, political and social structures quite distinct from other groups in sub-Saharan Africa. Their linguistic affinities link them with Berber and Arabic-speaking peoples of North Africa and the Sahara, rather than the West Atlantic and Mande languages of the Niger–Congo family. Numerous divisions, usually designated ''tribes'' or clans by commentators, existed within the three primary confederations (sometimes called ''nations'') that lived north of the Senegal River. In the French ethnographic literature, the three dominant confederations were conventionally paired with a particular Senegambian region. The Trarza and Brakna Moors interacted with states in the lower and middle Senegal valleys, respectively, while the Idawaish Moors operated on the upper Senegal.

Arabo-Berber clerics, traders and herders lived as ethnic minorities in precolonial Wolof and Futanke kingdoms, reflecting an economic and cultural symbiosis between savanna farmers and desert-edge herders. In the process of the colonial conquest, French strategy involved driving a wedge of geographical isolation and political suspicion between the two. Moors were obliged to reside north of the river and blacks south, so that they could be separately pacified. (See BORDERS.) Once the conquest was completed, however, Moors again found a place in the meat marketing and petty commerce of the colony of Senegal.

After independence, the Moors controlled a large proportion of commerce in Senegal. Moorish traders lived throughout the country, sometimes even in remote villages. In 1984, the Mauritanian Embassy estimated there were at least 50,000 Mauritanian citizens in Senegal, not counting ethnic Moors born Senegalese. The government of Mauritania, which reportedly tortured black African citizens, frequently accused Senegal of planning coups and harboring fugitives from Mauritania. Yet the border remained open, and Moors and Senegalese continued to live and work in both countries.

Violent clashes between Mauritanians and Senegalese in April 1989 dramatically changed relations between the two groups. While tensions had been high along the Senegal River, a territorial dispute in the upper valley near the village of Diawara led to violence and killings. Underlying ethnic tensions, and Senegalese resentment toward Moorish merchants, exploded. The clashes quickly spread to Dakar where there was a large Moorish population. Likewise, violence erupted in Nouakchott, the capital of Mauritania, and Senegalese merchants and other citizens were expelled from the country. Senegal expelled all Mauritanian citizens. Their shops were looted and burned, and the border was closed indefinitely. It remains to be seen what long-term effect these clashes and mass exodus have on the Senegalese economy and its relations with Mauritania.

In July 1991, the two countries agreed to set up a joint commission to review the situation, reinitiate contacts and discuss returning property and compensation on both sides.

MURID BROTHERHOOD. (Ar.: Muridiyya; Fr.: Mouride). Sufi
sect founded at the turn of the last century by *Shaix* Amadu
Bamba Mbake (q.v.). An offshoot of the Qadiriyya (see
QADIRI BROTHERHOOD), it rapidly grew to be the most
cohesive, influential brotherhood in Senegal. Today the
Murid brotherhood numbers about 700,000 adherents in
Senegal. Murids dominate the rural areas of western Senegal,
while the railroad centers and colonial towns became primarily Tijaniyya (q.v.) strongholds. It tends to be known as the
Wolof brotherhood, because the remnants of the old Wolof
kingdoms of Kajor, Jolof and Bawol (each q.v.) formed its
initial core, and most Murids are Wolof. Today, however,
many Serer, Fulbe, Malinke and Jola adhere to the brotherhood.

Although Amadu Bamba's teachings began in the 1880s,
the institution of the brotherhood is usually dated to 1903,
when Bamba gave it a separate initiation prayer (*wird*),
setting it apart from the Qadiriyya. During the lifetime of its
founder, the structure of the order was uncomplicated.
Spiritual leadership and ultimate authority in all matters were
in his hands, while two of his brothers, Mam Thierno and
Ibra Faty, dealt directly with disciples. The former was in
charge of those who wanted to study and work in the
traditional clerical fashion, while the latter supervised those
who only wanted to labor. The option of earning salvation
through hard manual labor, accompanied by neither prayer
nor fasting, is a Murid innovation, well suited to the early
cedo (q.v.) clientele. An idiosyncratic branch of Muridism,
the Bay Fal, followers of *Shaix* Ibra Fal (q.v.), have built a
distinct ethos around this tradition. Other non-Murid Muslims are sharply critical of this deviation from traditional
Islamic practice. In addition, the Murids encourage the
annual *magal* (q.v.) to the great mosque at Touba.

In the early colonial period, the brotherhood was viewed
as a refuge for those who wanted to continue to resist
colonization, and French authorities kept the founder in

almost continuous exile or supervised residence. In 1910, however, Amadu Bamba made his official peace with the colonial administration, and the brotherhood entered a phase of collaboration. During the military drafts preceding and accompanying World War I, colonial conscriptors were well satisfied with both the numbers and disciplined quality of the recruits sent them by Murid *marabouts* throughout the groundnut basin. The French also came to rely on the clerics to accelerate peanut production to aid the wartime economy. After the war, expansion of the peanut basin and expansion of the Murid brotherhood went hand in hand. Marabouts were freely granted choice agricultural land, because they were the only effective rural institution through which export farming could be increased.

After the founder died in 1927, there was a strong tendency toward decentralization of authority within the brotherhood. Mamadu Mustapha Mbacke (q.v.), Amadu Bamba's eldest son and heir, symbolized the unity of the brotherhood by taking the title of *Xalifa-Général*. But other leading marabouts founded fiscally independent lines, each headed by a *shaix* (pl. *shuyux*). In public, Murid *shuyux* usually defer to the *Xailfa-Général,* but in private, factionalism is widespread. The Murids have continued to attract followers and influence many political decisions. Murid support for presidents Senghor and Abdou Diouf (both q.v.) have been instrumental in the PS remaining in power.

MUSA MOLO. See BALDE, MUSA MOLO.

- N -

NASIR AL-DIN. (d. 1674) Seventeenth-century religious reformer whose movement, the Tubenan, and teachings have had a major impact on Senegalese Islam. A Berber cleric, he became prominent in the early 1670s when he led a group of southern Mauritanian clerics in casting off their Brakna Moor (q.v.) overlords. He subsequently invited all of the kings to the south, in Futa Toro, Walo and Kajor (each q.v.), to join his movement. When they declined, he went into Futa Toro and preached from village to village, asking people to overthrow their rulers who had been corrupted by the slave trade (q.v.) and had deviated from Islam. In the single dry season of 1673–74, first the Denanke (q.v.) of Futa Toro and then the rulers of Jolof, Kajor and Walo in turn capitulated and were exiled or killed. Nasir al-Din replaced them initially with his clerical followers, and then after a few months with members of the original royal families who swore allegiance to his movement. He was killed in battle in August 1674 and succeeded by his brothers in turn. The fragile unity he had forged collapsed, as French slave traders joined his multiple African enemies to restore the traditional dynasties.

NATIONAL PARKS. See NIOKOLO-KOBA NATIONAL PARK.

NAVETAN (Fr.: navétane). Wolof term for a migrant farmer. The term derives from the Wolof word, *nawet,* for rainy season.

During the colonial period, large numbers of *navetan* arrived from neighboring Mali, Guinea-Conakry and Guinea-Bissau to farm in the groundnut basin of central Senegal. Atrracted by the Senegalese cash economy based on a groundnut marketing system, they began arriving before World War I, with as many as 60,000 to 80,000 during a growing season. While the population was still sparse, land abundant in the groundnut basin, and the colonial government eager to expand production as rapidly as possible, the movement was encouraged by all concerned. The Senegalese host farmer typically housed, fed and lent land to the navetan in exchange for three to four days' labor per week on his own larger fields. Since independence, however, the population of the central groundnut basin has reached saturation, and the governments of the countries concerned discourage migration, now seen as inconsistent with national programs of development. Rainy season migrants, however, continue to flood into Senegal.

NDIAYE, VALDIODIO. (1923–) Lawyer and politician prominent at independence, but imprisoned from 1962 through 1974 for complicity with Mamadou Dia (q.v.) in the constitutional crisis of 1962 (q.v.). After earning his doctorate in law at the University of Montpellier in 1951, he entered politics in Senegal in 1952 as a territorial assembly representative from Kaolack. In 1957 he was chosen Minister of the Interior, and in 1958 elected UPS Deputy to the Legislative Assembly (which, after independence in 1960, became the National Assembly). In 1960 he added the functions of Mayor of Kaolack, and from August 1960 until May 1961 he was also head of defense.

His political career came to an abrupt end when he sided with Dia in the 1962 showdown. He spent 12 years in prison in Kédougou in the southeastern corner of the country. After his release in 1974, he returned to private practice, and now is retired.

NEGRITUDE. Philosophical movement asserting black African pride and cultural values, led primarily by Senegalese poet and President Léopold Senghor (q.v.). Since its beginnings in the 1930s, it has had widely different emphases, related to the changing intellectual and political climate.

Among West Indian and African students in Paris in the 1930s, it began as an assertion of black dignity and culture, in the face of French and Nazi contempt. Its original intellectual lights were a trio of poets and writers, Senghor and West Indians Léon Damas and Aimé Césaire. They attacked European technology, capitalism and faith in discursive reason, in favor of African instinctive reason, communalism, music, religion and dance. Senghor wrote in 1961:

Négritude is the whole of the values of civilization—cultural, economic, social political—which characterize the black peoples, more exactly, the Negro-African world. It is essentially instinctive reason, which pervades all these values. It is reason of the impressions, reason that is "intuitive." It is expressed by the emotions through an abandonment of self and a complete identification with the object, through the myth of the archetype of the collective soul, and the myth primordial accorded to the cosmos. In other terms, these are traits of Négritude, that we find like an indelible seal on all the world and activities of the black man (cited in Markowitz: 1969: I, 41).

After World War II, during the struggles for civil rights and greater political autonomy, *négritude* became the foundation for nationalist, anticolonial sentiment as well as for pan-Africanism. It had limited appeal outside Senegal, however, particularly among Anglophone African leaders and intellectuals offended by Senghor's continuing attachment to France.

With independence, négritude became the quasi-official ideology of Senegal, forming the basis for national unity, and the guiding inspiration for economic development and cultural growth. As the political climate changed, the concept lost its anti-European tone, and Senghor spoke increasingly of the "civilisation de l'universel" to which both European and African civilizations contributed. With the decline of pan-African unity, négritude became associated almost exclusively with Senegal and Senghor. For some, "militant de la négritude" became a euphemism for a loyal party member or, on the international level, a close ally of Senegal. On the philosophical level, however, it has proved a flexible ideology of unity, cultural self-confidence, generosity and tolerance in the face of modernization and growth without development.

NIANI. Mande kingdom on the north bank of the Gambia River in eastern Senegal, opposite modern Georgetown (the Gambia).

Founded in the fourteenth century by migrants from the Mali Empire, it had already gained its independence before the first Portuguese (q.v.) started trading there in the latter fifteenth century. Besides agriculture and pastoralism, Niani and neighboring Wuli (q.v.) became major commercial entrepôts for slaves and gold originating along interior routes from Bambuk (q.v.), Futa Jalon (q.v.) and the upper Niger. In exchange, European slave traders provided cloth, metal, luxury goods and firearms and ammunition. In the eighteenth and nineteenth centuries, the kingdom remained independent, but was frequently raided by Bundu (q.v.), its larger and more powerful eastern neighbor. Most of the kingdom was incorporated into the Gambia by the British, but the northern part came under French dominion. The Senegalese portion, southwest of Tambacounda (q.v.), is today host to the *Terres Neuves* (q.v.) agricultural resettlement areas.

NIASS, IBRAHIMA. (1902–76) Son and successor of Abdulahi Niass (q.v.), *marabout* and charismatic leader of a Tijani (q.v.) brotherhood branch headquartered in Kaolack. Although he was a learned cleric, Niass's reputation in Senegal was ambiguous. His relations with other Senegalese marabouts were cool, and his following and reputation were always greater outside of Senegal. The apocalyptic style of his teaching alienated many local Muslims. There may also have been an element of caste (q.v.) prejudice, because the family's blacksmith origins continue to be mentioned despite several generations of clerical family tradition. Rivalry underlay relations between Niass's Tijanis and the other major Senegalese Tijani leader in Tivaoune, headed by the Sy family. In the 1930s, a political rivalry was superimposed on the religious, with both Tijani branches allied to the then-Deputy Galandou Diouf (q.v.), whereas the Murid (q.v.) brotherhood supported the opposition Socialists (see PARTI SOCIALISTE) and Lamine Guèye (q.v.). After World War II, when Senghor broke with Guèye, the Murid marabouts went with Senghor, becoming his earliest and most influential supporters.

Niass inherited the Xalifat, or head of the brotherhood, in 1922 from his father, Abdulahi Niass (c.1850–1922), at the age of twenty. In 1931, he formed his followers into an order named the *Jamaat al-Faidah al-Tijaniyya* (Congregation of the Tijani Spiritual Flood). Tijani traditions prophesy that there will be one major religious revival per century, and Niass's choice of this name indicated that he saw his movement as fulfilling that prediction in this century. He also began building a new headquarters on the outskirts of Kaolack, which he named the *zawiya al-Madinat al-Jadi* (Retreat of the New City). Shortly after World War II, he renamed his movement, which by then had attracted followers from throughout West and North Africa, the *Jamiyaat Ansar al-Din* (Society of the Upholders of the Faith). Politically, Niass was active as a conservative in defense of the faith, against innovations that threatened it. In 1958 he joined with Saydou Nioro Tal and Cheikh Mbake (each q.v.) to organize the pro-French Comité pour la Ve République, in opposition to the advocates of immediate independence. In the early Sixties he opposed modernizing socialist legislation, including the *Code de la Famille* and the Law on the National Domain (q.v.). Though these laws were eventually passed, his opposition deterred acceptance and enforcement.

After Ibrahima's death in 1976, succession passed to his son, Abdulahi (not to be confused with Ibrahima's father and founder of the branch).

NIOKOLO-KOBA NATIONAL PARK. The largest and most visited national game park in Senegal. It is located in southern Sénégal-Oriental (eastern Senegal) on the upper reaches of the Gambia River, and covers 800,000 hectares. Animals include monkeys, baboons, wild pigs, antelope, gazelles, hippopotamuses, crocodiles, elephants, lions and scores of birds. The park is reached with difficulty by road via Tambacounda, or by air to Simenti.

NJAY, ALBURY. (c.1848–1901) Hero of the resistance in Jolof (q.v.), the oldest surviving kingdom in Senegal and one of the last to fall to the French. French invasions of Senegambian kingdoms began in earnest in 1855, when Albury was only seven years old, and he was raised and trained in warfare along with his older second cousin, Lat Jor Jop (q.v.). When the cleric Shaixu Amadu Ba (q.v.) conquered Jolof and ousted the ancient Njay dynasty in 1872, *Damel* Lat Jor of Kajor helped Albury mobilize resistance and conferred on him the title of *Barjak Kajor.* The two allies were able to enlist French support, and in 1875 they defeated the Tijani regime of Shaixu Amadu Ba, who was killed.

From 1875 to 1890 Albury ruled over Jolof, not as a traditional ruler, but as a charismatic military and religious leader. Unlike the old, nominally Muslim secular nobility, who had seen militant Islam as a potential threat to their rule, Albury embraced it and enforced a new puritanical ethos throughout the country. Like his mentor, Lat Jor, Albury was never ritually installed as king; he allowed first one of his uncles and then another to bear the title. It is unclear whether this was from religious disdain for secular authority or a sign that his hereditary claim was weak.

Albury's first six years were spent consolidating his rule. He married into the great Jolof families, bestowed titles, trained his slave guard and built himself a *tata,* or headquarters, outside Yang-yang in the style of *al-Hajj* Umar Tal (q.v.). He won over the clerics who remained after the Tijani defeat by obliging everyone, warriors, women and children included, to study the Quran, and by banning alcohol among his entourage.

From 1881 on, Albury turned to international affairs, in particular to the French, who were trying to establish a permanent military and commercial presence in central

Kajor by building a railroad (q.v.) through it. Albury helped Lat Jor fight the railroad, and when French forces drove Lat Jor out in 1882, Albury gave him asylum. A few months later the two sought revenge by pillaging Budhi, Walo, in French territory. The French withdrew their recognition of Albury as *Bur-ba,* and until 1885, debated and threatened an invasion. They were encouraged when Albury's cousin and close companion, Samba Laobe Penda Njay, defected, taking with him several notables and the bulk of the munitions, and asked the French to help him become Bur-ba. They held back, hoping he could oust Albury without needing a French expedition. Albury managed to retain his internal support in Jolof, and allied with Abdul Bokar Kan (q.v.) of Futa Toro.

In 1885, when both sides were dissatisfied with the disruption of trade and border conflicts, the French and Albury negotiated the first treaty in Jolof's history. Although never ratified in Paris, it endorsed the status quo. It also caused the French to call Samba Laobe away from the Jolof border and back to Saint-Louis. In exchange Albury obliged Lat Jor to move from central Jolof to the border area between Jolof and Kajor.

In 1886, another Samba Laobe Fal of Kajor (not to be confused with Samba Laobe Penda Njay), the Damel who replaced Lat Jor, picked a quarrel with Albury that precipitated the demise of both Kajor and Jolof. Albury reportedly had divorced Samba Laobe Fal's sister without returning her dowry. Samba Laobe Fal marched on Jolof only to be defeated, and the victorious Albury claimed the throne of Kajor. This alarmed the French, who intervened to negotiate a settlement. They agreed to guarantee Samba Laobe's payment to Albury of 300 cattle as indemnity. A few months later French expeditions "accidentally" killed first *Damel* Samba Laobe and then Lat Jor, and Kajor was partitioned into cantons. The French then assumed direct payment of the fine.

Increasing French encroachments, and the loss of his mentor, led Albury to plan in earnest the final retreat he had already begun to consider—a massive emigration to join *al-Hajj* Umar Tal's son Amadu at Segu. Many Muslims argued that one could not live in good conscience under Christian rule. Because the loss of Jolof seemed inevitable, Albury's last weapon was to take the people away and leave it a wasteland. He delayed as long as possible, holding off the French with protestations of friendship and trying to forge an Islamic defenders league with Saer Maty Ba (see BA, MA) in Rip and Abdul Bokar Kan in central Futa.

As had happened before in the Senegambia, the negotiation of a final treaty immediately preceded the invasion of Jolof. The treaty of 1889 recognized Albury as Bur-ba, promised mutual military aid and payment of the remaining fine from 1885, and regulated the terms of trade. The next year it was declared violated, and simultaneous French invasions of Jolof and Futa Toro began. In his hasty retreat, the massive exodus that Albury had envisioned dwindled to a trickle. By the time Albury reached Abdul Bokar in Futa, the two were stunned to learn that their destination, Segu, had also fallen to the French. Albury went on alone to find Amadu at Nioro, his second line of defense.

Thus began the famous exile of Albury Njay. Over the next 11 years he and Amadu were to retreat across the Sudan to Hausaland, fighting brilliant rear-guard actions that stayed, but could not stop, the inexorable French advance. Albury first found Amadu in 1890 at Nioro and distinguished himself as the outstanding general in defense of that redoubt. When it fell, Albury led a refugee force of 20,000 Senegambians eager to return home. As he neared the Senegal River, Abdul Bokar Kan of Futa Toro joined him. French Colonel Dodds attacked, forcing the two to retreat in Mauritania. There Abdul Bokar was killed by Moors, and Albury rejoined Amadu in his refuge near Jenne. When Jenne fell in 1893, they moved on to Dori near Say. The 1897 capture of

Say forced Amadu on to Sokoto where he died in 1898. Albury, however, stayed at Dosso, harassing French allies. In 1901 he was killed in battle near Dosso.

Unlike his powerful contemporary Samori Ture, who was driven back with an enormous army by the same French advance, Albury headed only a small party of cavaliers—a few hundred at the beginning, probably less than 100 at the end. But he won a place in people's hearts wherever he stayed—something that could not be said for Samori Ture. Albury has kept a hero's place in ballads and oral traditions all across the Sudan.

NJAY, NJAJAN. (fl. sometime between 1150 and 1350) Legendary founder of the Jolof Empire (q.v.) and progenitor of the Njay dynasty, which ruled continuously until the French conquest in the 1890s.

Oral traditions first recorded in the fifteenth century give many versions of Njajan's story. Most portray him emerging from a pond along the Senegal River (possibly the Lac de Guiers [q.v.]) to settle a quarrel among fishermen disputing the division of their catch. He silently disappeared back into the water. The incident was repeated a few days later, but this time the fishermen, presumably impressed with Njajan's ability to bring order and justice, seized him and begged him to be their king. The mysterious marine origin of Njajan suggests that kingship was originally considered sacred among the Wolof. Further evidence can be found in coronation rites, which included sacred baths, ritual seclusion and intercourse and enthronement on a hillock of eternity. Other, presumably later, embellishments to the legend make Njajan a Muslim ruler. Some say he was the son or grandson of Abu Darday, an Almoravid (q.v.) conqueror. Others report that he emerged from the water with a Quran in his hand, thus basing justice on Islamic law.

Traditions also relate the Mboj dynasty of Walo to Njajan, in a version that would conveniently rationalize Walo's (q.v.) long subjection to Jolof. It is said that after Njajan's father left, his mother contracted an alliance with a slave, Barka Mboj, despite her son's disapproval. The Mboj rulers who descended from that union were thus symbolically slave half brothers of their Jolof masters.

- O -

OFFICE DE COMMERCIALISATION AGRICOLE (OCA, Agricultural Marketing Office). Government agency created in 1960 to nationalize the purchase and sale of groundnuts for export. Bitter peasant resentment of French and Lebanese (q.v.) commercial and credit practices made new rural structures a top priority at independence. The OCA reached the farmers through seven Centres Régionaux de l'Assistance pour le Développement (CRADs, Regional Development Assistance Centers), providing seed, small equipment, fertilizer and pesticides on credit. Farmers were required to deal with the CRADs and the OCA. Each cooperative had to settle its members' debts before the OCA would collect and pay for its crop. This system has undergone periodic waves of reorganization, but has not overcome the basic exploitative system set in the colonial period. Groundnut profits collected by the bureaucracy ostensibly for investment in development have subsidized food imports (mainly consumed in urban areas) and government salaries instead of rural development.

In 1966 the first major reorganization divided the functions of the OCA by subsuming its domestic services under the new umbrella Office National de Cooperation et de l'Assistance au Développement (ONCAD, q.v.). That same year France stopped purchasing the Senegalese groundnut crop at subsidized prices, and the Senegalese government established a new Office de Commercialisation Agricole du Senegal, charged with international marketing.

OFFICE NATIONAL DES CENTRES DE L'ASSISTANCE POUR LE DEVELOPPEMENT (ONCAD, National Office of Development Assistance Centers). Government groundnut marketing and agricultural agency, created in 1966 to supervise the functions of the Centres Rurals de l'Assistance pour le Développement and to collect the groundnut harvest. It inherited the latter function from the Office de Commercialisation Agricole (q.v.). The agency was headed by a director-general responsible to the Ministry of Rural Development. Following the colonial tradition, it bought groundnuts (q.v.) from peasants at prices fixed before sowing; advanced seeds, equipment and pesticides to them on credit; and then marketed the harvest only after cooperatives had settled their debts. Abdou Diouf abolished ONCAD in 1983 as part of his economic reform plans.

ORGANISATION COMMUNE AFRICAINE, MALAGACHE, ET MAURITIENNE (OCAAM, African, Malagasy and Mauritanian Common Organization). Pan-Francophone-African international organization. Founded in 1965, it succeeded the Union Africaine et Malagache. Both organizations served as forums for coordinating Francophone African cultural and political interests with France. Since 1971 the member states have been associate members of the European Economic Community. During his term as president of Senegal, Senghor, an early and determined advocate of Francophone cooperation, was a pillar of the organization. In 1972, however, the EEC indicated a preference for negotiating with geographic rather than linguistic groupings, precipitating the withdrawal of Zaire and Congo that year; Cameroon, Chad and Madagascar the next, and subsequently Mali and Mauritania. In addition, the Organization of African Unity (OAU) is seen as a more effective international forum.

ORGANISATION POUR LA MISE EN VALEUR DU FLEUVE GAMBIE (OMVG, Organization for the Development of the

Gambia River Basin). Organization comprising Senegal and the Gambia, started in 1978 to coordinate the development of the Gambia River Basin. The initial development plan called for salt-intrusion dams on the lower reaches of the river, and at least one hydroelectric irrigation dam in Senegal on the upper river. After a brief flare-up, it was decided to let future studies determine whether there should be a simple bridge on the Senegalese trans-Gambia highway at Farafeni, or a more expensive bridge-dam as the Gambians have insisted. The bridge-dam option has since prevailed, but there has been little actual progress on the project. Vehicles on the highway continue to be ferried across, a slow and laborious process. With confederation in late 1981, it appeared there would be more cooperation in developing the Gambia River Basin. Yet, the general failure of the Confederation of the Senegambia (q.v.) has hampered OMVG efforts. The headquarters of the OMVG are in Kaolack.

ORGANISATION POUR LA MISE EN VALEUR DU FLEUVE SENEGAL (OMVS, Organization for the Development of the Senegal River Basin). Organization consisting of Mauritania, Senegal and Mali, formed to coordinate development planning and political questions surrounding the Senegal River. Created in 1972, it has predecessors dating back to the 1920s. Included in the current plan, in order of priority, are: a salt-intrusion dam at Diama in the delta; a hydroelectric and flow-regulating dam at Manantali, Mali; irrigated perimeters in Senegal, Mauritania and Mali; plans to make the river navigable as far as Kayes, Mali; and new port facilities at Saint-Louis and Kayes. In 1977 and 1978 the three presidents of OMVS countries travelled to OPEC countries, Europe and America seeking funds, and received enough pledges to begin construction on the dams at Diama and Manantali. Both were nearing completion in mid-1991. The 1970s drought in the Sahel persuaded local leaders that mastery of water resources was the only hope for future development, and the OMVS has been considerably more successful than its predecessors. Since the ethnic clashes between Mauritanians and Senegalese in 1989 (see MOORS), however, and the cessation of diplomatic contacts between the two countries, the OMVS has not been able to function effectively.

ORIGINAIRE. Legal and sociological term in use during the early part of the twentieth century, designating an African born in one of the four urban *communes* (q.v.) of Senegal: Saint-Louis, Gorée, Rufisque and Dakar. These towns had inherited electoral institutions from the precolonial period. *Originaires* struggled to maintain their historic rights, confirmed since the liberation of slaves and introduction of formal elections during the revolution of 1848. In the early twentieth century, with the establishment of colonial structures, originaires' rights were threatened. Under the leadership of Blaise Diagne (q.v.), they won legal recognition of their full French citizenship, the right to vote, and the right to enlist in the regular French army instead of being drafted into colonial units. They also received the right to Muslim, French or customary law rather than the arbitrary *indigénat* (q.v.) that served the remainder of the colony. Most originaires were Muslim, in contrast to the predominantly Catholic *métis* (q.v.) community called *habitants* (q.v.), living in the same towns and primarily engaged in commerce.

During the colonial period, originaires became a self-conscious African elite, serving as political and commercial intermediaries between the French and métis above them, and African *sujets* (q.v.) in the Protectorate. Having cast their lot with the French well before conquest, they were among the first to experience and express the contradictions of colonial rule. For example, they won exemption from military draft while their rural countrymen were going off to World War I in large numbers. Rural residents may have sympathized with their urban counterparts' struggle, but they bitterly resented the privileges that resulted. Urban residents, on the other hand, frequently flaunted their status. Once their own rights were assured, however, they campaigned to see them extended to the countryside. The term *originaire* fell into disuse after World War II, when rights were extended to rural residents as well, but the political legacy of urban/rural tensions continued to mark the politics of the early independence (q.v.) period.

- P -

PARTI AFRICAIN DE L'INDEPENDANCE (PAI, African Independence Party). From 1957 to 1960, a small intellectual Communist Party of Senegal. Founded in 1957 by Majmout Diop, a young pharmacist and author, it was allied with the French Communist Party. In the unity movement that witnessed the merger of most Senegalese political parties between 1956 and 1958, the PAI and another small intellectual group, the Mouvement Populaire Sénégalaise, refused to give up their separate identities. When the governing Union Progressiste Sénégalaise (q.v.) leaders decided to advocate acceptance of the de Gaulle form of union with France in 1958, the PAI bitterly attacked them for betraying the independence movement. The PAI favored immediate independence. In 1960, the party was banned as subversive. It remained intellectually active underground for more than a decade, during which it split into two factions. Then, with the constitutional reform of 1973 (q.v.), and the movement toward democratization and a multiparty system that followed, one branch—still under Majmout Diop's leadership—was again legalized. The PAI has published two party papers, *La Lutte* (The Struggle, in French) and *Momsarev* (lit., Own your country, in Wolof). In the elections of 1983 and 1988, the PAI ran candidates but received only a tiny percentage of votes. The democratic revolutions in Eastern

Europe in 1990 and the general decline of Communist influence throughout the Third World contributed to the general demise of the PAI. In 1991, the name was changed to the Parti de l'Independance et Travail (PIT).

PARTI DEMOCRATIQUE SENEGALAIS (PDS). Center democratic opposition political party founded in 1973 as part of the democratization of Senegal's constitution. Through its newspaper, *Le Démocrate,* and electoral politics it has emerged as the largest opposition party in a country with a single-dominant-party tradition. In the 1978 Assembly and Presidential elections, it took 17.7 percent of the votes, running well in the Casamance (q.v.) and urban areas. In 1983, the party increased its share of votes to about 18 percent. In 1988, the perennial PDS presidential candidate, Abdoulaye Wade (q.v.), who officially received 25 percent of the total vote, claimed the ruling PS had stolen the election. The increasing popularity of the PDS reflected the growing dissatisfaction with President Adbou Diouf and Senegal's deteriorating economic situation, rather than endorsement of Wade and his policies. When Wade entered the government as a minister of state in 1991, the PDS entered a brief period of "cohabitation" (q.v.) with the majority PS.

PARTI DU REGROUPEMENT AFRICAIN (PRA). An interterritorial grouping of political parties throughout French West Africa, organized in 1958 as a rival to Houphouet-Boigny's already established interterritorial party, the Rassemblement Démocratique Africain (q.v.). The PRA and the Cotonou conference of July 1958 that launched it were the culmination of the unity movement that had brought about the merger of political parties in Senegal. But it was short-lived. At the Cotonou conference, some delegates belonging to the UPS (q.v.) voted for immediate independence from France in the upcoming referendum (see INDEPENDENCE). Their votes were cast against the wishes of Senghor and Dia (both q.v.), who sought accommodation and the union option. When Senghor and Dia returned from the conference still refusing to commit the UPS to the independence vote, the dissenters left the party to establish their own Parti du Regroupement Africain-Sénégal (q.v.).

PARTI DU REGROUPEMENT AFRICAIN-SENEGAL. Short-lived Marxist, but not orthodox Communist, party, founded by a group of dissident intellectuals led by Abdoulaye Ly and Assane Seck. Many of the leaders had belonged to earlier opposition parties, and then all had joined the Union Progressiste Sénégalaise (q.v.) during a brief flurry of unity in 1956–58. When the UPS leaders refused to call for independence in the 1958 referendum, however, they split to form their own proindependence party. The party paper was called *Indépendance Africaine*. In the referendum, they were able to mobilize only 22,000 *no* votes in Senegal, against 870,000 supporting Senghor's *yes* position. Independence (q.v.) came quickly thereafter, nevertheless, and in 1966, the PRA-Senegal leaders rejoined the UPS in a formal party merger.

PARTI SOCIALISTE. (PS, Socialist Party). Since 1976, the name of the dominant political party in Senegal, formerly called the Union Progressiste Sénégalaise (q.v.). The name change reflects a rapprochement with European socialist parties, French in particular, which Senegal has been pursuing. The Senegalese have also been urging other African socialist countries to pursue a similar path. With the change in party name and the constitutional reform introducing multiparty democracy, Senghor was able to bring his party into the Socialist International in 1978. Shortly thereafter, he was elected its vice-president and then hosted its 1978 Congress.

Constitutional and administrative reforms accompanied this move, but there were no major changes within the party platform. Senghor and his successor, Abdou Diouf (q.v.), maintain that they practice a form of African socialism (q.v.).

The PS faces no serious opposition within Senegal since the vast majority of government workers at all levels owe their jobs to the party. Other socialist parties in Senegal's history include the PSS (q.v.) and the SFIO, Fédération Sénégalaise (q.v.). The election of François Mitterand and the Socialist Party in France helped relations between France and Senegal improve from good to excellent.

PARTI SOCIALISTE SENEGALAIS. (PSS, Senegalese Socialist party). One of the first modern political parties in Senegal, founded in 1929 by Lamine Guèye (q.v.). It had an urban intellectual membership, including local French socialists. It unsucessfully contested the 1928 by-election results in which Galandou Diouf (q.v.) defeated Guèye. In 1937 Guèye founded a Senegalese branch of the French socialist party, the Section Française de l'International Ouvrière, which absorbed most of the PSS the following year. A small group of mainly French radicals held on to the PSS name until after World War II, when it died out.

PASTORALISTS. People whose economic and social institutions are centered on livestock. Herding people usually raise cattle and/or camels plus smaller animals, including sheep, goats and chickens. Many were seasonally nomadic, with young men or small families travelling in set transhumant (q.v.) cycles from dry-season to rainy-season pastures and water sources. Most pastoralists today settle permanently along market roads and around deep wells, combining farming with livestock where feasible. An estimated 2 percent of the population in Senegal is dependent on livestock for a living, mainly Fulbe and Moors (both q.v.). Most Fulbe and Moors practice mixed farming and herding, however. Some Wolof, Serer, Soninke and Mande also mix herding and farming, or exchange grain with pastoralists for milk products (sour milk and butter).

PEANUTS. See GROUNDNUTS.

PETITE COTE. The section of the Atlantic coast of Senegal stretching from the Cape Verde Peninsula (q.v.) south to the Salum estuary. During the era of the slave trade (q.v.), it was dotted with small trading posts, usually manned by *métis* (q.v.) or African agents of European companies. These outposts were linked to the major European trading bases at Gorée (q.v.), the Cape Verde Islands and the mouths of the Senegal and Gambia rivers. Today the *Petite Côte* has been developed for tourism, with several luxury hotels. Fishing is also an important industry along the coast.

PIR SANOXOR. The most famous precolonial Muslim educational center in Senegal, located in Kajor (q.v.) near the modern-day town of Pire-Gourèye. It was founded in the late seventeenth century, at the same time that the revolution of the Tubenan clerics shook the region. The cleric who established the center, Amar Fal (q.v.), was a fifth-generation descendant of the founder of independent Kajor, *Damel* Amari Ngone Sobel Fal. His mother was the daughter of a prominent Futanke cleric from Futa Toro.

Pir became one of the educational and ideological links between the seventeenth-century Tubenan and later clerical reform movements. Among Pir's most illustrious students were Malik Dauda Sy (q.v.), founder of Bundu; *Almamy* Abdul Bokar Kan (q.v.) of Futa Toro; Matar Ndumbe Jop (q.v.), founder of Koki (q.v.); and perhaps also Sulaiman Bal (q.v.). Some traditions claim that Pir also hosted Abdul Karim of Futa Jalon, who initiated *al-Hajj* Umar Tal (q.v.) and his father, Asciid Tal, into the Tijaniyya. This may very well be historical embellishment, however. The subjects taught at Pir included *tafsir* (Quranic exegesis), *fiqh* (law), *nahw* (grammar) and *tawhid* (theology).

As a religious center, Pir was immune from war and conflict until the colonial conquest. In May 1869, the French sacked and burned it, in revenge for what they regarded as treachery on the part of the reigning *Serin Pir,* Bubakar

Penda Yeri Fal. They asserted that he had asked for and had been given arms and powder to protect himself from the exiled *Damel* Lat Jor Jop (q.v.), but had turned the munitions over to him instead. Most of the books used at Pir were buried and saved from the fire, but the town itself was destroyed and never rebuilt.

PLATEAU. The section of Dakar (q.v.) where the colonial government buildings were constructed, and where most Europeans lived before independence. It includes the Place de l'Indépendance (formerly Place Faidherbe), the President's Palace (formerly the Governor-General's Palace), the Supreme Court, the Cathedral, the Ministries, several embassies and the major shopping avenues Lamine Guèye and Georges Pompidou (formerly Maginot and William Ponty respectively). In modern Senegalese usage it still connotes the "European" city, although wealthy Senegalese and diplomats able to afford the escalating real-estate market also live there.

PONTY, WILLIAM. (MERLEAU-PONTY, AMEDEE WILLIAM). (1860?-1915) Governor-General of French West Africa from 1908 to 1915, and one of the best-remembered holders of that office. Starting in the colonial service in 1890, he made his name as a resourceful administrator and promoter of African colonial interests. In 1904, he was appointed governor of the French Sudan (modern-day Mali), and in 1908 he was chosen to replace Ernst Roume in Dakar as governor-general. He pursued several initiatives, including the development of educational institutions and the construction of the Dakar-Bamako railroad (see RAILROAD). He was determined to demonstrate to metropolitan skeptics that the AOF could fill its anticipated role as a manpower reserve in World War I. When he died in office in 1915, his memory was preserved in the Ecole Normale William Ponty (q.v.) and the naming of a major avenue

William Ponty (now renamed Avenue Georges Pompidou but usually referred to by its former designation).

PORTUGUESE. Merchant explorers under Portuguese Prince Henry the Navigator's sponsorship were the first modern Europeans to come into contact with Senegal and initiate the trans-Atlantic slave trade. In 1444, Dinis Dias first passed the mouth of the Senegal River and discovered the Jolof Empire (q.v.). Initial contacts were frequently hostile, with Portuguese raiding African coastal kingdoms. The Portuguese king, however, made formal diplomatic overtures to the Jolof king, the *Bur-ba Jolof,* and ordered his men to engage only in peaceful trade. A regular trade was established in which Portuguese brought iron bars, brass minalls, horses and cloth in exchange for hides, ivory, slaves and beeswax. From bases at Arguin (now in Mauritania), the Cape Verde Islands and in Guinea-Bissau, coastal agents called *lançados* served as the middlemen in the trade. Slaves gradually became the dominant export, initially to Portugal itself, then to Spanish colonies in the Americas, and finally, in the seventeenth century, to other European possessions in the Caribbean and North America.

The Portuguese arrival affected Jolof both directly and indirectly. Direct Portuguese interventions in the Jolof Empire include an incident in 1489–90, when a claimant to the Jolof throne, *Buumi* Jelen, took asylum and asked the Portuguese to help him gain the throne. He was taken to Portugal, given full diplomatic honors, converted to Christianity, swore allegiance to Joao II and was sent back to Jolof, supported by a large fleet of caravels. The Portuguese commander, however, quarreled with Jelen, killed him and abandoned plans to build a Portuguese trading fort on the Jolof coast. Gradually, Portuguese agents, or *tangomaos,* built trading posts in the interior on the Senegal, Gambia and Casamance Rivers. Their agents used their commercial influence in local politics, although they had no military capacity.

Indirect Portuguese influence, though less obvious, was more important in the long run. Trade ports on the coast reoriented communications and later political power on the mainland away from inland Jolof toward the coastal and riverine provinces. Between 1490 and 1550 the provinces broke off to form independent states, leaving Jolof an isolated interior kingdom. The gap between the warrior nobility and peasants widened, with the increase in wars and raiding for slaves for export.

In the late sixteenth and early seventeenth centuries, Portuguese traders lost many of their posts to the Dutch, and by the eighteenth century the British and French had in turn taken over from the Dutch. The Portuguese, however, conserved their contacts with Afro-Portuguese on the Cape Verde Islands and at trading ports along the Petite Côte (q.v.) from the Cape Verde Peninsula (q.v.) to the Southern Rivers (present Guinea-Bissau). Portuguese names, terms, clothing and a syncretistic form of Catholicism attest to their cultural influence even today.

- Q -

QADI (Wolof variants XADI, XALI). Arabic term for a judge, often reserved for the supreme justice or head of an Islamic community.

QADIRI BROTHERHOOD. The first Islamic order, or brotherhood, to be introduced into West Africa. It traces its origins to Sidi Abd al-Qadir al-Jilal (1079–1166) of Baghdad. It was popularized in West Africa in the late fifteenth and early sixteenth centuries by Muhammad ibn Abd al-Karim al-Maghili and his disciple Sidi Ahmad al-Bakkai al-Kunti. The main modern Senegalese Qadiri brotherhood was founded by Abu Naam Kunta, who came to Kajor from the Niger River Bend area as a missionary in 1809. The *Xalifa* or head of the

Qadiri in Senegal today, who resides at Njasan near Tivawan, is his great-grandson. The Qadiri order at Njasan has a few hundred members in Senegal and several thousand more adherents in Mali and Mauritania. Other Qadiri branches were introduced by students of two famous nineteenth-century Mauritanian *marabouts,* Cheikh Sidiyya al-Kabir (1780–1869) and Cheikh Muhammad al-Faidil (1780–1896). The latter's followers are sometimes called Fadili, with the understanding that the Qadiriyya is the parent order. Another and more prominent offshoot of the Qadiriyya is the Murid brotherhood (q.v.). It is likely that Abdul al-Qadir (see KAN, ABDUL QADIR), consolidator of the 1776 clerical movement in Futa Toro (q.v.), was an early Qadiri missionary. His movement resulted in the founding of a political rather than a religious order, however.

- R -

RAILROADS. The two major railroads in Senegal were built during the colonial period. One line links the ports of Saint-Louis and Dakar, while the other, much longer line links Dakar and Bamako, the capital of Mali.

Railroads were a key factor in the conquest, pacification, administration and economic exploitation of the Senegal region. The first line, from Dakar to Saint-Louis, was planned in 1879, and built from 1882–1886. The project to construct a railroad, ostensibly to promote economic development, was one way local French military administrators could persuade the home government to finance troops for the conquest. Once completed, it would also make troop movements more efficient, assuring French domination. French merchants also anticipated gaining control, from Wolof and Moor traders, of the profitable groundnut export trade. The railroad realized all these expectations. Its construction through Kajor (q.v.) provoked the final campaigns of resistance (see JOP, LAT JOR), and the last two kings were killed within a few months of its completion, by troops brought in on the rails. Railroad towns grew up around the major stops. The colonial government allocated prime commercial land around the stations to French import-export merchants. A link begun simultaneously in 1880 from Kayes on the Senegal River headwaters to Bamako on the Niger River was slower being built, but also freed the needed credits for the conquest of the Sudan.

The second and far more important line was the so-called Ocean-Niger railroad linking Dakar on the coast to Bamako on the Niger River. The Senegal section of the line, which connected to the Kayes-Bamako portion, was built between 1906 and 1923. With its completion, the line became the main commercial and strategic axis of French West Africa. As conceived by Governor-General Roume in 1902, it was to be the beginning of a great transversal system, linking up with port-to-interior spurs in Guinea, Ivory Coast and Dahomey. This grandiose plan echoed a series of tran-Saharan projects, which aroused colonial enthusiasm during the conquest, but never proved feasible. The Dakar-Bamako line became a very important economic axis making the Sudan an economic hinterland for Senegal. It also replaced the Senegal River as the dominant axis into the interior, and contributed to the rapid growth of both Dakar and Bamako, and simultaneously the decline of Kayes and Saint-Louis. The line was superimposed directly on precolonial caravan routes and towns, with the added refinement that it deliberately passed close enough to the British-controlled Gambia to siphon trade destined for its headwaters, but not close enough to facilitate freight transshipment to the Gambia's cheaper ocean route. The other links to the railroad were never built. Thus, by independence, the infrastructure, like colonial economics and politics, favored the Balkanization of French West Africa.

Senegal and Sudan tried to unite at independence in the Mali Federation (q.v.), based partly on their common interest in maintaining economic links via the railroad. When they broke relations after the collapse of the Federation in August 1960, however, they also closed the railroad. It reopened after three years, but had been allowed to disintegrate. Although Mali's present economic links are stronger with the more prosperous Ivory Coast than with Senegal, there has been an ongoing project to upgrade Dakar-Bamako rail service. The railroad remains the primary land route between the two countries, but within Senegal, roads have largely replaced train transport. The Dakar–Saint-Louis link also still functions, but at a reduced volume.

RAINY SEASON. See HIVERNAGE.

RASSEMBLEMENT DEMOCRATIQUE AFRICAIN (RDA, African Democratic Assembly). First Pan-Francophone-African political movement founded at the Bamako Congress of 1946, and led by Ivory Coast's Félix Houphouet-Boigny. All French territories and metropolitan parties were invited to send representatives, but at French urging, Senegal's Lamine Guèye and Léopold Senghor (both q.v.) stayed away. Non-Communist metropolitan parties, similarly intimidated by government fear of Communist influence, also declined to attend, leaving the French Communist Party until 1950 the unique formal ally of the RDA. Despite official repression, the RDA seized the initiative in all of French West Africa except Senegal. Senghor's rival Pan-Francophone Indépendants d'Outre-Mer, founded in 1948, never achieved a mass following. For a decade, the RDA fought for Francophone African federation and independence, but when the crucial vote came on the Fifth Republic constitution (q.v.) in 1958, no unified stand was developed. Guinea's and Niger's leaders came out against the constitution, preferring immediate independence, while Houphouet-Boigny and the other leaders called for a *yes* vote. As a result, the RDA fell apart.

RASSEMBLEMENT NATIONAL DEMOCRATIQUE (RND, National Democratic Assembly). Contemporary political party led by historian-politician Cheikh Anta Diop (q.v.). It was denied legal standing when three other parties were given it under the Constitutional Reform of 1977 (see CONSTITUTION OF THE SECOND SENEGALESE RE-PUBLIC). In October 1977, in response to RND initiative, 300 Senegalese intellectuals signed a petition in *Le Monde* of Paris demanding legal recognition of all political parties in Senegal. Senghor insisted that the RND was a personality cult, not a political alternative, and refused to consider its legalization. The party functioned as an interest group, however. Senghor's successor, Abdou Diouf (q.v.), legalized all opposition parties in 1983, and the party operated openly. It won one seat in the National Assembly in 1983. The Wolof journal *Taxaw* (Stand Up!), which Diop published, had some influence on local politics, occasionally inspiring rejoinders from the government mass-circulation daily, *Le Soleil* (q.v.). With Diop's death, the RND disintegrated.

RELIGION. Islam is the dominant and longest-established world religion in Senegal, having been introduced in the eleventh century and currently claiming 80 to 85 percent of the population. Muslims are not required to belong to a brother-hood (q.v.), although most Senegalese Muslims join a broth-erhood. The major ones in Senegal include the Murid, Tijani and Qadiri (each q.v.), while smaller groups include the Layennes of Cape Verde and the Hamallists, originally from western Mali.

Christians comprise about 6 percent of the population, almost entirely Catholic. They are concentrated in the cities and among ethnic groups that were not strongly influenced by Islam by the time of colonial conquest. Most Christians belong to the Serer, Jola and smaller groups of Casamance and eastern Senegal.

In isolated rural areas, especially in southern and eastern

regions, some groups have retained traditional religions. Education, migration and missionaries (Muslim and Christian) are rapidly eroding them, however. Yet, many Muslims and Christians do retain elements of their traditional religions.

RESISTANCE. The French struggle to establish hegemony and eventually rule over the Senegambia, and the corresponding period of African resistance, lasted longer in Senegal than in almost any other area of Africa. Excluding the 1819–27 French attempt to establish an agricultural colony in Walo (q.v.), the first major invasions of the mainland began in 1855 with General, and later Governor, Louis Faidherbe (q.v.). The last expeditions to "pacify" the Jola (q.v.) in southern Senegal continued well after the end of World War I. Senegambian leaders and groups responded to French aggression with a variety of tactics, from military resistance on the battlefield to guerrilla-style harassment, diplomatic defiance and insults to negotiated collaboration or cooperation, nationalism, Pan-Islamic anti-Christian ideology, and opportunism. The active resistance to military intervention was followed by a long tradition of passive resistance to administrative measures, such as tax imposition and French army conscription.

The centralized Wolof kingdoms were the most powerful militarily but, ironically, were the first to be defeated by the French. French military, communications and medical technology had made such rapid advances in the Industrial Revolution that Wolof armies that had easily kept eighteenth-century French off the mainland could not stand up to their mid-nineteenth-century successors. Because the Wolof and Serer of Sin and Salum (both q. v.) had standing armies and hereditary kings, they were easier targets than the independent villagers of the Casamance. Nevertheless, only the small, exposed and internally divided kingdom of Walo fell quickly in 1855. Faidherbe attacked the kingdoms one by one, using imported Algerian troops and drafting Africans to supplement his meager French forces. By the time of his departure in 1865, he had defeated most of the kingdoms at least once, but had unsettled rather than conquered them. Confidence in traditional dynasties and the hereditary style of rule was shaken. Yet, the kingdoms quickly regrouped around a new style of leadership, based on Islam, which measured its success by military prowess. The most renowned heroes of the resistance were all of this type, including Lat Jor Jop in Kajor, Albury Njay in Jolof and Abdul Bokar Kan in Futa Toro (each q.v.). Until the railroad (q.v.) campaigns of the 1880s, they were regarded as the most powerful legitimate rulers in the area and the hope for successful resistance to the French. Each combined diplomatic negotiation and periods of peace or even alliance with the French with active military resistance. All were eliminated between 1886 and 1890, when the French were determined to establish their rule by force.

Another style of resistance to French aggression came from Muslim clerics (q.v.). The greatest of these leaders and the model for all others was *al-Hajj* Umar Tal (q.v.), whose teachings, beginning in 1845, and empire-building, starting in 1852, reverberated throughout the Senegambia and the Western Sudan. It is important, however, to caution that his jihad was directed more consistently and fiercely against corrupt, ineffectual traditional dynasties than against the French. But it was by far the most pervasive source of hostility that the French had to face. Ma Ba, Shaixu Amadu Ba and Mamadu Lamine Drame (each q.v.) all claimed authority to wage jihad directly from *al-Hajj* Umar. Other clerical resistors of the same era modeled their careers on *al-Hajj* Umar even though they were distant or even hostile to his movement, including Musa Molo Balde and *Fodé* Kaba Dumbuya (each q.v.), the two great Casamance rivals.

The last of the active military leaders was eliminated from central Senegal in 1890, and from the Casamance in the early twentieth century. Then began a phase of withdrawal from the French, ranging from actual physical withdrawal and refusal to cooperate, sometimes involving cultural and religious defiance. The main leaders of this phase were also clerics, first Amadu Bamba Mbake and secondly *al-Hajj* Malik Sy (each q.v.). By the time of World War I, both had accepted the inevitability of French occupation. They counseled their followers to pay their taxes, and even to serve in the army, but educated them carefully to avoid French learning and stay with Islamic law and culture. They also helped finance, and cooperated with, French-educated African politicians like Blaise Diagne and Galandou Diouf (each q.v.), who were launching a new style of resistance in African nationalism. This strain of thought continued throughout the colonial period and has echoes of unreconciled tension even in the postindependence era.

ROYAL AFRICA COMPANY. English joint-stock slave trading company, given monopoly rights on the African coast from Sali (Petite Côte, q.v.) to the Cape of Good Hope by royal charter, from 1672 to 1698. The company was charged with the maintenance of factories and forts within its territory, thus acquiring quasi-governmental authority. Like other slave trading companies, it administered justice to its own employees and persons living around the forts and conducted foreign relations with local sovereigns. In the Senegal area, this applied chiefly to the area around James Fort, Gambia, though the British took and held Gorée and Saint-Louis (both q.v.) at intervals during the eighteenth century. From their Gambian posts the British tapped the same commercial region as the French on the Senegal River, making the two perennial rivals in the region.

The company lost its monopoly in 1698, when private English shippers were allowed to trade in exchange for a 10 percent prime per slave. In 1712, the prime was suppressed, and beginning in 1730 Parliament voted an annual subsidy to the company for the maintenance of the forts. In 1751 the Royal Africa Company was dissolved, to be replaced by the Company of Merchants Trading to Africa (q.v.).

- S -

SAINT-LOUIS. Capital of the Fleuve Region (q.v.) and centered on an island at the mouth of the Senegal River (q.v.), it is the historic port town and colonial capital of Senegal. Wolof speakers refer to the city as N'Dar. Saint-Louis was one of the earliest European outposts in Africa and the first town in the Senegambian region. It served as the starting point for almost all military expeditions, which gradually spread French rule through Senegal, the Sudan and the Upper Niger valley.

Portuguese, Dutch and English traders frequented the area but did not establish a permanent settlement. It was only in 1638 that French slave traders built a small post on the nearby island of Bocos, and in 1659 transferred their operations and built a permanent fort on the present island of Saint-Louis (N'Dar). Since the British gained firm control of the easily navigable Gambia River, the French gradually settled their headquarters at Saint-Louis. A sandbar and dangerous surf across the mouth of the Senegal made access from the sea difficult, and the river was navigable to Bakel (q.v.) upriver for only four months a year (mid-July through mid-November). Despite these obstacles, in the eighteenth century a permanent settlement of boatmen, fishermen, *métis* (q.v.), and French traders and their slaves gradually grew up around the fort. The British captured Saint-Louis during the Seven Years War in 1758 and held it until 1778, leaving the French without a base, until they moved their headquarters to Gorée (q.v.) from 1763 to 1778. During the Napoleonic Wars the French posts again fell to the British, who controlled Saint-Louis from 1809 until 1817.

During the eighteenth century, representative institutions, a mayor and a council had developed, and during the second British occupation received official recognition from the governor. When the French reoccupied in 1819, they were unable to replace a mayor they disliked since the tradition of local politics clearly had a firm footing. For the first half of the nineteenth century, the métis mayor and council members conducted diplomatic and commercial relations with neighboring kingdoms on behalf of the French and themselves.

By mid-century, immediately before the conquest of the mainland, local merchants were forced out of the middleman trade by larger French companies and replaced in their diplomatic functions by directly hired French agents. In 1848, against the wishes of local notables, slaves (q.v.) residing in Saint-Louis and Gorée were freed, and for the rest of the century the two locations became a rather uncertain sanctuary for escapees. Depending on French relations with the kingdom of origin and the vagaries of the courts, slaves were either given asylum, drafted into the local militia or returned to their masters. The census taken prior to emancipation showed that the population of Saint-Louis in the mid-1840s was three-quarters slave. A telegraph line linking Saint-Louis with Gorée was completed in 1862, while the railroad connecting Saint-Louis with Dakar was finished in 1885.

When the headquarters of the government-general of French West Africa was installed at Dakar in 1902, Saint-Louis remained the capital of the territory of Senegal, and the home of its governor. The decline of the gum arabic (q.v.) trade in the late 1890s, and the growth of the Senegalese groundnut basin in central Senegal reduced the town's importance. In addition, the inadequacy of its port meant that it was quickly replaced by Rufisque and Dakar as a peanut-exporting center. The completion of the Dakar–Bamako railway in 1923 cut off its economic hinterland, putting it into a decline from which it has not recovered. In 1957, with independence approaching, the capital of Senegal was moved to Dakar, leaving Saint-Louis a backwater. The city retains its historic significance for the Senegalese people, however, and its colonial architecture rivals that of any city in the former French colonies in West Africa.

In 1989, the government announced plans to construct a university near Saint-Louis and by mid-1991, several buildings were under construction. The town has a permanent population of about 90,000; during the dry season, the population increases markedly.

SALUM. Serer (q.v.) kingdom in the center of Senegal, founded in the late fifteenth century by the Gelwar matrilineage, an offshoot of the royal family of Kabu (q.v.). The capital was at Kawon (Fr.: Cahonne), and through seaports at Kaolack on the Salum estuary and Kaur on the Gambia, it conducted a steady commerce with European slave traders. Originally part of the Jolof Empire (q.v.), Salum won its independence in the late sixteenth century. With military supplies purchased from European traders—first iron and horses, later firearms—it became one of the more powerful kingdoms on the coast. The militaristic aristocracy monopolized foreign trade and used the slave trade to bolster its power internally. A crown-slave bureaucracy developed alongside slave troops, and the nobles used both to recruit more slaves through war and raids. An ethos developed to protect loyal citizens from enslavement, but disobedient subjects, prisoners of war, and non-Muslims could be sold. In the nineteenth century, when French and British traders stopped buying many slaves in Salum, the country continued to sell slaves to Moors (q.v.) and other Africans and began exporting groundnuts to Europe.

In the mid-nineteenth century, European invaders and Muslim clerics began threatening the kingdom at almost the same time. In 1859 General Faidherbe (q.v.) led a relatively uneventful military promenade through Salum, and tried subsequently to impose a protectorate. But beginning in 1862, it was conquered by Ma Ba (q.v.), a Tijani cleric strongly influenced by *al-Hajj* Umar Tal (q.v.). He founded a new capital at Nioro du Rip and consolidated his rule. After his death in battle in 1867, his succession was disputed between his brother Mamur Ndari and his son Saer Maty. The two clashed with French conquerors from the north and British from the south. In 1898 the French finally dissolved and absorbed Salum, the northern portion of Ma Ba's legacy, and the British claimed Rip (Badihu) in the south. Unlike most Senegalese kingdoms, the precolonial Gelwar dynasty was allowed to continue appointing a nominal *Bur Salum* until 1969.

The Dakar–Bamako railroad, begun in 1906, ran through the center of the kingdom. It supplanted the old overland trade routes and traders, bringing an economic boom to new groups in its wake. Salum became the heart of the groundnut basin, and the colonial export economy that created it. Migrant farmers (see NAVETAN) from other regions moved into the area, with government help, and cultivated peanuts. They earned cash to pay their taxes and buy imported cloth and other goods. The westernmost part of the region is densely populated and soil depleted today, but eastern Salum is still receiving new settlers. Kaolack developed as a railroad town, farm market and port, to become the second largest city in Senegal. Since independence, however, it has lost its function as a farm market (owing to the government monopoly, ONCAD, q.v.) and some of its dry season affluence. (See SIN.)

SARAKHOLE or SARAXOLE. See SONINKE.

SECK, BU AL-MOGDAD. (1826–80) *Tamsir* and *Qadi* (q.v.) of Saint-Louis (q.v.) during the period of the French conquest, he served as explorer and principal diplomatic emissary to the kingdoms of the interior. A Saint-Louisien by birth, Bu al-Mogdad began his service to the French with Governor Protet in the early 1850s. In 1861 Governor Faidherbe (q.v.) sponsored him on a pilgrimage to Mecca (see HAJJ), hoping thereby to endow him with prestige equal to that of *al-Hajj* Umar Tal (q.v.). Caste prejudice, and the political transparency of the move in the context of French imperialism frustrated that hope.

But al-Mogdad's universally acclaimed intelligence and good Arabic education won him the position of personal attendant to the governors from 1868 on. In addition to numerous missions in Mauritania and the Sudan (Mali), he is credited with persuading Lat Jor Jop (q.v.) to sign the 1879 treaty authorizing the construction of a railroad through Kajor (q.v.), assuring the king that he had ridden on one and they were harmless. Bu al-Mogdad's officially recognized French titles included Tamsir (Officier de l'instruction publique), Qadi (Chef de la justice musulmane et française à Saint-Louis), Officer de le Légion d'honneur, Chevalier du Médjidié and Interprète principal. One of his sons, Bu al-Mogdad II, fulfilled similar exploring missions in the 1890s and 1900s, but by then the French administration was better established and did not depend so strongly on Muslim mediators.

SECTION FRANÇAISE DE L'INTERNATIONAL OUVRIERE (SFIO), FEDERATION SENEGALAISE (French Section of the Worker's International, Senegalese Federation). Senegalese branch of the French Socialist Party from 1936 to 1957. When the Popular Front came to power in France in 1936, Lamine Guèye (q.v.) brought the Parti Socialiste Sénégalais (q.v.) into the movement. The Senegalese SFIO won the municipal elections in Saint-Louis in 1937 and in other towns by 1939.

After the Second World War, the SFIO regrouped and emerged the strongest party in Senegal. It won the 1945 and

1946 elections, with Lamine Guèye representing the urban constituencies and Léopold Senghor (q.v.) chosen by Guèye to run for the newly enfranchised rural population's deputy seat. Tensions between Guèye and Senghor emerged quickly, however, and in 1947 the latter formed his own party, the Bloc Démocratique Sénégalais (q.v.). In the 1951 and 1952 elections, the BDS won all seats except those in Dakar and Saint-Louis. For the next five years, the SFIO struggled to overcome its narrow, urban elite orientation and alliance with the French socialists. In 1957 it broke with the French SFIO, and renamed itself the Parti Senegalais d'Action Socialiste. In 1957, the BDS and the PSAS, along with several smaller groups, merged to form the Union Progressiste Sénégalaise (q.v.).

SEMBENE, OUSMANE. (1923–) Writer and leading Senegalese film director, producing films in both Wolof and French designed for African audiences but also winning international acclaim.

Born to a Lebu (q.v.) fishing family in Ziguinchor (q.v.), Sembène was drafted into the French army during World War II. Embittered by discrimination during his service, and the massacre of protesting veterans at Thiaroye (q.v.) immediately after the war, he returned to France to work the docks at Marseilles. He taught himself to write in French and became a union representative. His longshoreman's experience appears in his early novel, *The Black Docker,* and the life of African migrants to France is the subject matter of several other works. Upon returning to Senegal in 1947, he helped organize the railway workers' strike at Thiès, the first effective strike in French West Africa. These events were later re-created in his best-known novel, *God's Bits of Wood.*

Sembène continued to write in French, but turned to cinema to reach a larger audience. He won a fellowship to the Moscow Film School in 1961. His first short, *Borom Sarret,* depicted a noble degraded by colonialism, forced to make a living by driving a horse cart in Dakar. In his internationally successful *Mandabi* (*The Money Order*), the recipient of a postal money order from a young relative sweeping streets in France is hounded by both the bureaucracy and his family and neighbors. In *Xala*, he openly satirizes the political and business elite of modern Senegal. Sembène has also turned to historical themes: religion in the film *Emitai,* and the precolonial Wolof military aristocracy in *Ceddo,* which remains banned in Senegal but has played to international acclaim. The Senegalese government insists that the title should be spelt with one *d* in accordance with a decree on national languages published by Senghor, whereas Sembène uses two *d's,* as it is pronounced. Obviously, the film's subject matter, which is harshly critical of Islam and Christianity, is the primary reason for its banning. Sembène has recently finished a film on the massacre at Thiaroye (q.v.), titled *Camp de Thiaroye.* (See LITERATURE in the Bibliography.)

SENEGAL ORIENTAL. Eastern Senegal is the largest and most sparsely populated and isolated region of Senegal. It stretches from the upper Casamance to the Faleme and Senegal rivers and shares borders with Mauritania, Mali and Guinea. The region has always been and continues to be a crossroads of people from other areas, most notably Fulbe pastoralists, Futanke and Khassonke farmers, as well as Soninke, Jakhanke and Mande merchants. They occupy the area along with the indigenous Tenda and Bassari peoples, who are concentrated in the southern section near the Guinea border. The major precolonial states were Bundu and Gajaaga to the north, Bambuk to the east, and portions of Kabu to the south (each q.v.). Today the region is partly pastoral and partly agricultural, with millet, cotton, groundnuts and corn dominating production. The region's capital is at Tambacounda (q.v.), which is linked by railroad and paved road to Kaolack, and by railroad to Kayes (Mali).

SENEGAL RIVER. The river that gave the country its name and the first part of the region to be reached by Portuguese (q.v.) explorers in the mid-fifteenth century. Today the river forms the northern and eastern border with Mauritania.

The rich flood plains of the river supported early agriculture, and the river itself served as an avenue of trade for medieval Sudanic states. The first trade mentioned in Arabic sources from the eleventh century was salt from the river mouth, passing upstream in exchange for gold from the interior Sudanic states. During the nineteenth century, gum arabic from upstream dominated river trade. With railroad construction and groundnut expansion, the Senegal River lost its importance as a trading axis from interior to coast. Sizable vessels can navigate only as far as Dagana year-round, and to Bakel (q.v.) from mid-July through mid-November. The Gambia River to the south had considerably more commercial potential.

Flood-recession agriculture was practiced the length of the floodplain, which is widest in the area between Podor and Matam. Salt-sea intrusion limits agriculture in the delta area from Saint-Louis to Dagana, but the region was an important dry-season refuge for livestock and an abundant source for fish. The Lac de Guiers (q.v.), connected to the river near Richard Toll, fills with fresh water during the flood season, and is then dammed as a reservoir. Salt mines at Ganjkol at the mouth were an important source of wealth for Kajor, and still function today.

During the colonial conquest, the French divided the right and left banks, generally obliging Moors (q.v.) to stay north and blacks to the south, and administering the two as separate territories. At independence, the river became an international border between the Arab-dominated Mauritania, and the black African-dominated Senegal. This division also diminished the river's commercial importance. Since the 1930s, the male population of riverine areas has tended to migrate in substantial numbers in search of better economic opportunities in cities and the groundnut basin. The Organisation pour la Mise en Valeur du Fleuve Senegal (q.v.) has been working to reverse this trend by damming the river upstream, irrigating the entire floodplain and making the river navigable as far as Kayes, Mali.

In April 1989, ethnic clashes between Moors and Senegalese erupted over disputed land situated on the Senegal River. Both groups claimed historic possession of the land. The clashes spread to Dakar, Nouakchott and other towns in both Senegal and Mauritania. There was a mass exodus and confiscation of property on both sides. The border was closed and joint development projects between the two countries have been suspended. (See also FLEUVE; MOOR.)

SENGHOR, LEOPOLD SEDAR. (1906–) The founding father and first president of the Republic of Senegal from 1960 to 1980. Senghor is one of the continent's outstanding intellectual and political figures. He has remained an international statesman, instrumental in the establishment of the Organization of African Unity (OAU), the Organisation Commune Africaine, Malagache et Mauritienne (q.v.) and various regional organizations. He is also a renowned poet, the main promoter of the concept of *négritude* (q.v.) and in 1983 became the first African elected to the *Academie Française.*

Senghor was born October 9, 1906, in Joal on the Petite Côte (q.v.). He was descended from a Catholic Serer family that also had Mande and Fulbe elements. This contrasted with the dominant Wolof, Muslim orientation of contemporary politicians. Furthermore, he was the first major political figure not to have come from one of the four *communes* (q.v.) where Africans had French citizenship and special privileges. He attended the Ngasobil Catholic Mission School and prepared for the priesthood at Libermann Seminary in Dakar. He decided not to pursue a religious career, however, and transferred to the Public Secondary School in Dakar (later Lycée Van Vollenhoven). By all accounts, he was an exceptional pupil. In 1928, he realized a life-long dream and went to France to study, enrolling at the Lycée Louis le Grand in Paris. Among his classmates was Georges Pompidou, later president of France.

As a student during the Depression years in Paris, Senghor lost many of his illusions about Europe. He plunged into an intense intellectual interaction with West Indian, black American, African and European writers and thinkers, and began to produce a poetry that helped launch the concept of *négritude* (q.v.). Inspired partially by the romantic vision of Africa in Harlem Renaissance authors and early European ethnographers, Senghor exalted African culture. He contrasted African ways with all that was wrong with the West—rationalism, mechanization, capitalism, materialism, bourgeois values, individualism, competition and a stiff, cold ugliness. He became one of the first black intellectuals to express discontent with French cultural assimilation. He retained an admiration of French culture, however, including the French language and literature, philosophy and artistic achievements.

In 1931 Senghor received his *Licence es Lettres.* In 1935 he became the first black African to pass the *Agrégation* competitive examination, but only after he had become a naturalized French citizen, largely through the efforts of Lamine Guèye (q.v.). The following year he was drafted into the army. After military service, he taught in *lycées* in Tours and outside of Paris. During a vacation in Dakar in 1938, he gave his maiden political speech, making his first important statements of what was to become his characteristic point of view, and his reputation began to grow in Senegal and among political circles in France. In the opening months of World War II, Senghor was again called up. After being captured and nearly killed by German troops, he spent two years as a prisoner of war. Released in 1942, he returned to teaching near Paris, and worked with the French resistance.

With the end of the war, his literary career reached fruition with the publication of his first volume of poetry, *Chants d'Ombre*. He also decided, despite the primacy that he reserved for cultural matters, that politics could not be ignored. Offered a place on Lamine Guèye's ticket as the candidate of the newly enfranchised rural voters, Senghor was elected a Deputy to the French Assembly with the support of the French Socialist Party (SFIO).

In 1946, Senghor participated in the French Constituant Assemblies, which shaped the Fourth Republic. Like his counterparts in other African territories, he became increasingly concerned with the issue of African self-government. The same year, a group of political leaders from France's West and Central African territories met in Bamako, Sudan (Mali), to form the Rassemblement Démocratique Africain (RDA, q.v.), an interterritorial political party. Senghor and Guèye were persuaded by their French socialist allies to boycott the conference for fear that it was Communist-dominated. The RDA thus came to be controlled by Felix Houphouet-Boigny, whose ideas on the future of Africa differed radically from Senghor's.

Senghor remained subservient to Guèye until 1947, when differences in style and political philosophy led to a break between the two men. Senghor felt that Guèye neglected the common people of the countryside and did not work actively for African issues. The following year, Senghor founded the Bloc Démocratique Sénégalais (q.v.), which promoted an "African socialism" (q.v.) based on traditional village cooperation, religious faith and a new nationalism. That same year, he and Alioune Diop launched *Présence Africaine,* a Paris magazine that promoted African culture.

Sweeping electoral victories in 1951 and 1952 confirmed Senghor's appeal to the rural population, as opposed to Guèye's reliance on an urban elite constituency. The UPS affiliated with other parties in France's African territories, but outside Senegal it was not strong enough to counter Houphouet's RDA. Senghor's group believed that the Francophone territories should unite in some sort of federation. Houphouet called for complete autonomy for each territory under the French umbrella. In the 1956 elections to the French legislature, the RDA defeated Senghor's affiliates everywhere but in Senegal. France's 1957 enactment of the *loi cadre* (q.v.), giving autonomy to the territories individually instead of collectively, was a bitter disappointment. In its first legislative elections later that year, Senghor formed the new government. He invited Lamine Guèye to participate as well.

When given the choice in 1958 of voting yes for autonomy and continued association with France, or no for immediate independence, Senghor and most of the rest of French West Africa chose autonomy and continued assistance. Several intellectual leaders favored immediate independence, and UPS unity was undermined. In addition, Guinea's no vote in the referendum set off a chain reaction of events that resulted in independence for all of Francophone Africa within the next few years after all.

As events moved rapidly, Senghor struggled to preserve the essentials of regional cooperation and Francophone cultural exchange in the new context. His 1959 call for a voluntary Francophone West African federation initially enlisted Sudan (now Mali), Upper Volta (Burkina Faso) and Dahomey (Benin), but the latter two dropped out within the year, under pressure from Houphoet-Boigny. Senghor negotiated independence for what remained of the Mali Federation (q.v.) of Senegal and Sudan by June 1960. As the first elections approached in August, Senghor realized that the Sudanese allies were opposing his election as president and seeking support for their party in his territory. The Sudanese leaders were also trying to convince Senegalese intellectuals that Senghor would maintain close ties to France. The federation quickly fell apart, and Senghor declared Senegal an independent republic. He was elected president, with responsibility for policy and international affairs. Prime

Minister Mamadou Dia (q.v.) was charged with the daily administration of the government. During the first two years of independence, Senghor nationalized groundnut marketing, initiated rural cooperatives and instituted a national system of agricultural credit, extension services and cooperative administration. Land tenure laws were also modified. Senghor also carefully courted the various Muslim leaders in the country, particularly the powerful Murid brotherhood (q.v.).

Tensions arose between Senghor and Mamadou Dia over the implementation of reforms, with conservatives, moderates and the Murid leaders supporting Senghor's gradualism as opposed to Dia's plan for immediate implementation, by force if necessary. In December 1962, there was a showdown (see CONSTITUTIONAL CRISIS OF 1962). Senghor prevailed, sending Dia and his top ministers to jail for an attempted coup d'état. The constitution was rewritten to provide for a single strong executive, and Senghor ruled with an iron hand for the next eight years. Opposition parties were eliminated nonviolently either by absorption or banning, and freedom of the press and association was severely limited. Senghor overcame electoral unrest (1963) and student riots (1968) by force and by maintaining a broad-based coalition of supporters. He was reelected President unopposed in 1963, 1968 and 1973. (See ELECTIONS.)

Senghor's political position allowed free reign for his statesmanship as well as for the promotion of African culture. The arts were well-funded in Senegal, and the Festival of Negro Arts in Dakar in 1966 (q.v.) crowned his promotion of négritude. His contribution to the founding of the Organization of African Unity (OAU), the Organisation Commune Africain, Mauritienne et Malagache (q.v.) and the various Senegal and Gambia River Basin development associations won him respect as an elder statesman. Senegal's economic base did not expand, and Senghor relied increasingly on his personal dynamism and historic role.

In 1970, Senghor felt confident enough to reintroduce the office of prime minister, filling it cautiously with a young technocrat Abdou Diouf (q.v.). Beginning in 1973 he also initiated far-reaching administrative reforms (q.v.) and political reforms. Two opposition parties were legalized, and in the 1978 election Abdoulaye Wade (q.v.) was allowed to stand against Senghor for President. Senghor won in a landslide. He also changed the name of his party from the Union Progressiste Sénégalaise (q.v.) to the Parti Socialiste (q.v.), and brought it into the Socialist International. The 1970s were a difficult period for the Senegalese economy with a major drought in the mid-1970s and declining prices for and production of groundnuts (q.v.), the country's main export. In the multiparty elections of 1978, Senghor's Parti Socialiste received 81.7 percent of the vote; only 43 percent of the eligible voters in Senegal voted, however. This contrasts with the 90 percent who voted in earlier elections. Clearly, Senghor's popularity was on the wane. Abdou Diouf increasingly managed the government, and on December 31, 1980, Senghor resigned in favor of Diouf. Senghor thus became the first African leader installed at independence to resign voluntarily his position.

During his retirement, Senghor has pursued his career as one of Africa's most respected elder statesmen. He has remained on the international political scene, becoming involved with the Socialist International and the Palestine Liberation Organization. He now spends most of his time in France.

SERER. One of the largest ethnic groups in Senegal, comprising about 19 percent of the population. They occupy the most densely populated area of the groundnut basin in central Senegal, inland from Cape Verde (q.v.) to the Kaolack-Kaffrine area.

According to their oral traditions and archaeological evidence, they originally lived as far north as the Senegal River

Valley, adjacent to their "cousins," the Fulbe (q.v.). In the eleventh century, they began migrating into their present homeland in Bawol, Sin, and Salum (each q.v.). Adhering to their traditional religion, they became concentrated in their present area through centuries of pressure from more powerful Muslim Futanke, Wolof and Mande neighbors. The main body formed itself into the small but powerful kingdom of Sin in the twelfth or thirteenth century, while the neighboring kingdom of Salum had emerged by the late fifteenth century. Both were absorbed, along with the Wolof kingdoms, into the Jolof Empire (q.v.). Small groups of Serer, trying to preserve a decentralized egalitarian political tradition, were enclaved in the hills of southern Kajor (q.v.) and eastern Bawol. The kings of those states raided them for slaves and obliged them to pay tribute. The Serer were among the few groups in Senegal north of the Gambia River to convert in some numbers to Christianity, mainly Catholicism.

The Serer are conventionally divided into Serer-Sin (from the Sine-Saloum Region) and Serer-Bawol from the area around Diourbel. Interestingly, the acephalous Serer-Non and Serer-Ndut, the original inhabitants of the area frequently grouped with the Serer, are not related either linguistically or culturally to the Serer of Sin and Salum. The Serer generally practice mixed farming, raising cattle and smaller livestock, groundnuts and food crops. By the late 1960s population density had reached a crisis stage around Fatick—no land remained for fallowing, balanced rotation broke down and production declined. The drought (q.v.) of 1968–73 accentuated the problem. A resettlement scheme was launched in the *Terres Neuves* (q.v.) southwest of Tambacounda (q.v.), but proved expensive and inadequate to solve the demographic problem. A more common response recently has been urban migration to Dakar, Kaolack, Thiès and Diourbel. In the cities, the Serer tend to assimilate to Wolof culture and Islam, although a strong minority has become Christian since the early colonial era.

SIGNARE. Senegambian term of Portuguese origin for wealthy women traders in Saint-Louis, Gorée and other European trading stations along the coast. *Signarés* are portrayed in precolonial literature and sketched in Abbé Boilat's book (see Bibliography) as charming, sophisticated and wealthy merchants who intentionally grew as portly as possible (reportedly a sign of wealth) and decked themselves in gold jewelry and imported finery. They were often mistresses or common-law wives of French traders, combining amorous liaisons with business partnerships. They maintained commercial networks of relatives, friends and longtime customers on the mainland, through which they acted as middlemen for their French partners. Most were of mixed ancestry. (See METIS.)

SIN. Precolonial Serer (q.v.) kingdom situated on the north bank of the Salum estuary, and today part of the Region of Sine-Saloum (Kaolack). The capital was Jaxao, and the main seaport Joal on the Petite Côte (q.v.). It was ruled by the Gelwar matrilineage, founded by Maisa Wali Jon, a refugee from Kabu (q.v.). Maisa Wali Jon is believed to have fled to Sin about the time of the founding of the Jolof Empire (twelfth to fourteenth century?) and accepted Jolof as overlord. The Serer population of the region, which had been migrating to the area from Futa Toro (q.v.) since the eleventh century, probably outnumbered the autochthonous Non, Nominka and Njeghem. A new influx of Serer arrived in the late fifteenth century led by Elibana, who had been defeated by Koly Tengela Ba (q.v.). The Jolof Empire (q.v.) was engaged in a civil war, and toward the mid-sixteenth century, Sin gained its independence from Jolof. Unlike the Muslim Wolof and Futanke monarchs to the north, the Sin rulers apparently adapted to Serer traditional religion, using it to enforce their authority. Even in the mid-nineteenth century, Sin was a stronghold of resistance to the clerical reformer Ma Ba (q.v.), who died in 1867 trying to conquer it.

Unlike other Senegalese monarchs, the *Burs* of Sin and Salum were allowed to keep their titles throughout the colonial period, although they became French civil servants. The dynasty lost official recognition in 1969.

SLAVES. Most Senegalese societies were based on some form of indigenous slavery. Slaves were exported into the trans-Saharan trade as early as the tenth century, and after the mid-fifteenth century, much larger numbers were exported into the trans-Atlantic slave trade. This prolonged intensive demand swelled the domestic dependence on slavery. During the latter nineteenth century, 50 years of colonial and indigenous religious wars resulted in enslavement on an unprecedented scale. When slavery was legally abolished in Gorée and Saint-Louis (both q.v.) in 1848, a French census showed that slaves comprised over three-quarters of the towns' populations. As newly conquered areas were added to the colony, the colonial administration liberated slaves living there. This was the major reason that the rural areas of Senegal were generally incorporated under French rule as a protectorate rather than a colony, for within the protectorate, slavery could be eliminated gradually. In the Senegambian region generally, according to French estimates, one-half to two-thirds of the population was of slave descent in the 1890s. Vestiges of slavery still remain today; in prejudice against freeborn-slave marriages, restrictions on slaves advancing in the religious hierarchy, some occupational distinctions, occasional inheritance of former slaves' goods by former masters' families, prestations and landlessness. Although persons of slave descent are usually easily identifiable within Senegalese societies, it is illegal to refer publicly to someone's origins, or to hinder his or her advancement because of it. The law of the national domain (q.v.) theoretically gives everyone access to land.

Owing to the diversity of the practice of slavery among the different ethnic groups in Senegal, it is difficult to generalize about the work and lives of slaves. Slavery was a much more versatile tradition in precolonial Senegal than in the New World. Male and female slaves worked in all sectors of the economy. The only common attribute of slaves was that they could not inherit land or titles, as they were owned by masters and considered "perpetual outsiders" of foreign origin. Slave status was generally inherited from the mother, regardless of the father's status. Domestic slaves usually fed themselves from their own plots, which they worked along with their masters' fields. They were rarely sold after the first generation, and in certain areas could escape an intolerable master by cutting the ear of their desired new master, his child, or his horse. The offending slave would then be given as compensation to the new master. Slaves could, however, hold high office and have property and clients of their own, including casted persons, concubines and other slaves. Crown-slaves formed royal bodyguards in the Jolof Empire and early Wolof kingdoms. From the eighteenth century on, as the Atlantic slave trade intensified, these corps swelled to form standing armies and fill a panoply of offices in royal bureaucracies. As owned persons, they were the king's main weapon for strengthening his political position vis-à-vis hereditary nobility. By the seventeenth century, clerics complained that the king's *cedo* (q.v.) harassed and enslaved the population. Clerics offered slaves a somewhat more liberal alternative, in which adherence to Islam and descent from a Muslim father were theoretically sufficient grounds for manumission. This became one of the recurrent tensions in Senegambian history, not finally resolved until the colonial era.

SLAVE TRADE. The area of modern Senegal exported slaves into and across the Sahara Desert regularly from about the eighth century CE onward. The arrival of the Portuguese (q.v.) in the mid-fifteenth century inaugurated a new European branch of the slave trade, which quickly became the single most important feature of coastal and riverine Senegambian history. From the mid-fifteenth century until the end of the sixteenth century, the Senegambia provided most slaves to Europeans in West Africa. The Portuguese purchased slaves both from the Senegambian coast and from the trans-Saharan trade at Arguin, where in the late 1400s, they purchased 800 to 1,000 slaves annually. Under the pressure of this rapidly growing trade, the Jolof Empire (q.v.) broke up, and wars among the constituent kingdoms made Wolof the major victims. The expansion of Kabu (q.v.) in the south made Casamance (q.v.) and Bissau another major supply area well into the sixteenth century.

In the seventeenth century, European attention shifted to more densely populated areas of West and Central Africa, but the Senegambia remained a steady source of 2,000 to 3,500 slaves annually until the end of the eighteenth century. The destinations of exported Senegambians varied over time, and according to which ship or company purchased them. In the fifteenth century, most went to Portugal itself, and later to Portuguese Atlantic islands. In the sixteenth century the Portuguese carried them to Spanish colonies in South and Central America. In the seventeenth, first Dutch and then English and French began taking them to sugar plantations in the Caribbean and tobacco estates in North America.

As the Atlantic slave trade reached its peak between the mid-seventeenth and mid-eighteenth centuries, the economic, social and political impact on Senegambian kingdoms was also greatest. Crown-slave armies grew, and nobles used them against one another or to raid small pockets of non-Muslims. The slave trade was an issue in the domestic politics of coastal and riverine kingdoms from at least the seventeenth century on. Reform clerics (q.v.) listed the enslavement of Muslims among the oppressions that they fought. Even when clerics succeeded in taking over the government, however, they were unable to reduce the volume of the slave trade—in fact, the wars they initiated resulted in increased rather than decreased total exports.

The volume of the Atlantic slave trade began to decline in British trade zones in the late eighteenth century, as England moved into the Industrial Revolution, but the slave trade in French zones did not fall off until the nineteenth century. It decreased sharply in the Senegambia, but did not end when the British banned their traders from exporting slaves in 1807 and obliged the French to do the same in 1815. Gum arabic (q.v.) and later groundnuts (q.v.) replaced slaves as the primary exports of the Senegambia in the nineteenth century. The French continued to purchase slaves, but gave them contracts for military or other service for fixed periods of time—usually 20 years. Very few of these *èngagés à temps,* as they were euphemistically called, ever gained their freedom. The Saharan and Sudanic slave trades also continued unabated into the early twentieth century.

Senegambian economics were transformed from slave-based agricultural and commercial systems to colonial producers for export by a series of early colonial policies. The maintenance of an adequate supply of cheap labor was one of their major goals. Forced labor, conscription and indenturing were required throughout the early colonial period. After World War II, abolition of these was among the first reforms to be demanded and instituted. By then the cash economy had so thoroughly penetrated the Senegambia that an adequate labor supply could be anticipated from migrant peasants.

SOCIETE COMMERCIAL DE L'OUEST AFRICAIN (SCOA, Commercial Corporation of West Africa). One of the major French import-export houses in colonial Africa (see also CFAO). Founded in 1906 by a group of French colonial merchants linked with banking and industrial interests in Lyon and Geneva, it was soon operating throughout French West and Equatorial Africa. International headquarters were in Paris, and Conakry (Guinea) was the West African base. Turnover and profits reached a peak immediately after World

War II, when it also initiated its first tentative ventures into industrialization. In the early Fifties it abandoned the trading-post format and blossomed into a modern conglomerate with interests in retail (Printania, Priscoa and rural general stores), transportation, automobiles and export of primary produce. With independence, groundnut (q.v.) exports were nationalized, and SCOA was obliged to retreat somewhat from colonial commerce. It branched out in Europe and then reorganized its Senegalese interests, introducing African participation. It formed SOSECOD in 1964, which in 1965 was absorbed by SONADIS, or Société Nationale de Distribution au Sénégal, the national retail corporation.

SOCIETES DE PREVOYANCE. (Savings and Loan Associations). Rural credit and marketing cooperatives sponsored by the colonial government and under the direction of local administrators. They spread through Senegal in about 1910, despite the resentment of the major French firms, and then throughout French West Africa.

SOLEIL, LE. The only daily newspaper in Senegal, it has been published since 1970 by a joint government and private agency. It replaced the earlier daily, *Dakar-Matin* (q.v.), which had been published by an exclusively French firm.

SONINKE. (also Sarakholle or Saraxolle). Ethnic group centered on the upper Senegal River from Matam to Bakel (q.v.) and south of the confluence of the Falémé River. They also live in Mauritania and Mali. The Soninke comprise about 5 percent of the total population of Senegal.

The Soninke heartland, primarily limited to an area of cultivable savanna along the desert fringe, occupied approximately 800 kilometers from the upper Senegal to the Niger bend. The Soninke ruled the ancient empire of Ghana (called Wagadu in indigenous traditions), the first known major state in the Western Sudan. The empire's decline in the late eleventh century caused a Soninke diaspora, particularly of clerics and merchants, resulting in the formation of the Jaxanke (q.v.), Gajaaga Soninke and the Juula (Dyula). The majority of Soninke remained in the transitional zone between the Sahara Desert and the Sudanic belt, however. In the upper Senegal, the Soninke, also called the Serawoolies, Saracolets, Sarakholles and Marka, inhabited and dominated the states of Gajaaga and Gidimaka (both q.v.). They also formed an important merchant minority in Niani and Wuli (each q.v.).

Predominantly agriculturalists, they also engaged extensively and profitably in commerce, benefitting from the symbiotic relationship between the desert and savanna economies and the proximity of the Senegal River. The Soninke converted relatively early to Islam; in some places, the word ''Saracolet'' became synonymous with ''marabout'' (q.v., or religious teacher). According to traditions, the Soninke, though sharing the tripartite social division of other savanna peoples, contained a separate category of mercenaries and warriors who captured the slaves used by merchants and agriculturalists. The Soninke constituted a significant and integral component of the greater Mande (q.v.) formation that, along with the Fulbe (q.v.), dominated the middle and upper Senegal and Niger River valleys before the arrival of the French.

Since the colonial era the Soninke have emigrated in large numbers to coastal Senegal and to France. They enlisted in the French military and merchant marine, and since 1960 have come to form, along with Mauritanian and Malian Soninke, three-quarters of the African migrant worker population in France. From 20 to 70 percent of the active male population of Soninke villages are absent, leaving women, old men and hired workers to tend their fields and herds. Absences that tended to last two to four years on the average are tending, despite French opposition, to become permanent. Remittances from France allow families left behind to have concrete houses and consumer goods in greater quantities than their neighbors, but are not being reinvested in the economic development of the region.

SUFI, SUFISM. Islamic mystical orders called Sufi brotherhoods emerged within the first century of the founding of Islam, amid an orthodox legalistic religious tradition. They are typically founded by a single great mystic, whose extreme veneration by his followers offends some Muslims. The first order to be introduced into West Africa was the Qadiri (q.v.) brotherhood in the fifteenth century. The Tijani (q.v.) sect was founded in Morocco in the late eighteenth century and quickly spread throughout West Africa. In the nineteenth century many leaders of the jihads (q.v.) founded Tijani branches, including the most famous, al-Hajj Umar Tal (q.v.).

At the beginning of the twentieth century a Wolof cleric, Amadu Bamba Mbacke (q.v.), founded the first black African order, the Murid brotherhood (q.v.). The Tijaniyya and the Muridiyya are the largest Sufi brotherhoods in Senegal, with the Qadiriyya a distant third. Two other orders have small followings in Senegal, the Layenne on Cape Verde and the Hamalliyya, largely among Malian immigrants.

SUJET (SUBJECT). The legal status of an African born in the protectorate of Senegal or any other part of French Africa except the four urban *communes* (q.v.), in the colonial period until 1946. Subjects lacked legal protection of human and civil rights and came instead under the *indigénat* (q.v.). The legal distinction between natives of the communes, who were considered French *citoyens* (q.v.), and those of the empire, who were subjects, evolved during the conquest and early colonial era around the turn of the twentieth century. In the flush of conquest, many French administrators would have preferred to consider all Africans subjects, but residents of the communes, who had been voting in government-organized elections since 1848, refused to be leveled. The hated status of subject was abolished in 1946, when both subjects and citizens were reclassified "citizens of the French Union."

SY, ABDUL AZIZ. (c.1905–) *Xalifa* of the Tijani (q.v.) brotherhood at Tiwawan since 1957. He is the third son of the founder, *al-Hajj* Malik Sy (q.v.), and succeeded the first son Abu Bakr Sy (q.v.) in office. The succession was contested by Abu Bakr's third son, Cheikh Tidiane Sy. President Léopold Senghor (q.v.) supported Abdul Aziz and consulted cordially with him on religious affairs. President Abdou Diouf (q.v.) has also maintained friendly relations with Abdul Aziz as well. Abdul Aziz has exerted intellectual rather than political leadership and generally allied with Saidu Nourou Tal (q.v.) when political questions arose. In 1964, when the Grande Mosque of Dakar was consecrated, Saidu Nourou Tal wanted Abdul Aziz named Imam, but a coalition of rival marabouts with government backing insisted that the current Imam of Dakar, *al-Hajj* Amadou Lamine Diène, retain the honor.

SY, ABU BAKR (or ABOUBACAR). (c.1890–1957) *Xalifa* of the Tijani order at Tiwawan from 1922 to 1957. The first son of the founder, *al-Hajj* Malik Sy (q.v.), Abu Bakr inherited his father's title. During his 35-year reign, the Tijaniyya continued to grow, and his school remained the best in Senegal. Only the rivalry of his next two younger brothers, Mansur and Abdul Aziz (q.v.), troubled him. In the last decade of his Xalifat, the fraternal factionalism was complicated by competing political alliances and became overt. Abu Bakr supported, and was supported by, Léopold Senghor and the dominant Bloc Démocratique Sénégalaise (q.v.), while his younger brothers allied with Lamine Guèye's Socialists (q.v.). Abu Bakr died March 25, 1957, and Mansur, four days later, leaving the third son Abdul Aziz to inherit the Xalifat.

SY, AL-HAJJ MALIK. (c.1855–1922) Prominent cleric who founded the main Senegalese lodge at Tiwawan (Tivaouane). Born near Dagana on the Senegal River, of a noted Futanke family, he was raised in Wolof country, where he became an assimilated Wolof. As the Wolof kingdoms and Tijani resistance were being crushed in the mid-1880s, he began the life of an itinerant teacher in Kajor, Jolof and Walo. In 1889 he went to Mecca, and upon his return he established a school in Saint-Louis. From 1895 to 1902 he taught in Marne and Kajor, and then in 1902 he settled permanently and established a lodge in the booming railroad town of Tiwawan. He had been initiated into the Tijaniyya order by his uncle, Mayoro, whose own initiation had been confirmed by *al-Hajj* Umar Tal (q.v.).

Despite his spiritual mentor's long military career, Malik conducted his jihad on a spiritual and cultural plane only. The French considered Malik Sy a reliable leader, in contrast to Amadu Bamba Mbacke (q.v.), who worried them. With tacit French cooperation, he became the most effective proselytizer of the Tijaniyya among the Wolof. His adherents were largely drawn from the burgeoning cities and towns along the railway. Those who studied at his center of higher learning in Tiwawan introduced a new level of sophistication into Islam among the Wolof. His teaching emphasized an enlightened approach to Islam, criticizing mysticism, petty intolerance and evocations to blind obedience among Senegalese marabouts. At his death in 1922, he was succeeded by his son Abu Bakr Sy (q.v.), who took the title *Xalifa*. A splinter group organized around a favorite disciple, *al-Hajj* Aghwan Ngon of Saint-Louis, and refused to recognize Abu Bakr's authority, but it never attracted a large following.

SY, BOKAR SAADA. Ruler of Bundu (q.v.) in the upper Senegal valley from the late 1850s until his death in 1885. Bokar was the son of Almamy Saada Sy, ruler of Bundu from 1820 until 1845, and a descendant of the first *almamy* of Bundu, Malik

Dauda Sy (q.v.). When Almamy Saada died, Bundu was plunged into civil war, followed by the upheaval caused by the Umarian jihad (q.v.). Bokar Saada initially supported the jihad of *al-Hajj* Umar Tal (q.v.), but then, for a variety of reasons, turned against him. Realizing he would play a limited role and wield little influence in a Umarian political formation, Bokar Saada professed his opposition to Umar and his loyalty to the French, who were engaged in a military campaign against Umar Tal in the upper Senegal valley. Governor Faidherbe (q.v.) saw the opportunity to restore the French advantage in Bundu that had existed during the reign of Almamy Saada and informally recognized Bokar as almamy in 1855, with official recognition bestowed in 1858.

The new almamy initially had little indigenous support, but French weapons and ammunition and the logistical aid of the Bakel (q.v.) and Senudebu commanders enhanced his position. Successful raids for slaves and booty into Bambuk (q.v.) and the area around Bakel soon won Bokar Saada a loyal following. Assisted by the Senudebu garrison, the almamy was able to limit Umar's recruitment efforts in Futa Toro (q.v.) and block Umarian access to Gambian and Bambuk trade routes that passed through Bundu. Faidherbe hoped Bokar would also help the French secure Bambuk and its reputedly extensive gold deposits.

Bokar Saada gave legitimacy to colonial operations in the upper Senegal valley while manipulating French support to his own advantage. He sought to extend his hegemony and increase his wealth, prestige and position by allying with rulers in other parts of Senegal, including Abdul Bokar Kan (q.v.) of eastern Futa Toro. Bokar Saada conducted numerous raids into Bambuk, the upper Gambia and the Ferlo (q.v.) with French approval and, frequently, encouragement. In the 1860s, Bokar Saada, almost exclusively through raiding, expanded the sphere of influence and extended the borders of Bundu by annexing parts of the surrounding polities.

By the 1870s, discontent with Bokar Saada was rampant.

His heavy taxations and forced labor demands grew more oppressive, and migration increased to southern and western areas. Defeats at Gamon in the south in 1881 and 1884 seriously demoralized the Bundunke military. With the almamy's health deteriorating, divisions within the Sissibe ruling lineage were more pronounced. When Bokar Saada died in December 1885, he was succeeded by his brother Umar Penda, who had little support. Mamadu Lamine Drame (q.v.), the Soninke leader, rapidly gained control of Bundu. When Lamine was killed, Bokar Saada's descendants were again installed as rulers of Bundu.

SY, MALIK DAUDA. (c.1640–c.1700). Founder of Bundu (q.v.) in the upper Senegal valley. Born in Futa Toro of Fulbe ancestry and into a clerical family, Malik Sy received a Quranic education in Futa and at Pir-Sanoxor (q.v.) in Kajor (q.v.). He became an itinerant teacher and about 1690 received a grant of land from the *tunka,* or king, of Gajaaga (q.v.). By 1693, Malik Sy and his growing following quarreled with the king and declared their independence. Sy's leadership rested primarily on religious prestige, and he took the title of *almamy* as did his descendants who belonged to the Sissibe lineage.

- T -

TAL, AL-HAJJ SAIDOU NOUROU. (c.1890–1981) *Marabout* grandson of *al-Hajj* Umar Tal (q.v.), who led a Tijani (q.v.) branch in Dakar, with a largely Futanke following. He was closely related to the Sy branch of the Tijani at Tiwawan since the days of the founder *al-Hajj* Malik Sy (q.v.), to whose care and teaching Saidou was conferred as a child and whose daughter he subsequently married. Tal was often seen as the statesman and mediator of the clerical community of Senegal, a role for which he was well-suited by temperament, age and distinguished lineage. During the middle decades of the colonial era, he served frequently as mediator between the colonial government and marabouts, or between different marabouts, traveling throughout West Africa at government expense, settling disputes and advocating the extension of peanut cultivation for colonial markets. By 1957 he had been decorated for outstanding services 24 times.

He led a Futanke ethnic association, the Union Générale des Originaires de la Vallée du Fleuve (q.v.), which gave him a substantial political power base in Dakar and the Fleuve (q.v.). In the competition between Lamine Guèye and Léopold Senghor (both q.v.) in 1948–52, he sided with Senghor, at least in part because the latter made Futanke politician Mamadou Dia (q.v.) important in his organization. When Dia was ousted in 1962, however, Tal remained loyal to Senghor. As self-government approached in the late Fifties, Saidou Nourou organized the Conseil Supérieur des Chefs Religieux (q.v.) to ensure protection of religious interests in the constitution and government. Although it never achieved the controlling voice he sought, it has remained influential.

One effort to which Saidou Nourou contributed substantially was the construction of the Grande Mosquée of Dakar, which was first proposed in the 1930s and finally consecrated in 1964. It was to be the largest mosque in Senegal, outshining that at Touba (see MURID). Saidou Nourou wanted the Tijani *Xalifa* Abdul Aziz Sy (q.v.) named Imam, but a coalition of rival marabouts with government backing insisted that the current *Imam* of Dakar, *al-Hajj* Amadou Lamine Diène, retain the honor.

Nevertheless, Saidou Nourou's relations with the government remained cordial until his death. He invested substantial amounts, accumulated through years of prominence and mediation, in the highly lucrative real-property market in Dakar, and he built a comfortable estate.

TAL, AL-HAJJ UMAR (also called SHAIXU UMAR or AL-HAJJ UMAR). (c.1794–1864). Fulbe cleric from Futa Toro (q.v.) who led a series of holy wars, or jihads, (q.v.) against traditional nobilities of the upper Senegal-Niger area and the French from 1852 until his death in 1864. He popularized the Tijani order (q.v.) and inspired, either directly or indirectly, a host of lesser Tijani jihadists, whose activities stretched from the Casamance and Futa Jalon (Guinea) to the south to the Senegal River basin in the north, and east across the Sahel to Hausaland (Nigeria). His teaching and style of leadership set the pattern for resistance throughout the Senegambia.

Born at Halwar in Toro province in western Futa, Umar received his early education there and was initiated by visiting Idawali Moorish clerics into the new Tijani brotherhood. Fifteen years of travels in North and West Africa and Arabia completed his education in grand style. He spent several months with Muhammed Bello in the Sokoto Caliphate in Hausaland before continuing to Mecca and Medina. Umar gained enormous prestige from his pilgrimage to Mecca. After intensive travels and studies, he was invested by Tijani leader Muhammad al-Ghali Abu Talif as *Xalifa* of the Tijaniyya for the Western Sudan. On his return to West Africa in 1832, *al-Hajj* Umar stayed seven years in Sokoto, taking three wives in Bornu and Hausaland, including one of Bello's daughters, and acquiring considerable political prominence. Bello died in 1837, and Umar moved to Masina on the middle Niger with his large following of *talibe* (q.v.) and slaves (q.v.). After nine months there, and a brief detention among the Bambara of Segu, he went on to settle in Futa Jalon, passing only briefly through his native Futa Toro. Umar established a base at Jagunko in Futa Jalon, attracting many followers from Futa Toro, Bundu (q.v.) and Futa Jalon. He built his following into a zealous, prosperous and influential Tijani mission. In 1849, he broke with the *almamy* of Futa Jalon and moved his headquarters to Dingiray in the Mandinka kingdom of Tamba, which bordered Futa Jalon. In

1852, the ruling elite of Tamba, threatened by the growing number of the interloper's followers, attacked Dingiray, and Umar reacted by declaring a jihad, or holy war.

Al-Hajj Umar took advantage of existing political divisions and economic crises in the upper Senegal valley. In July 1854, he mobilized approximately 2,000 men and moved up from Dingiray along the Tambura ridge in Bambuk (q.v.) to avoid Kartan influence in the east and the French at the fort of Senudebu (Bundu) to the west. By late 1854, Umar had successfully crushed the Mandinka of Bambuk and established his capital at Farabanna (q.v.). Besides its strategic location above the confluence of the Senegal and Faléme Rivers, Farabanna, populated almost exclusively by refugee slaves, had been an unwelcome symbol of resistance to the traditional rulers of nearby polities.

Umar rapidly gained the support of the ruling classes in eastern Senegambia. Supporters from all over the region joined the Umarian army, which rapidly swelled to about 10,000 men. From his headquarters at Farabanna, Umar carefully maintained and consolidated his control over the upper valley. A French arms embargo imposed in 1855 was the first sign of hostility from the French, who were his main competitors for control of the region. When Umar did turn against the French, his religious charisma and military ability made him a focus of the resistance across the whole Western Sudan. Many recruits answered Umar's call to jihad in 1857–58, coming from Gidimaka, Kamera (both q.v.) and Khasso. In 1857, when his rule in Khasso was fairly secure, Umar moved his capital to Konykary and attacked and blockaded the French fort at Medina (Khasso). After three months, Faidherbe (q.v.) broke through to relieve the siege, and Umar was obliged to retreat.

In 1858 Umar went to Futa Toro and Kajor, urging people to abandon this territory, which had fallen under French influence, and emigrate to Karta to join him in a united resistance. This was the beginnings of the *fergo nioro,* which lasted into the 1880s, and set the pattern of recruitment in the west and war in the east that would characterize Umar's jihad. Some 40,000 followed him, leaving a trail of famine in their wake along the river valley. They enabled him to expand his horizons anew. On his way back to Nioro, Umar garrisoned the fort at Gemu that cut off Moorish caravans trying to trade with the French at Bakel (q.v.). Then he turned his attention to war on Segu, his old enemy. When the French retook and razed the fort at Gemu in October 1859, Umar opened negotiations for a truce with them so that he could continue to recruit men and secure material from the Senegal River to support his campaign against Segu. Although no formal treaty resulted, French trade was allowed to resume unmolested. Umar's recruiters in Futa Toro and Wolof country were resisted by French agents but not harassed.

From 1860 until his death in battle in 1864, Umar was almost continually directing campaigns in the Karta-Segu area against a variety of kingdoms and states. In 1861 Umar defeated the combined forces of Segu and Masina, enabling him to occupy Segu. By mid-1862, Umar had invaded and conquered Masina. Yet, some Masina forces remained and besieged Umar at his capital in Hamdallhi. Finally in February 1864, Umar fled into a cave in the Bandiagara cliffs. There are several stories concerning Umar's death, but most likely he died in a fire in the cave after troops discovered his hideout.

Umar's eldest son, Amadu Tal (q.v.), had been installed in Segu during Umar's absence in Masina. He claimed the succession as Commander of the Faithful and tried to establish central authority over all of the conquered territories. His claim to supreme central authority was challenged by other sons and commanders, however. A nephew of Umar, Amadu al-Tijani, gained control of Masina, and like the brothers and lieutenants commanding other parts of the region, retained considerable autonomy.

The tradition of purification and resistance launched by Umar did not die with him. It was taken up by Tijani leaders near and far, deputized directly by him or his descendants. Among the best known in the Senegambia were Ma Ba, *Shaixu* Ahmadu Mahdiyu Ba, *Alfa* Molo Balde and Mamadu Lamine Drame (each q.v.).

TAL, AMADU (also called AMADU SHAIXU or SHAIXU AHMADU). (c.1833–95). Son and successor to *al-Hajj* Umar Tal (q.v.) and ruler of a large state centered on Segu in the middle Niger valley. Amadu inherited his father's title of *Commander of the Faithful* and was a feared opponent of the French advance into the Western Sudan. Although his state was centered in present-day Mali, Amadu's family and the core of his army and followers were from Futa Toro (q.v.). He remained in close contact with the homeland and regularly sent his disciples to recruit followers. This drain on the manpower of the Futa was bitterly resented by both the ineffectual *almamies* of the period and the local resistance leader Abdul Bokar Kan (q.v.), who needed soldiers for the first-line defense of the homeland. When the French mounted the final invasion of Futa Toro in 1890, however, Abdul Bokar, his ally Albury Njay (q.v.) of Jolof, and their followers fled toward Amadu's territory, which became the second line of defense. When the middle Niger fell to Colonel Archinard in 1893, Amadu retreated east across the Sahel to Hausaland (Nigeria), where he was killed in 1895.

TALIB (pl. TALIBE). Arabic term for a disciple or student of a cleric, or *marabout* (q.v.). Both the term and the institution are widespread in the Senegambia. Senegambian Muslims often gave up their existing allegiances and occupations to go and study with a teacher. Grown men used to do so, but today it is more commonly children aged three through twenty, who are conferred on a marabout by their parents.

Poor children often become total dependents of the marabout and work long days for him, with only early morning and late evening hours for study or begging. In rural areas, they farm the cleric's fields and tend his herds, learning humility by begging their suppers, bowls in hand going from one home to the next. In urban areas begging is usually for cash and becomes a full-time occupation. Parents in urban areas generally prefer to keep their children at home if they can afford it, paying a marabout to teach them the Quran and discipline on certain days of the week. Life is customarily and intentionally difficult for the student—both academic and personal discipline are rigid, authority is absolute and may be arbitrary, and food, clothing and shelter are minimal. The child's experience of discipleship is a common theme in Senegalese autobiographies. Cheikh Hamidou Kane portrays a deeply moving, essentially positive experience in *Ambiguous Adventure,* contrasting sharply with the harrowing childhood in Amar Samb's *Matraqué par le destin.*

TAMBACOUNDA. The capital of the region of Senegal-Oriental (q.v., Eastern Senegal). Tambacounda was a small village in eastern Niani (q.v.) until the early twentieth century and the arrival of the Ocean-Niger railroad (q.v.). It was also situated on the major trade route into southeastern Senegal and the Guinea rain forest zone. With the expansion of the groundnut basin and the *Terres Neuves* (q.v.) just to the west, Tambacounda experienced a rapid growth, primarily migrants from the upper Senegal valley and the Sudan. The town often served as a temporary stop for migrants from the east on their way to Dakar, the groundnut basin in central Senegal, or the Gambia. Many Fulbe fleeing the repressive government of Sekou Toure in Guinea-Conakry also moved into Tambacounda. After the droughts of the late 1960s and early 1970s, however, the town lost some of its permanent population, which in 1990, was estimated at 40,000. Yet, during the rainy season, or hivernage (q.v.), the population increases markedly. Today it is still the major town in the eastern part of Senegal and the site of all regional offices.

TANDA (TENDA). Ethnic group that includes the modern Bassari (q.v.), Konagi (q.v.), Bajaranke and Bedik, centered in Senegal-Oriental, especially along the Guinea border. They number only about 40,000 today and are believed to be the original inhabitants of most of southeastern Senegal. The Tanda were concentrated in the foothills of Futa Jalon, and their linguistic and cultural ties were with groups in Guinea. They had little contact with their northern Muslim savanna neighbors. Yet, they were raided for slaves by more powerful states to the north and to the south from medieval times on, particularly by Futa Jalon and Bundu (both q.v.) in the eighteenth and nineteenth centuries. They took refuge in the hills and mesas of southeastern Senegal and adjacent areas of Guinea-Conakry and Guinea-Bissau.

TATA. Garrisoned fort, traditionally built by Mande rulers and adopted by the Fulbe and other jihadists during the nineteenth century. Earthen walls usually surrounded an inner enclosure made of sunbaked brick walls several feet thick. *Tatas* were very effective against traditional cavalry and even cannon, but when exploding mortars were introduced in the latter nineteenth century, they fell easily. The remains of many can be traced today, especially in the upper Gambia and Senegal valleys.

TEKRUR (or TAKRUUR). A state and its people that flourished in the central Senegal River Valley in the eleventh through thirteenth centuries. The people were most likely predecessors to the Fulbe, who now dominate the area of Futa Toro (q.v.). It is the first known state in the Senegambian region.

The origins of the state are obscure. Archaeological sites indicate the development of concentrated settlements, probably early Tekrur, in the river valley from modern Dagana to

Matam, beginning in the fourth century CE and using metal technology from the sixth century on. By the time travellers from North Africa reached the area in the tenth century, the state was already well-established. Tekrur was the southern terminus to the westernmost trans-Saharan trade route and also commanded the east-west trade on the Senegal. Arab sources confirm that Islam was introduced into the area by the eleventh century, before the Almoravid (q.v.) movement, which Tekrur helped to launch. Propagation of Islam provided a justification for its wars on neighbors and raids on non-Muslims to the south. Captives were then sold north into slavery. Pilgrims from Tekrur are reported in the Middle East beginning in the tenth century, and it became customary to refer to any West African pilgrim as a Tekruri. (See HAJJ.)

In the eleventh century Tekrur reigned over neighboring Silla and was itself a tributary of the Ghana Empire, centered to the east. The decline of Tekrur is difficult to trace, because the area continued to be called Tekrur, at least until Koly Tengela Ba (q.v.) invaded and founded Futa Toro (q.v.) in its place in the fifteenth century. Tekrur is reported variously as a tributary of the Mali Empire and the Jolof Empire (q.v.) in its late period.

TERRES NEUVES. New lands for groundnut (q.v.) cultivation, opened up during the colonial period in central Senegal. In the 1930s the name referred to the area of central and eastern Salum (q.v.) then being colonized, frequently by the Murids (q.v.) and their disciples. The colonial government, eager to expand groundnut exports, their only source of capital, provided tracts of forest reserves, credit and market transport to Murid clerics. In exchange, the clerics sent their highly disciplined Wolof *talibe* (q.v.) to clear the land, dig wells, plant, build and reap. The area of "new lands" pushed into far eastern Sine-Saloum Region, eastern Senegal around Tambacounda (q.v.) and the upper Casamance. The new settlers occasionally displaced indigenous inhabitants, however, especially Fulbe herders who used the areas for pasture.

There were a few violent clashes, and a reservoir of ill will toward the new arrivals. The government tended to support the claims of the Murids, and some Fulbe moved further into Senegal Oriental (q.v.).

Terres Neuves is also the name of a modern development scheme, launched in 1972 by the government of Senegal with World Bank financing, to try to improve on this historic tendency. Avoiding marabouts and Wolof, it resettled Serer peasants from the Fatick district, the most densely populated rural area in the country. The individuals resettled found it an improvement, but it proved so expensive that it failed to provide a solution to the larger problem of population pressure in the groundnut basin. Urban migration, especially to Dakar and the Cap Vert peninsula, continues to be the major outlet for population pressures throughout the rest of the country.

THIAROYE. Now situated on the outskirts of Dakar's sprawling shantytowns, Thiaroye was the site of an important confrontation in 1944 between Senegalese veterans of World War II and the colonial government. The incident was fresh in the memory of many Senegalese in the years immediately prior to independence and disrupted Franco-African harmony at that critical period.

Thiaroye was the site of the repatriation center for Senegalese troops returning from Europe. On December 1, 1944, at least 24 Africans were killed, 11 wounded and another 34 put into detention. What actually happened remains obscure. Africans claimed that the French were trying to cheat them out of pay earned during the war. They merely objected to this unfairness, and in return, were fired upon by colonial troops. For several days before this, however, rumors had been circulating in nearby Dakar that there was danger of an uprising. Some Frenchmen felt that a frightened French commander, determined to show that the postwar administration of the colony would be firm, lost his nerve and fired on the Africans to make them an object lesson. Whatever the events that triggered the violence, the deaths outraged the African population of the colony. Leaders like Lamine Guèye (q.v.) were further angered that the events were hushed up. No word appeared about them in the local press. In his poem *Tyaroye*, Léopold Senghor (q.v.) expressed his disillusionment with the colonial administration. Ousmane Sembene (q.v.) made a film, released in 1990, based on the events at Thiaroye, which was harshly critical of the French.

THIES. Important railway center east of Dakar. Thies was the headquarters of the railroad administration, since the Saint-Louis branch linked up with the Dakar-Bamako line at Thies.

TIJANI BROTHERHOOD. Islamic Sufi (q.v.) order founded in Fez, Morocco, by Ahmad al-Tijani (c.1737–1815), and the largest brotherhood in Senegal today. The sect was popularized throughout the Senegambia by *al-Hajj* Umar Tal (q.v.) (fl. 1845–64) and his deputies and successors. As a simplified, purified order of Islam, it had much more popular appeal than the older Qadiri (q.v.) order. The Tijaniyya claimed to bypass the long spiritual chains of authority traced by some other orthodox brotherhoods. Ahmad al-Tijani's authority came from direct revelations from God and Muhammad. Under *al-Hajj* Umar's leadership the Tijaniyya became a rallying force against Christian imperialism in the Senegambia. After Umar's death in 1864, the banner of holy war and Tijani proselytism was taken up by Ma Ba (q.v.) and later by Shaixu Ahmadu *Madiyu* Ba (q.v.). When the French conquest had become a reality, *al-Hajj* Malik Sy (q.v.) preached the Tijani way as a form of cultural resistance, building an enormous following in the trading centers and towns that sprang up along the railroad.

Several minor and three major branches of the Tijani exist in Senegal today: the Sy family *Xalifat* at Tiwawan (see *AL-HAJJ MALIK SY*); Saidou Nourou Tal's (q.v.) following in Dakar and the Fleuve; and the Niass (q.v.) lodge in

Kaolack. Al-Hajj Mamadu Saidu Ba (q.v.) of Medina-Gonasse also belonged to the Tijani brotherhood.

TORODO (pl. TORODBE). The Muslim clerical estate among the Futanke (see CLERICS). Like other groups in Fulbe society, the Torodo constituted a vocationally defined, endogamous, culturally distinct group within society. Although they were generally freeborn, Islamic law allowed them to consider the children of slave (q.v.) or caste (q.v.) women and Torodo men as free, contrary to the rule among the other nobility. Torodo developed as a clerical community as early as the eleventh century in Tekrur (q.v.) and sent pilgrims to the Middle East. Historically, they were responsible for most of the clerical reform movements of the nineteenth century, not only in the Senegambia but across West Africa. The leaders of successive reform movements remained in contact with one another from the Atlantic to the Nile River.

TRAITANT. Petty trader in the precolonial and colonial eras. *Traitants* were usually *métis* (q.v.) who took goods on credit from the French *commerçant,* or merchant, sold them in the interior and returned with produce from the interior for his patron.

TRANSHUMANCE (adj. TRANSHUMANT). Cyclical movement by herding people or pastoralists (q.v.) from rainy-season grazing lands to dry-season pastures. Each band generally has usage rights and rights of passage defined by customary law. Often pastoralists had seasonal symbiotic relations with farming communities, grazing their cattle and sheep (in some cases, camels) on stubble left after harvest, fertilizing the fields with manure and exchanging milk for grain. In the last few decades of rapid population growth, farmers have expanded into former herder drought refuges and become so land hungry that the old symbiosis is breaking down. Transhumance is being abandoned as herders are obliged to sedentarize along roads and around deep wells, taking up mixed farming.

TUBAB. Term used throughout Senegambia and the Western Sudan for white people, and, by extension, anyone who goes to school, dresses and/or lives in the European manner.

TUKOLOR (TOUCOULEUR, TOKOLOR). Pulaar-speakers or Fulbe (q.v.) who live in the region of Futa Toro (q.v.) and are also known as Futanke. In Wolof, French and common Senegalese usage, the *Haalpulaar'en,* or speakers of Pulaar, are called Toucouleurs, derived from Tekrur or Takruur (q.v.), the name of the ancient state contemporary with the Ghana Empire.

Nineteenth-century French ethnographers divided *Haalpulaar'en* into two groups: Toucouleurs (or Tukolors) originally from Futa Toro, and Peuls (or Peuhls), consisting of Fulbe from other areas. By the mid-nineteenth century, Toucouleur had become the standard designation in the French literature for Fulbe considered "Muslim fanatics," openly hostile to European commercial and military activity and in favor of the establishment and maintenance of an Islamic state. In the 1850s, *al-Hajj* Umar Tal (q.v.), a Muslim Fulbe from Futa Toro, given his tense relations with the French and his call to jihad, reinforced this stereotypical image. The Toucouleur were contrasted with the seemingly more docile and cooperative Peuls and Mande-speakers.

Many Futanke have migrated to new areas and, as minorities, have tended to lose their language in favor of Wolof and gradually to assimilate Wolof cultural identity.

- U -

UNION GENERALE DEMOCRATIQUE DES ORIGINAIRES DE LA VALLEE DU FLEUVE (UGOVF, General Union of

People of the River Valley). Nationwide federation of Fu-tanke/Fulbe ethnic associations, founded in Dakar in 1947. Originally based on mutual-aid societies formed by urban migrants concerned about the economic decline of their homeland, the organization quickly spread to the valley itself. Sections were organized, one per canton in the valley, one per town in the rest of Senegal. In Dakar, migrants from each canton had their own section, capped by a citywide central bureau. The well-organized sections often succeeded in getting improvements for their place of origin: roads, wells, dispensaries and agricultural development aid. In the highly politicized years following World War II, however, this unique nationwide organization quickly became a political machine. Encouraged by the Futanke marabout Saidou Nourou Tal (q.v.), they endorsed Léopold Senghor's Bloc Démocratique Sénégalais (q.v.) in its split with Lamine Guèye (q.v.), a major factor in the BDS victory.

In 1953 the organization split over the high-handed tactics of the Tal family. Saidou Nourou had engineered the ouster of an elected president, replacing him with a relative. A faction that attributed the move to prejudice against the caste (q.v.) origin of the elected president founded the rival Union Générale Démocratique des Originaires de la Vallée du Fleuve. In 1959 the government banned all ethnic-political organizations, to dampen sectionalism and ethnicity in preparation for independence. The sections generally transformed themselves back into mutual-aid societies, changing their name to *Amicale*. Politics rapidly reentered, but on the local rather than national levels.

UNION MONETAIRE DE L'OUEST AFRICAIN (UMOA, West African Monetary Union). Currency union that issues and controls the CFA franc (q.v.) for the member countries: Senegal, Ivory Coast, Mali, Burkina Faso, Togo, Niger and Benin. Of the former French West African countries, Guinea declined to join from the inception at independence. Mali withdrew in 1962 and then reentered in 1983. In the mid-1970s, Mauritania withdrew to issue its own currency.

UNION PROGRESSISTE SENEGALAISE (UPS, Senegalese Progressive Union). From 1958 through 1976, the name of the dominant political party in Senegal, under the leadership of Léopold Senghor (q.v.). It was formed in 1958, when Senghor's Bloc Démocratique Sénégalais (q.v.) absorbed Lamine Guèye's (q.v.) Socialists. The merger represented the culmination of a campaign to create a single unified party, in preparation for self-government. The first issue the UPS faced was the 1958 constitutional referendum. Young radicals, who had recently joined the party, organized a congress of allied parties at Cotonou that voted to endorse independence. Senghor and Lamine Guèye, however, refused to go along, with the result that they lobbied for approval of a French Union. The radicals left the UPS to form the PRA-Senegal (q.v.). Trade union leaders also defected, despite UPS wooing.

The UPS platform in the years before and immediately after independence in 1960 was based on what Senghor and Mamadou Dia (q.v.) called "African socialism" and *négritude* (each q.v.). Village-level cooperatives were introduced, theoretically as an African adaptation of communalism to modern economic modes. Groundnut marketing and the rural credit system were nationalized, and mixed government and private (French and Senegalese) corporations were established in most sectors of the economy. Close ties were retained with France, which remained the major source of aid and trade, as well as a touchstone for Senegal's political and cultural life.

One of the first issues facing the party organization after independence was internal discipline. The French mass parties, on whose organization it was modeled, required deputies to vote the party line. But the UPS, as a single party, needed some room for internal dissent. The constitutional crisis of 1962 (q.v.) brought the issue into the open, when members of the UPS voted to censure their own prime minister, a move that he deemed illegal. He lost that point when he was tried and imprisoned, and the issue remained unresolved. In practice, unity is expected but not always enforceable.

The party structure included sympathizers who could be counted upon to vote the party line, card carriers (who in the mid-Sixties were also obliged to subscribe to the party paper *Unité africaine*) and militants who staffed the local, district, regional and national committees. At the national level there was also a political bureau that functioned as an executive body between meetings of the full committee. There was also a youth movement, a student association at the university, a women's section and, from 1968 on, an officially allied trade union.

In the years immediately following independence, Senghor favored a single-party system on the grounds that the body politic was too fragile and the need for rapid development too great to permit the luxury of political opposition. In the early 1960s, those parties that had not been merged were gradually banned. After a decade of single-party rule, however, a tentative trend toward multiparty democracy has begun. Abdoulaye Wade's Parti Démocratique Sénégalais (q.v.) was legalized in 1974, and has run slates in every election since 1978. In 1976 the constitution was reformed to allow closely restricted multiparty democracy. Three ideological tendencies were allowed to be represented by one party each: Marxist, socialist and liberal-democratic. Senghor and the UPS leaders chose the socialist slot, the tendency that they felt they had represented all along and the "middle road." There was some confusion, however, since they had once opposed Lamine Guèye (q.v.) and his socialist party at the polls. To clarify their role and move into international socialist politics, they changed their name in 1977 to the Socialist Party (Parti Socialiste) (q.v.).

Abdou Diouf took over control of the PS when Senghor resigned the presidency and party chairmanship on December 31, 1980. The PS remains the dominant party in Senegal, and Diouf generally continues the policies of Senghor. For most of the 1980s, the opposition was splintered among a proliferation of small parties. The strongest challenge to Diouf and the PS has traditionally been the PDS, led by Abdoulaye Wade (q.v.). In 1991, Wade was invited to join the Diouf government as minister of state. Wade continues to head the PDS.

UNIVERSITY OF DAKAR, now UNIVERSITY CHEIKH ANTA DIOP. The university system of Dakar. In 1988, the name was changed to honor Cheikh Anta Diop (q.v.). When the university at Saint-Louis (q.v.) is completed (c. late 1992), the Dakar university will no longer be the sole university, but it will remain the largest.

The university comprises four faculties (Law and Economics; Sciences; Letters and Humanities; and Medicine, Pharmacy and Dental Surgery), and five professional schools (the Ecole Normale Supérieur [Teachers' College], the Institut Université de Technologie [University Institute of Technology], the Institut des Sciences et Médecines Vétérinaires [Institute of Veterinary Medicine], the Ecole des Bibliothecaires, Archivistes et Documentalistes [Librarians', Archivists' and Documentalists' College] and the Centre d'Etudes des Sciences et Techniques de l'Information [Center for the Study of Communications]). In addition, there are several affiliated research institutes, the oldest and most comprehensive of which is the Institut Fondamental d'Afrique Noire/ Cheikh Anta Diop (Institute for Fundamental Research in Black Africa). The University grew out of the School of Medicine of Dakar, founded in 1918, and IFAN, founded in 1938, to become in 1950 the Institute for Higher Studies. In 1957 it was made a full university in the French system, and in 1960 it reverted to nominal Senegalese control. Enrollment went from 1,018 students, of whom only 39 percent were Senegalese in 1960–61, to 8,014 (73 percent Senegalese) in 1976–77. The French, who still subsidize the university, insisted that it serve all Francophone West Africa, but other countries have been building and expanding their university systems.

- V -

VETERINARY MEDICINE. Beginning with the 1932 campaign against trypanosomiasis, the French colonial government established veterinary research and training facilities in Dakar for all of French West Africa. The laboratory at Dakar-Hann developed and supplied vaccines and dips for cattle-epidemic control but had little direct communication with herders. The weak extension-program pattern persists in recent years, while central institutions continue to develop. With French government subsidy, the major countries of the former AOF have cooperated to found the Ecole Interétats des Sciences et Médecine Vétérinaires (EISMV, International School of Veterinary Sciences and Medicine) at the University of Dakar/Cheikh Anta Diop (q.v.). The school is under the Ministry of Higher Education, while field programs are administered by the Ministry of Rural Development in collaboration with prefects and subprefects. (See ADMINISTRATION.)

- W -

WADE, ABDOULAYE. (1925–) Leader of the largest opposition party, the Parti Démocratique Sénégalais (q.v.) and, since early 1991, a *Ministère d'Etat* in the Diouf (q.v.) government.

A lawyer by profession, Wade was a long-term supporter

and party delegate under President Senghor (q.v.) until the constitutional reform of 1973. When Senghor decided to move from a single-party to a multiparty system, he and Wade reportedly agreed amicably that the latter would attempt to form the first opposition party. Three ideological platforms were recognized in the new constitution, and each was allowed to be represented by a single party. Wade's PDS was recognized as representing the center-democratic ideological stance. After 1973, Wade became an increasingly strident critic of the government, frequently attacking the government groundnut-marketing agency, ONCAD (q.v.), and other aspects of state socialism. In the 1978 election Wade, as the only opposition presidential candidate, won 17.7 percent of the vote, running particularly well in the Casamance and urban areas.

Following Senghor's resignation in December 1980, Wade increased his following and became even more outspoken in his criticism of President Abdou Diouf. Diouf, however, legalized several opposition parties, which detracted from Wade's support. In the 1983 election, Wade received about 18 percent of the vote. In the bitterly contested 1988 election, which included several opposition parties, Wade's totals officially reached 25 percent. Wade and his supporters charged massive election fraud, however, and claimed victory. Diouf imposed a state of emergency to quell disturbances in Dakar. Wade and some other opposition leaders were arrested, tried and convicted. Soon afterward, under a general amnesty the leaders were freed. Because of his conviction, however, Wade was unable to return to his seat in the National Assembly. Talks continued between Wade and the government. In a surprise move in early 1991, Diouf asked Wade to join the government as a minister of state, instituting a period of "cohabitation" (q.v.).

WALO. Wolof kingdom comprising the delta of the Senegal River from the outskirts of Saint-Louis to Dagana, north and south of the river. The royal Mboj patrilineage traces its reign to Njajan Njay (q.v.), founder of the Jolof Empire (q.v.), probably in the early fourteenth century. Legend makes Mboj the younger half brother of Njajan by a slave father, and his country vassal to the Jolof Empire. When the empire was rent by civil war in the mid-sixteenth century, *Brak* Yerim Kode led Walo to independence.

The socioeconomic situation of Walo was more fragile than the other Wolof kingdoms, as it was directly exposed to European slave traders, Moorish raiders and traders and its powerful neighbors, Kajor and Futa Toro (both q.v.). It also lacked good agricultural land owing to salt intrusion and unreliable rainfall, depending instead on fishing, herding, hunting and commerce. The slave trade transformed the nobility into a parasitic class, providing slaves through the use of their own slave armies, and collecting gifts and tolls from European and Moorish traders. Unlike their southern neighbors, they were unable to provide basic security to their own population.

Walo was therefore fertile ground for clerical reformers offering hope of a more stable, ethical society. It fell to the Tubenan in 1673–77, the invasion of *Almamy* Abdul Qadir (q.v.) in the 1770s and conquest by Dile Cam (q.v.) and under Njaga Isa Jop (q.v.) in 1828–29. Each time the traditional nobility, with the help of the French and sometimes other neighbors, was restored. Even after the French had occupied Walo in the mid-nineteenth century, however, the country was deeply moved by the religious leadership of *al-Hajj* Umar Tal (q.v.) and the 1868–75 movement of *Shaixu* Ahmadu Mahdiyu Ba (q.v.).

The loss of national sovereignty began much earlier in Walo than anywhere else in the Senegambia. In the eighteenth century, Trarza Moor (q.v.) and Moroccan troops raided the country frequently, and by the end of the century it was in collapse. The early nineteenth century witnessed civil wars, exacerbated by competition between French and

Trarza Moors, each seeking to establish hegemony. The French experimented unsuccessfully between 1819 and 1828 with the agricultural colonization of Walo. When Dile Cam conquered the country in the name of Islamic reform in 1828, the French had only their honor and commercial passage left to defend—the plantations had long been abandoned. They intervened and killed Dile Cam but retreated immediately to Saint-Louis, leaving a political void. Trarza Moor (q.v.) chief Muhammad al-Habib then married the *Linger* Njembot (q.v.) of Walo, threatening to produce an heir eligible to rule both Walo and Trarza. Two years of war (1833–35) and devastation by the French persuaded the newlyweds to renounce their son's succession on paper. In the late Forties, however, the son, Eli Njembot, claimed the throne of Walo. His cousin, Sidia Ndate Yala, contested his claim, in what had become chronic civil war. The coup de grace was dealt Walo as a result of the French decision of the early 1850s to dominate the river valley. Walo succumbed early in 1855, within a few weeks after Louis Faidherbe (q.v.) was appointed governor with a mandate to impose a military solution. Both factions of nobility went into exile, Eli to the north and Sidia to the south. But surrender did not spare Walo. It became a continuous battleground for French raids on Moors and Futanke during the next five years, and sporadically into the 1890s. Repeated French invitations to refugees to return to the "pacified" territory had only a desultory response.

In the colonial period, the exodus toward the towns, notably Saint-Louis and Dakar, completed the depopulation of the area, and demands for firewood eliminated the once abundant game forests. The government of independent Senegal found the delta so sparsely populated in the late 1960s that it was declared a "pioneer zone" under the Law of the National Domain (q.v.) and turned over in its entirety to the SAED, a mixed government-private corporation. SAED recruited peasants for pilot irrigated perimeters from

throughout Senegal, aiming to commercialize rice and vege-
table production. Results were disappointing, and the program was terminated.

WOLOF. The dominant ethnic group and *lingua franca* of
Senegal, comprising nearly 40 percent of the population.
They are overwhelmingly concentrated in the western part of
the country. Historically, the Wolof formed the core population of the Jolof Empire and its successor states, Walo, Kajor,
Bawol and Jolof (each q.v.). They were also an important
minority in the Serer kingdoms of Sin and particularly Salum
(both q.v.). Only a handful of Wolof traders lived in areas of
eastern Senegal or the Casamance (q.v.). The Wolof constitute the bulk of the Murid brotherhood (q.v.).

During the colonial period, groundnut (q.v.) cultivation
expanded almost to the exclusion of the traditional millet
(q.v.) and sorghum in Wolof areas. Peasants under the
tutelage of the powerful Murid brotherhood (q.v.) colonized
the new expanding southeastern frontier. The colonial capital
of Saint-Louis, the modern capital of Dakar and major
railroad towns like Thies (each q.v.) were all in the Wolof-
speaking areas. Wolof is spoken in towns throughout the
country and in many rural areas. Non-Wolof urban migrants
tend to adopt the Wolof language and ethnicity within a
generation or two.

The traditional social structure of the Wolof shared a
tripartite division similar to other savanna peoples: freeborn,
caste and slave. Each category was further subdivided into
endogamous estates. Freeborn included nobility, clerics and
peasants. Caste (q.v.) groups included artisans and *griots*
(q.v.), who were endogamous: blacksmiths and jewelers,
carvers, tanners and cobblers, gourd workers, weavers and
bards. Fishermen and herders were similar to castes, though
not usually listed with them. Owned persons were classed as
slaves (q.v.), although those belonging to the nobility could
attain wealth and power as officials of the crown and

soldiers. With modernization, the caste system is eroding, and the major Wolof social distinctions are becoming urban versus rural. The former dominate the government bureaucracy and all modern sectors of the economy, while peasants are the productive backbone of the groundnut basin.

The groundnut economy eroded Wolof extended-family farming early in the colonial era, so that today only food crops are sometimes cultivated. Traditional cooperative work groups of men and women are being adapted by government policy to an official cooperative system. Family structure shows increasing fragmentation, particularly in urban areas. Polygamy continues in law and practice. Inheritance is generally patrilineal, although matrilineal inheritance was historically important for nobility. Islamic law is the norm in rural areas, interpreted by clerics in accordance with Wolof custom. Those who wish may also appeal to the ever-increasing body of civil law, administered by the government courts, which is inspired more by French than by Islamic law or Wolof custom.

WULI. Mande kingdom on the north bank of the Gambia River upstream from Niani (q.v.) and west of Bundu (q.v.). Founded in the fourteenth century by Mandinka (q.v.) migrants from the Mali Empire, it had become independent by the time Portuguese (q.v.) traders arrived in its port on the Gambia in the mid-fifteenth century. Soninke and Mande traders travelling the caravan routes between the Gambia, Senegal and Niger River basins made Wuli a major entrepôt during the era of the Atlantic slave trade (q.v.). Most of the kingdom was incorporated into the Gambia by the British, but the northern part came under French dominion. The imposition of an international frontier between Senegal and Sudan (Mali), and the construction of colonial railway systems (see RAILROADS) destroyed Wuli economically. At independence, the area was sparsely populated, and the government of Senegal selected it for the *Terres Neuves* (q.v.) agricultural colonization project. Today it contains several large villages, but no major towns.

- X -

XALIFA (KALIFA, KHALIFA). Wolof/Pulaar title, adapted from the Arabic, for the head of a community of Muslim believers. In Wolof usage, it generally applies to the head of a Sufi (q.v.) brotherhood, or one of its branch lodges.

- Z -

ZIGUINCHOR. Capital of the Casamance (q.v.) region, located on the south side of the Casamance River about 40 miles from its mouth on the Atlantic coast. The city has a commercial history dating to at least the fifteenth century, having originated as the port of trade for the kingdom of Kasa (q.v.), with which the Portuguese (q.v.) traded. It is connected by the trans-Gambian highway with Dakar (q.v.), but the ferry across the Gambia River and the two Gambian border crossings make it a long trip. Geographic isolation has been a major factor in the city's political and economic evolution. In 1982, 1983 and 1990, the city was the scene of clashes between government forces and Casamance separatists. Although located in the area with the richest agricultural potential, and offering good port potential, it has remained a relatively small provincial capital. The permanent population in 1990 was approximately 80,000, although in the dry season there is a large influx of rural migrants.

INTRODUCTION TO THE BIBLIOGRAPHY

Compared with other sub-Saharan African countries, Senegal has an abundant and diverse scholarly literature, including written and oral accounts. Therefore, the following list is presented as an introduction to the printed literature on Senegal and is by no means exhaustive. Most written works on Senegal are in French and English, and these languages predominate in the bibliography. Yet, there is also a sizable Arabic corpus as well as works in other European languages. In addition, there is a growing body of literature in the main indigenous Senegalese languages, including Wolof, Serer, Pulaar, Soninke and Mandinka.

The earliest written documents concerned with Senegal date from approximately the tenth century A.D., and consist primarily of travellers' accounts in Arabic. Muslim traders and voyagers from North Africa crossed the Sahara Desert into the Western Sudan and Senegambia and left written descriptions of the region. After the mid-fifteenth century, Europeans sailed along the West African coast and up the Senegal River. Portuguese, Dutch, English and French trading posts on the coasts and along the river in the sixteenth through the early nineteenth centuries offer four centuries of correspondence and reports. The eighteenth and early nineteenth centuries were a period of intense geographical interest, especially throughout the Senegal River valley and along the Atlantic coast. Owing to its coastal and desert-side location, Senegal is in the comparatively unique position of having first-hand accounts in both Arabic and European languages for the precolonial era.

During the colonial period in the nineteenth and early twentieth centuries, circumstances fostered a scholarly focus on Senegal. As the cornerstone of the Federation of French West Africa, Senegal attracted early efforts at colonial economic development and the resultant literature. Dakar, the federation capital, was also the site of the archives, research institutions (e.g., IFAN, the medical-research laboratories, and later ORSTOM) and the university. The scholar-administrators of the colonial era—Faidherbe, Gaden, Delafosse, Hardy, Marty, Culturu, Delavignette, Brunshwig, Deschamps, Mauny and Boutillier—often remain the only or most frequently used sources.

Prior to independence in 1960, Senegalese scholars emerged in a variety of disciplines, offering quite different perspectives from those of colonial commentators. Historian Cheikh Anta Diop's theory of the African origin of Egyptian and much of European civilization challenged the entire curriculum of European history. Leopold Senghor's philosophies of *négritude* and African socialism were revolutionary ideologies in the 1930s and 1940s. Early novels by Ousmane Socé, Abdoulaye Dadji and Cheikh Hamidou Kane also raised awareness of the impact of colonialism, penetrating into the dilemmas of individual lives under colonial rule. Many of the early Senegalese authors were "renaissance men," trained in one field but using their general education to analyze and explore others. Thus Senghor moved from romantic poetry into politics and diplomacy; Abdoulaye Ly from colonial commercial history into economic and political development. Economist Mamadou Dia wrote in his field and tried to apply it as prime minister. Veterinarian Birago Diop is best known for his short stories based on collections of oral traditions, and pharmacist Majhemout Diop has become one of Senegal's foremost Marxist theoreticians. Geographer Assane Seck moved into politics and economic development, and historian Mokhtar Mbow focused on education and international administration. Ousmane Sembene essentially educated himself to become Senegal's most renowned writer and filmmaker.

The younger generation of Senegalese scholars tend to stay in a single discipline and to cover smaller topics in greater depth. Among those who figure in the bibliography are historians Boubacar Barry, Abdoulaye Bathily, Mamadou Diouf and Oumar

Kane; sociologists Abdoulaye Bara Diop, Fatou Sow, Yaya Wane and Ousmane Silla. Bakary Traoré, Mamadou Lo, Alioune Diop, Mamadou Diallo and Mamadou Diarra have joined the list of publishing political theorists, whereas economists Doudou Thiam and Babacar Ba managed to combine careers as Ministers with scholarly publication.

Another important trend in indigenous scholarship since independence has been the reemergence of an Islamic literary tradition. Scholars like Amar Samb, Cheikh Tidiane Sy and Rawane Mbaye, who have combined a traditional Islamic education with French training, are publishing religious, religious historical and educational works in Arabic and/or French for a flourishing market. They follow in the tradition of such colonial-era Arabists as Shaikh Musa Kamara and Siré Abbas Sow.

Oral history has always been important in Senegal and, like the Islamic tradition, is experiencing a renaissance. *Griots* and nobles, as well as historians publish Wolof, Serer and Pulaar oral traditions translated into French and English and, increasingly, in their primary languages. This follows the practice of their colonial-era predecesors, Yoro Diao (Jaw), Ahmadu Wade, Siré Abbas Sow and Saikh Musa Kamara.

Independence also permitted the diversification of scholarship by non-Senegalese scholars. Francophone Marxists, such as Jean Suret-Canale, Samir Amin and Jean Copans, found expression alongside those more philosophically attuned to the colonial tradition and those with a new focus on the practical problems of development. British scholars, and later a host of Americans, began to bring knowledge of Senegal to the English-speaking world and new methodological and theoretical approaches to the subject. For the convenience of English-speaking readers, the list of English-language works is as complete as possible, including, for example, many unpublished dissertations of merit. Dutch, Belgian, German and Russian scholars have also taken an interest in Senegal.

Perhaps the greatest gap in the literature on Senegal is in the area of general and reference works. No comprehensive history of

Senegal has been published since Cultru's 1910 work, which covers only up to 1870. Philip Curtin's monumental *Economic Change in Precolonial Africa* (1975) is the most ambitious of recent works, but focuses closely on economics and ends with the 1840s. Reference works on Senegal are also minimal, although this situation is changing. The *Atlas National du Sénégal* and the *Area Handbook for Senegal* are currently the most useful reference works devoted exclusively to Senegal. General textbooks on Africa, many of which include good chapters on Senegal, are not included in the present bibliography.

The bibliography, designed to serve as an introduction to the more detailed literature on Senegal, is organized into broad subject headings. Each work is listed only once, even though it may be relevant to a number of categories. The number of subheadings has been kept relatively small to avoid confusion.

BIBLIOGRAPHY

I. GENERAL WORKS

A. *OFFICIAL AND SEMI-OFFICIAL PUBLICATIONS*

Annales sénégalaises de 1854 à 1885 suivies de traités passes avec les indigènes. Paris: 1885.

Annuaire du Sénégal et Dépendances. Paris: Ministry of Marine and Colonies, 1854–1902. Annually (irregular).

Annuaire Statistique du Sénégal. Dakar: République du Sénégal. 1960–1976. Annually. (irregular).

Atlas national du Sénégal. Paris: Institut de Géographie National, 1978.

Bulletin de l'Institut Française d'Afrique Noire. (BIFAN). Dakar: IFAN, 1950–1960. Later published as *Bulletin de l'Institut Fondamental d'Afrique Noire.* Most recently published as *Bulletin de l'Institut Fondamental d'Afrique Noire/Cheikh Anta Diop.*

Bulletin du Comité d'Afrique française, Renseignements coloniaux [BCAF/RC], 1890–1920.

Bulletin du Comité des études historiques et scientifiques de l'Afrique occidentale française [BCEHSAOF], 1917–1925.

Bulletin statistique et économique mensuel. Dakar: Direction de la Statistique. Monthly since 1962.

Le Sénégal en chiffres (1976-present). Dakar: Direction de la Statistique. Société Africaine d'Editions. Annual. [Replaced *Annuaire du Sénégal.*]

Le Soleil. Dakar, Senegal. 1970-present. Daily newspaper.

Moniteur du Sénégal et Dépendances (also entitled *Feuille officielle du Sénégal et Dépendances* and *Journal officiel du Sénégal* at times). Begun in 1856. Weekly Newspaper. Replaced by *Paris-Dakar* and, later, *Dakar-Matin* (1960–1970).

Revue coloniale, 1848–1858, and its successors, the *Revue algérienne et coloniale,* 1859–1860; the *Revue maritime et coloniale,* 1860–1898; and the *Revue maritime,* 1899–1928.

Sénégal. Direction de la Statistique. *Enquête démographique nationale, 1970–71: Résultats définitifs.* Dakar: 1971.

Sénégal. Direction de la Statistique. *Situation économique du Sénégal.* Dakar: Annually since 1962.

B. *BIBLIOGRAPHIES AND REFERENCE WORKS*

Abi-Saab, Rosemary. "Elements de bibliographie—le Sénégal, des origines à l'indépendance." *Genève-Afrique* 3 (1964): 288–297.

Archives nationales du Sénégal. *Bulletin bibliographique,* no. 39 (October 1964–71). Dakar: Centre de Documentation.

————. *Bibliographie du Sénégal.* Dakar: Archives Nationales, 1972.

Baudet, Danielle and Michel Condamin. *Bibliographie générale du Parc National du Niokolo-Koba et da sa région.* Memoire no. 84. Dakar: IFAN, 1969.

Brasseur, Paule and Jean-François Maurel. *Les sources bibliographiques de l'Afrique de l'Ouest et de l'Afrique equatoriale d'expression française.* Dakar: IFAN, 1970.

Carson, Patricia. *Materials for West African History in French Archives.* London: Athlone Press, 1968.

Chambre de Commerce, d'Industrie et d'Artisanat de la Région du Cap Vert. *Bibliographie séléctive d'études et articles relatifs à l'économie et au développement industriel et commercial en Afrique.* Dakar: Chambre de Commerce, 1973.

Charpy, Jacques. *Répertoire des archives du Gouvernement gén-*

érale de l'A.O.F. Rufisque: Imprimèrie du Gouverneur Général, 1955.

Collignon, Rene and Charles Becker. *Santé et population en Sénégambie des origines à 1960: Bibliographie annotée.* Paris: Institut National d'Etudes Démographiques, 1989.

Cruise O'Brien, Donal B. "Mouride Studies." *Africa* (July 1970): 257–60.

Cuoq, Joseph. *Recueil des sources arabes concernant l'Afrique occidentale du VIIIè au XVIè siècle.* Paris: Editions du Centre National de la Recherche Scientifique, 1975.

Diallo, Thierno, *et al. Catalogue des manuscripts de l'I.F.A.N., Fonds Vieillard, Gaden, Brevié, Figaret, Shaykh Moussa Kamara et Cremar en langues arabe, peule et voltaiques.* Dakar: IFAN, 1966.

Fage, John. *A Guide to Original Sources for Precolonial Western Africa Published in European Languages.* Madison: University of Wisconsin Press, 1987.

F.A.O. *La zone sahélienne: Bibliographie sélectionnée pour l'étude des problèmes.* Rome: Food and Agriculture Organization, 1973.

Johnson, G. Wesley. "Bibliographic Essays: Senegal." *Africana Newsletter* 2 (1, 1964): Entire issue.

Jones, Adam. *A Critical Review of Editorial and Quasi-Editorial Work on pre-1885 European Sources for Sub-Saharan Africa, 1960–1986.* Madison: University of Wisconsin Press, 1987.

Levtzion, Nehemiah and J. Hopkins. *Corpus of Early Arabic*

Sources for West African History. Cambridge: Cambridge University Press, 1981.

Markowitz, Irving L. "A Bibliographic Essay on the Study of Ideology, Political Thought, Development and Politics in Senegal, Parts I and II." *Current Bibliography on African Affairs* 3 (3, March 1970): 5–29; and 3 (4, 1970): 5–35.

Paricsy, Paul J. "Selected International Bibliography of Negritude, 1960–1968." *Studies in Black Literature* 1 (September 1970): Entire issue.

Pollet, Grace. "Bibliographie des Sarakolé (Soninke-Marka)." *Journal de la société des africainistes* 34 (2, 1964): 283–292.

Porges, Laurence. *Bibliographie des régions du Sénégal.* Dakar: Ministère de la Plan et du Développement, 1967.

————. *Bibliographie des régions du Sénégal: Complément pour la période des origines à 1965 et mise en jour 1966–73.* Paris: Mouton, 1977.

————. *Eléments de bibliographie sénégalaise, 1959–63.* Dakar: Archives Nationales, Centre de Documentation, 1964.

Seydou, Christiane. *Bibliographie du monde peul.* Niamey: Etudes Nigériennes, 1977.

Thomassery, Marguérite. *Catalogue des périodiques d'Afrique noire francophone (1958–1962) conservés à l'I.F.A.N.* Dakar: IFAN, 1965.

Zidouemba, Dominique H. *Les sources de l'histoire des frontières de l'Oeust Africain.* Dakar: IFAN, 1979.

C. *GENERAL STUDIES*

Bridges, R. C., ed. *Senegambia: Proceedings of a Colloquium at the University of Aberdeen, April 1974.* Aberdeen, Scotland: Aberdeen University, 1974.

Deschamps, Hubert J. *Le Sénégal et la Gambie.* 3rd ed. Paris: Presses Universitaires de France, 1975.

Gellar, Sheldon. *Senegal: An African Nation Between Islam and the West.* Boulder, CO: Westview Press, 1982.

Hargreaves, John D. *West Africa: The Former French States.* Englewood Cliffs, NJ: Prentice-Hall, 1967.

Lavroff, Dmitri-Georges. *La République du Sénégal.* Paris: Pichon et Durand-Auzias, 1966.

Lusignan, Guy de. *French Speaking Africa since Independence.* New York: Praeger, 1969.

Manning, Patrick. *Francophone Sub-Saharan Africa: 1880–1985.* Cambridge: Cambridge University Press, 1988.

Nelson, Harold D., *et al. Area Handbook for Senegal.* 2nd edition. Washington, DC: U.S. Government Printing Office, 1974.

Thompson, Virginia and Richard Adloff. *French West Africa.* Stanford: Stanford University Press, 1958.

Yansané, Aguibou Y. *Decolonization in West African States with French Colonial Legacy.* Cambridge, MA: Schenkman Publishing Co., 1984.

D. *TOURISM*

Carte d'Identité du Sénégal. Dakar: Grand Imprimérie Africaine, 1973.

Courrègues, Georges and Fadel Dia. *Saint-Louis-du-Sénégal.* Clermont-Ferrand, France: Editions SOPREP, 1982.

Dakar, Saint-Louis et leurs environs: collection des Guides Bleus. Paris: Hachette, 1958.

DuPay, André. *Le Niokolo-Koba: Premier grand parc national de la République du Sénégal.* Dakar: Grand Imprimèrie Africaine, 1971.

Gordon, Eugene. *Senegal in Pictures.* New York: Sterling Publications, 1974.

Guide de Dakar et du Sénégal. Dakar: Société Africaine d'Edition, 1977–1978.

Guide du musée historique de l'A.O.F., à Gorée. Dakar: IFAN, 1955.

Popvic, U. *Le tourisme au Sénégal.* Addis Ababa: Commission Economique des Nations Unies pour l'Afrique, 1974.

Rémy, Mylène. *Senegal Today.* Paris: Editions Jeune Afrique, 1974. Also published in French as *Le Sénégal aujourd'hui.* Paris: Editions Jeune Afrique, 1974.

II. CULTURE AND SOCIETY

A. *ANTHROPOLOGY, ETHNOLOGY AND SOCIOLOGY*

Ames, D. W. "The Economic Base of Wolof Polygyny." *Southwestern Journal of Anthropology* 2 (4, 1955).

————. "The Use of a Transitional Cloth Money Token among the Wolof." *American Anthropologist* 57 (1955): 1016–1024.

Angrad, Armand-Pierre. *Les Lébous de la presqu'ile du Cap Vert.* Dakar: Maison du Livre, 1946.

Audiger, J. "Les Oulofs du Bas Ferlo." *Cahiers d'outre-mer* 14 (1961): 157–181.

Aujas, Louis. "Les Sérères du Sine et du Saloum." *BCEHSAOF* 3 (1933): 293–333.

Balandier, Georges and P. Mercier. *Les pecheurs lebou: particularisme et évolution.* Etudes Sénégalaises no. 3. Saint-Louis: IFAN, 1952.

Bérenger-Féraud, L. "Etude sur les griots du peuplades de la Sénégambie." *Revue d'anthropologie* 50 (1882).

————. *Les peuplades de la Sénégambie.* Paris: Leroux, 1879.

Bonnel de Mejieres, A. "Les Diakhanke de Bani-Israila et du Boundou meridional (Sénégal)." *Notes Africaines* 41 (1949): 20–25.

Bourgeau, J. "Notes sur les coutoumes des Sérères du Sine et du Saloum." *BCEHSAOF* 1 (1933): 1–65.

Boutillier, Jean-Louis, et al. *La moyenne vallée du Sénégal: étude socioéconomique.* Paris: Presses Universitaires de France, 1962.

Boyer, Gaston. *Un peuple de l'Ouest soudanais: les Diawara.* Dakar: IFAN, 1953.

Copans, Jean. "From Senegambia to Senegal: The Evolution of

Peasantries." In M. Klein, ed., *Peasants in Africa* (London: Sage, 1980): 77–103.

Corre, A. "Les Sérères de Joal et de Portudal." *Revue ethnographie* 2 (1883): 1–20.

Courtet, E. *Etude sur le Sénégal: Productions, agriculture, commerce, géologie, ethnographie, travaux publics, main d'oeuvre.* Paris: Challamel, 1903.

Cruise O'Brién, Donal B. *Saints and Politicians: Essays in the Organization of a Senegalese Peasant Society.* Cambridge: University Press, 1975.

Cruise O'Brien, Rita. *White Society in Black Africa: The French of Senegal.* Evanston, IL: Northwestern University Press, 1972.

De Lestrange, Monique. *Les Coniagui et les Bassari.* Paris: Presses Universitaires de France, 1955.

Diage, A. M. "Contribution à l'étude des coutumes des Balantes de Sedhiou." *Cahiers d'outre-mer* 1 (March, 1933): 16–42.

Diarra, Fatoumata A. *Relations inter-raciales et inter-ethniques au Sénégal.* Dakar: Nouvelles Editions Africaines, 1969.

Diop, Abdoulaye Bara. *Société toucouleur et migration.* Dakar: IFAN, 1965.

———. *La famille wolof.* Paris: Karthala, 1983.

———. *La société wolof: tradition et changement.* Paris: Karthala, 1981.

Diop, Majhemout. *Histoire des classes sociales dans l'Afrique de l'Ouest.* Vol. 2: *Le Sénégal.* Paris: Maspero, 1972.

Dujarric, M. *L'habitat traditionelle au Sénégal.* Dakar: Nouvelles Editions Africaines, 1976.

Dupire, Marguerite. *Organisation sociale des Peul.* Paris: Plon, 1970.

Dupon, Jean-François. "Tambacounda, capitale du Sénégal orientale." *Cahiers d'outre-mer* 66 (1964): 175–204.

Fernaud, Daniel. "Etude sur Soninké ou Sarakolé." *Anthropos* 4 (1910): 27–49.

Fleury, M. F. "Un village Diakhanke du Sénégal-Oriental: Missirah." *Cahiers d'outre-mer* 37 (1984): 63–86.

Foltz, William J. "Social Structure and Political Behavior of Senegalese Elites." *Behavior Science Notes* 2 (4, 1969): 145–163.

Fougeyrollas, Pierre. *Ou va le Sénégal?* Paris: Anthropos, 1970.

Gamble, David P. *The Wolof of Senegambia.* London: Oxford University Press, 1967.

Garine, I. de. "Usages alimentaires dans la région de Khombole (Sénégal)." *Cahiers d'études africaines* 3 (10, 1962): 218–265.

Geismar, Louis. *Recueil des coutumes civiles des races du Sénégal.* Saint-Louis: Imprimerie du Gouvernement, 1933.

Girard, Jean. "De communauté traditionel à la collectivité moderne en Casamance: Essair sur de dynamis du droit traditionnel." *Annales africaines* 11 (1964): 135–165.

Gomila, Jacques. *Les Bedik (Sénégal-Oriental): Barrières culturelles et hétérogenéité biologique.* Montreal: Presses Université Montreal, 1971.

Gravrand, H. *Les civilisations sereer. Cosaan.* Dakar: Nouvelles éditions africaines, 1983.

Hauser, A. *Les ouvriers de Dakar: Étude psychosociologique.* Dakar: ORSTOM, 1968.

Holderer, P. "Note sur la coutume mandingue du Ouli (Tambacounda)." *Coutumiers juridiques de l'Afrique occidentale française* 1 (Paris, 1939): 323–348.

Kane, Francine. "Femmes prolétaires du Sénégal, à la ville et aux champs." *Cahiers d'études africaines* 17 (65, 1976): 77–94.

Mauny, Raymond and Denise Bouche. "Sources écrites relatives à l'histoire des Peuls et Toucouleurs." *Notes africaines* (Dakar) 31 (1946): 7–9.

Mercier, Paul. *L'agglomération dakaroise.* Saint-Louis: IFAN, 1954.

———. "Evolution of Senegalese Elites." *International Social Science Bulletin* 8 (1956): 441–451.

Odeye, M. *Les Associations en villes africaines: Dakar-Brazzaville.* Paris: Harmattan, 1985.

Pollet, Eric and Grace Winter. *La société Soninke.* Brussels: Université Libre de Bruxelles, Editions de l'Institut de Sociologie, 1969.

Saint-Pére, J. H. *Les Sarakholle du Guidimaka.* Paris: Larose, 1925.

Sanneh, Lamine. *The Jakhanke.* London: International African Institute, 1979.

Sarr, Moustapha. *Louga: La ville et sa région.* Dakar: IFAN, 1973.

Schmitz, Jean. *Sedentary Fulbe of the Senegal Valley.* Paris: ORSTOM, 1980.

Silla, Ousmane. "Persistance des castes dans la société Wolof contemporaine." *Bulletin de l'I.F.A.N.* 28 B (3–4, 1966): 731–770.

Smith, Pierre. "Les Diakhanke." *Bulletin et mémoire de la société d'anthropologie de Dakar* 8 (1965).

Sow, Fatou. *Les fonctionnaires de l'administration centrale du Sénégal.* Dakar: IFAN, 1967.

Sow, Ibrahima. "Le monde des *subalbe,* vallée du fleuve Sénégal." *Bulletin de l'IFAN* 44 B (3–4, 1982): 237–320.

Tautain, L. *Etudes critiques sur l'ethnologie et ethnographie des peuples du bassin du Sénégal.* Paris: Ernest Leroux, 1885. Also published in *Revue d'Ethnographie* 4 (1885).

Tauxier, Louis. *Moeurs et histoire des Peuls.* Paris: Payot, 1937.

Thomas, Louis V. *Les Diola: essai d'analyse fonctionelle sur une population de Basse-Casamance.* 2 vols. Dakar: IFAN, 1958–1959.

———. "Analyse dynamique de la parenté sénégalaise." *Bulletin de l'I.F.A.N.* 30 B (3, 1968): 1005–1056.

Van Dijk, M. P. *Sénégal: Le scrutin uniformel à Dakar.* Paris: Harmattan, 1986.

Wane, Yaya. *Etat actuel de la documentation au sujet des Toucouleurs.* Dakar: IFAN, 1963.

———. *Les toucouleur du Fouta Tooro: Stratification sociale et structure familiale.* Dakar: IFAN, 1969.

Ware, Theresa A. "Wolof Farmers and Fulani Herders: A Case Study of Drought Adaptation in the Diourbel Region of Senegal." Ph.D. thesis, University of Michigan, 1979.

Winder, R. Bayly. "The Lebanese in West Africa." *Comparative Studies in Society and History* 4 (April, 1962).

B. *ARTS*

Charters, Samuel. *The Roots of the Blues: An African Search.* New York: Putnam, 1981.

Contemporary Art of Senegal/ Art Contemporian du Sénégal. Hamilton, Ontario: Art Gallery of Hamilton, 1979.

Delange, Jacqueline. "L'art peul." *Cahiers d'études africaines* 14 (1964): 5–13.

Johnson, Marion A. "Black Gold: Goldsmiths, Jewelry and Women in Senegal." Ph.D. thesis, Stanford University, 1980.

———. "The French Impact upon African Art: The Case of Senegalese Goldsmiths." In G. W. Johnson, ed. *Double Impact* (Westport, CT., 1985).

Lassaigne, Jacques. *Art sénégalais d'aujourdhui.* Paris: Musée d'Art Modern, (Catalogue), 1974.

M'Bengue, Mamadou Seyni. *Cultural Policy in Senegal.* Paris: UNESCO, 1973.

Pfaff, Françoise. *The Cinema of Ousmane Sembene: A Pioneer of African Film.* Westport, CT.: Greenwood Press, 1984.

Pitts, Delia C. "An Economic and Social History of Cloth Production in Senegambia." Ph.D. thesis, University of Chicago, 1978.

Renaudau, Michel. *Musée de Dakar: Témoin de l'art nègre.* Dakar: Nouvelles Editions Africaines, 1973.

C. *DEMOGRAPHY, MIGRATION AND URBANIZATION*

Adams, Adrian. *Le long voyage des gens du Fleuve.* Paris: Maspero, 1977.

————. *La Terre et les gens du Fleuve.* Paris: Harmattan, 1985.

Amselle, Jean-Loup, ed. *Les migrations africaines.* Paris: Maspero, 1976.

Becker, Charles; M. Diouf and M. MBodj. "L'évolution démographique régionale du Sénégal et du bassin arachidier (Sine-Saloum) au vingtième siècle, 1904–1976." In D. Cordell and J. Gregory, eds. *African Population and Capitalism* (Boulder, CO: Westview Press, 1987): 76–94.

Cahiers de l'ORSTOM. No. 12 (1975). Entire issue on migration in Senegal.

Collomb, Henri and Henri Ayats. "Les migrations au Sénégal, étude psychopathologique." *Cahiers d'études africaines* 8 (1962): 570–597.

Colvin, Lucie G., et al. *The Uprooted of the Western Sahel: Migrants' Quest for Cash in the Senegambia.* New York: Praeger, 1981.

David, Philippe. *Les navetanes: Histoire des migrants saisonniers de l'arachide en Sénégambie des origines à nos jours.* Dakar: Nouvelles Editions Africaines, 1980.

Delaunay, Daniel. *De la captivité à l'exil: Histoire et démographie des migrations paysannes dans le moyenne vallée du fleuve Sénégal.* Paris: ORSTOM, 1984.

Diop, Abdoulaye-Bara. *Société toucouleur et migration.* Dakar: IFAN, 1965.

———. "Enquête sur la migration toucouleur à Dakar." *Bulletin de l'IFAN* 23 B (1960): 393–418.

Falade, Solange. "Women of Dakar and the Surrounding Urban Area." In Denise Paulme, ed. *Women of Tropical Africa* (London, 1963): 217–229.

Gerry, Chris. "Small-Scale Manufacturing and Repairs in Dakar: A Survey of Market Relations within the Urban Economy." In R. Bromley and C. Gerry, eds. *Casual Work and Poverty in Third World Cities* (New York, 1979).

———. "The Crisis of the Self-Employed: Petty Production and Capitalist Production in Dakar." In R. Cruise O'Brien, ed. *The Political Economy of Underdevelopment* (London: Sage, 1981): 126–155.

Laurent, O. "Une banlieue ouvrière: L'agglomération suburbaine de Grand-Yoff." *Bulletin de l'IFAN* 32 B (1970): 518–557.

Manchuelle, François. "Origins of Black Emigration to France: The Labor Migrations of the Soninke, 1848–1987." Ph.D. thesis, University of California at Santa Barbara, 1987.

Minvielle, Jean-Paul. *Paysans migrants du Fouta Toro (vallée du Sénégal)*. Paris: ORSTOM, 1985.

Ndoye, E. "Migration des pionniers Mourid Wolof vers les terres neuves: rôle de l'économique et du religieux." In Samir Amin, ed. *Migrations in Western Africa* (Oxford: Oxford University Press, 1974).

Nicolas, P. and M. Gaye. *Naissance d'une ville au Sénégal*. Paris: Karthala, 1988.

Salem, Gerard. "De la calebasse à la production en série: Les résaux commerciaux laobé au Sénégal et en France." In F. Cooper, ed. *Struggle for the City* (London: Sage, 1983): 195–246.

Sankalé, Marc, L. Thomas and P. Fougeyrollas, eds. *Dakar en devenir: groupe d'études dakarois*. Paris: Présence africaine, 1968.

Seck, Assane. *Dakar: métropole ouest-africaine*. Dakar: IFAN, 1970.

Vernière, M. *Dakar et son double: Dagoudane-Pikine*. Paris: Imprimérie Nationale, 1978.

Weigel, Jean-Yves. *Migration et production domestique des Soninké du Sénégal*. Paris: ORSTOM, 1982.

Zachariah, K. and N. K. Nair. "Senegal: Patterns of Internal and International Migration in Recent Years." In *Demographic Aspects of Migration in West Africa*. Washington, DC: OECD/World Bank, 1978.

D. *DICTIONARIES AND LINGUISTICS*

Ba, Oumar. *Le Fouta Toro: Au carrefour des cultures.* Paris: Harmattan, 1977.

Blondé, Jacques, P. Dumont and D. Gontier. *Lexique du français du Sénégal.* Dakar: Nouvelles Editions Africaines, 1979.

Canu, G. *Les systèmes phonologiques des principales langues du Sénégal: étude comparative.* Dakar: Centre de Linguistique Appliquée, Faculté des Lettres, n.d.

Centre de Linguistique Appliquée de Dakar. *Léxique wolof-français.* 4 vols. Dakar: Faculté des Lettres, 1978–79.

————. *Njangum wolof.* Dakar: Faculté des Lettres, 1978.

Cribier, J., M. Dreyfus and M. Guèye. *Léébu: Proverbes wolof.* Paris: Fleuve et Flamme, 1986.

Diagne, Pathé. *Grammaire de wolof moderne.* Paris: Présence Africaine, 1971.

Doneux, J. L. "Les liens historiques entre les langues du Sénégal." *Realités Africaines et Langue Française* 7 (1978).

————. *Systèmes phonologiques de la Casamance.* Etude #28. Dakar: CLAD, n.d.

Dumont, Pierre. *Le Français et les langues africaines au Sénégal: problèmes politiques, linguistiques et pédagogiques.* Dakar: CLAD, Faculté des Lettres, 1983.

Ezanno, P. *Dictionnaire sérère-français.* Joal, Senegal: Mission de Joal, 1960.

Faidherbe, Louis. *Langues sénégalaises: Wolof, arabhassania, soninke, sérère.* Paris: 1887.

Gaden, Henri. *Le Poular, dialecte peul du Fouta sénégalais.* Vol. I: *Etude morphologique, textes.* Paris: Leroux, 1913. Vol. II: *Lexique poular-français.* Paris: Leroux, 1914.

————. *Proverbes et maximes peuls et toucouleurs, traduits, expliqués, et annotées.* Paris: Institut d'Ethnologie, 1931.

Ka, Fary. *Le Pulaar au Sénégal: étude dialectologique.* Dakar: Université de Dakar, 1982.

Kane, Francine. ''Sociologie des langues au Sénégal.'' These de 3ème cycle, Ecole Pratique des Hautes Etudes, Paris, 1974.

Labouret, Henri. *La langue des Peuls ou Foulbé: Lexique français-peul.* Memoire no. 41. Dakar: IFAN, 1952.

————. *La langue des Peuls ou Foulbé. Lexique français-peul.* Dakar: IFAN, 1955.

Mansour, Gerda. ''The Dynamics of Multilingualism: The Case of Senegal.'' *Journal of Multilingual and Multicultural Development* I (4, 1980): 273–293.

Pichl, Walter. *The Cangin Group: A Language Group in Northern Senegal.* Pittsburgh: Duquesne University Press, 1966.

Plurilinguismes. Special Issue: ''La dynamique des langues du Sénégal.'' Number 2, December 1990. Paris: Revue du Centre d'Études et de Recherches en Planification Linguistique.

Republique du Sénégal. ''Laws, Statutes.'' *Transcription des langues nationales.* Rufisque: Imprimérie Nationale, 1972.

Sapir, J. D. *A Grammar of Diola-Fogny.* Cambridge: Cambridge University Press, 1965.

Sylla, Yero. *Grammaire moderne de Pulaar.* Dakar: Nouvelles Editions Africaines, 1982.

Wintz, Père. *Dictionnaire français-diola.* Abbeville: Imprimérie Paillart, 1909.

E. *EDUCATION*

Badiane, F. ''The Development of Learning Strategies for the Post-Literacy and Continuing Education of Neo-Literates in Senegal.'' In R. Dave, D. Perera and A. Ouane, eds. *Learning Strategies for Post-Literacy and Continuing Education in Mali, Niger, Senegal and Upper Volta* (Hamburg: UNESCO Institute for Education, 1984): 113–145.

Balans, J., C. Coulon and A. Ricard. *Problèmes et perspectives de l'éducation dans un état du tiers-monde: le cas du Sénégal.* Bordeaux: Centre d'Etudes d'Afrique Noire, 1972.

Belloncle, G. *La question éducative en Afrique noire: Les leçons de l'expérience Sahélienne.* Paris: Karthala, 1984.

Bolibaugh, Jerry B. *Educational Development in Guinea, Mali, Senegal and Ivory Coast.* Washington: U.S. Department of Health, Education and Welfare, 1972.

Bouche, Denise. ''Autrefois, notre pays s'appelait la gaule . . . remarques sur l'adaptation de l'enseignement au Sénégal de 1817 à 1960.'' *Cahiers d'études africaines* 8 (29, 1968): 110–122.

———. ''L'école française et les musulmanes au Sénégal de

1850 à 1920.'' *Revue française d'histoire d'outre-mer* 61 (1974): 218–235.

————. *L'enseignement dans les territories français de l'Afrique occidentale de 1817 à 1920.* Lille: Atelier Reproduction des Theses, 1975.

Chau, T. and F. Caillods. *Financement et politique educative: le cas du Sénégal.* Paris: Institut International de Planification de l'Education, 1976.

Clement, W. *The Economic Structure of Education.* Dakar: University of Dakar, 1967.

Dumont, Pierre. *Politique linguistique et enseignement au Sénégal.* Dakar: CLAD, 1975.

Flis-Zonabend, Françoise. *Lycéens de Dakar: essai de sociologie de l'éducation.* Paris: Maspero, 1968.

Fougeyrollas, Pierre. *L'éducation des adultes au Sénégal.* Dakar: IFAN, 1966.

———— and F. Valladon. ''Senegal.'' (Monographies africaines, no. 11.) Paris: UNESCO Institut International de Planification de l'Education, 1966.

Gaucher, Joseph. *Les débuts de l'enseignement en Afrique francophone: Jean Dard et l'Ecole Mutuelle de Saint-Louis du Sénégal.* Paris: International University Booksellers, 1968.

Hunter, Thomas. ''The Development of an Islamic Tradition of Learning among the *Jahanka* of West Africa.'' Ph.D. thesis, University of Chicago, 1977.

Le Brun, Olivier. "Education and Class Conflict." In R. C. O'Brien, ed. *The Political Economy of Underdevelopment* (London: Sage, 1981): 175–208.

Marty, Paul and Jules Salenc. *Ecoles maraboutiques du Sénégal: La médersa de Saint-Louis.* Paris: Léroux, 1914.

Obichere, Boniface. "Colonial Education Policy in Senegal: A Structural Analysis." *Black Academy Review* (Winter, 1970): 17–24.

Rajaoson, François. *Enseignement supérieur et besoins en main d'oeuvre: Le cas du Sénégal.* Dakar: U.N. Institute for Economic Development and Planning, 1972.

Samb, Amar. *Matraqué par le destin: ou la vie d'un talibe.* Dakar: Nouvelles Editions Africaines, 1973.

Yansané, A. Y. "The Impact of France on Education in West Africa." In G. W. Johnson, ed., *Double Impact* (Westport, CT., 1985): 345–362.

F. *LITERATURE*

Aire, Victor. "Didactic Realism in Ousmane Sembene's *Les bouts de bois de Dieu.*" *Canadian Journal of African Studies* 11 (2, 1977): 283–294.

Ba, Mariama. *Une si longue lettre.* Dakar: Nouvelles Editions Africaines, 1979. Also published as *So Long a Letter,* trans. by M. Thomas. London: Heinemann, 1981.

———. *Un Chant écarlate.* Dakar: Nouvelles Editions Africaines, 1982.

Ba, Sylvia Washington. *The Concept of Negritude in the Poetry of*

Léopold Sédar Senghor. Princeton: Princeton University Press, 1973.

Bérenger-Féraud, Laurent. J. B. *Receuil de contes populaires de la Sénégambie, 1839–1880.* Paris: Léroux, 1885.

Blair, Dorothy S. *Senegalese Literature: A Critical History.* Boston: Twayne Publishers, 1984.

Case, F. I. "The Socio-Cultural Functions of Women in the Senegalese Novel." *Cultures et développement* 9 (1977): 601–629.

Dadji, Abdoulaye. *Maimouna.* Paris: Présence Africaine, 1958.

Diallo, Nafissatou. *De Tilène au plateau: une enfance dakaroise.* Dakar: Nouvelles Editions Africaines, 1976. Also published as *A Dakar Childhood,* trans. by D. Blair. London: Longman, 1982.

Diop, Birago. *Les Contes d'Amadou Koumba.* Paris: Présence africaine, 1961; 1969. Also published as *Tales of Amadou Koumba,* trans. by D. Blair. London: Oxford University Press, 1966.

————. *Les nouveaux contes d'Amadou Koumba.* Paris: Présence Africaine, 1958; 1969.

Diop, Cheikh Anta. *Nations négres et culture.* Paris: Présence Africaine, 1955.

Diop, David. *Coups de pilon.* Paris: Présence Africaine, 1961. Also published as *Hammer Blows and Other Writings,* trans. by S. Mpondo and F. Jones. London: Heinemann, 1975.

Diop, Ousmane Socé. *Karim.* Paris: Nouvelles Editions Latines, 1948.

Dorsinville, Roger. *Gens de Dakar.* Dakar: Nouvelles Editions Africaines, 1978.

―――. "Littérature sénégalaise d'expression française." *Ethiopiques* 15 (1978): 41–51.

Fall, Aminata Sow. *La Gréve des Battu.* Dakar: Nouvelles Editions Africaines, 1982. Also published as *The Beggars' Strike,* trans. by D. Blair. London: Longman, 1989.

―――. *Le Revenant.* Dakar: Nouvelles Editions Africaines, 1976.

Fall, Malick. *La plaie.* Paris: Albin Michel, 1967. Also published as *The Wound,* trans. by C. Wake. London: Heinemann, 1973.

Guèye, Youssouf. *Les exilés de Goumel.* Dakar: Nouvelles Editions Africaines, 1975.

Hymans, Jacques L. *Léopold Sédar Senghor: An Intellectual Biography.* Edinburgh: University Press, 1971.

Irele, Abiola. ed. *Selected Poems of Léopold Sédar Senghor.* Cambridge: Cambridge University Press, 1977.

Ka, Abdou Anta. *Mal.* Dakar: Nouvelles Editions Africaines, 1975.

Kane, Cheikh Hamidou. *L'Aventure ambigue.* Paris: Juillard, 1961. Also published as *Ambiguous Adventure,* trans. by K. Woods. New York: Macmillan, 1969; London: Heinemann, 1972.

Kane, Mohamadou. *Essai sur les Contes d'Amadou Coumba.* Dakar: Nouvelles Editions Africaines, 1981.

Kébé, Mbaye Gana. *Kaala Sikkim*. Dakar: Nouvelles Editions Africaines, 1973.

Kesteloot, L., B. Dieng and S. Faye. *Contes et mythes du Sénégal*. Paris: Fleuve et Flamme, 1986.

Klein, Pierre. ed. *Anthologie de la nouvelle sénégalaise, 1970–1977*. Dakar: Nouvelles Editions Africaines, 1978.

Madubuike, G. I. "Form, Structure and Esthetics of the Senegalese Novel." *Journal of Black Studies* 4 (3, 1974): 345–359.

———. "The Politics of Assimilation and the Evolution of the Novel in Senegal." *African Studies Review* 18 (2, 1975): 89–99.

Mercier, Roger, M. Battestini and S. Battestini. *Birago Diop: Ecrivain sénégalais: Textes commentés*. Paris: Nathan, 1964.

Meyer, Gérard. *Contes du pays malinké*. Paris: Karthala, 1987.

Ndiaye, Sada Weinde. *La fille des eaux*. Dakar: Nouvelles Editions Africaines, 1975.

Samb, Amar. *Essai sur la contribution du Sénégal à la litterature d'expression arabe*. Dakar: IFAN, 1972.

Seck, Chérif Adrame. *Njangaan*. Dakar: Nouvelles Editions Africaines, 1978.

Sembène, Ousmane. *God's Bits of Wood*. Trans. by F. Price. London: Heinemann, 1970. Originally published as *Les bouts de bois de Dieu*. Paris: Le Livre Contemporain, 1960.

———. *Le dernier de l'empire*. 2 vols. Paris: 1981. Also

published as *The Last of the Empire,* trans. by A. Adams. London: Heinemann, 1983.

————. *Le docker noir.* Paris: Editions Debresse, 1956. Also Présence Africaine, 1973. Also published as *Black Docker,* trans. by R. Schwartz. London: Heinemann, 1987.

————. *L'harmattan.* Paris: Présence Africaine, 1964.

————. *O pays, mon beau peuple.* Paris: Amiot-Dumont, 1957.

————. *Tribal Scars and Other Stories.* Trans. by L. Ortzen. London: Heinemann, 1973.

————. *Véhi-coisane ou blanche genèse* suivi du *Mandat.* Paris: Présence Africaine, 1969. Also published as *The Money-Order* with *White Genesis,* trans. by C. Wake. London: Heinemann, 1972.

————. *Voltaiques.* Paris: Présence Africaine, 1971.

————. *Xala.* New York: Lawrence Hill, 1976. Also published in English as *Xala,* trans. by C. Wake. London: Heinemann, 1976.

Senghor, Léopold Sédar. *Ce que je crois.* Paris: Grasset, 1988.

————. *Chants d'ombre,* suivis de *Hosties noires.* 2nd ed. Paris: Seuil, 1956.

————. *Ethiopiques.* Paris: Seuil, 1956.

————. *Nocturnes.* Paris: Seuil, 1961. Also published in English as *Nocturnes,* trans. by J. Reed and C. Wake. London: Heinemann, 1970.

————. *Poèmes.* Dakar: Nouvelles Editions Africaines, 1977.

————. *Prose and Poetry,* trans. by J. Reed and C. Wake. London: Oxford University Press, 1965; Heinemann, 1969.

————. *Selected Poems,* trans. and introduced by J. Reed and C. Wake. London: Oxford University Press, 1964; New York: Atheneum, 1964.

Socé, Ousmane. *Karim, roman sénégalais,* suivi de *Contes et légendes d'Afrique noire.* Paris: Nouvelles Editions Latines, 1966.

————. *Mirages de Paris.* Paris: Nouvelles Editions Latines, 1965.

————. *Rythmes du khalam.* Paris: Nouvelles Editions Latines, 1962.

G. *RELIGION AND PHILOSOPHY*

Abun-Nasr, Jamil. *The Tijaniyya: A Sufi Order in the Modern World.* London: Oxford University Press, 1965.

Colvin, Lucie G. "The *Shaykh's* Men: Religion and Power in Senegambian Islam." *Asian and African Studies* 20 (1, 1986): 61–71.

Copans, Jean. *Les marabouts de l'arachide.* Paris: Le Sycomore, 1980.

Cruise O'Brien, Donal B. *The Mourides of Senegal.* Oxford: Clarendon Press, 1971.

Cruise O'Brien, Donal and Christian Coulon, eds. *Charisma and*

Brotherhoods in African Islam. Oxford: Clarendon Press, 1988.

Delcourt, Jean. *Histoire religieuse du Sénégal.* Dakar: Nouvelles Editions Africaines, 1976.

Dia, Mamadou. *Islam, sociétés africaines et cultures industrielles.* Dakar: Nouvelles Editions Africaines, 1975.

Dumont, Fernand. *La pensée religieuse d'Amadou Bamba.* Dakar: Nouvelles Editions Africaines, 1975.

Fisher, Humphrey. *Ahmadiyyah: A Study in Contemporary Islam on the West African Coast.* London: Oxford University Press, 1963.

Froelich, J. C. *Les musulmans d'Afrique noire.* Paris: Orante, 1962.

Gouilly, Alphonse. *L'Islam dans l'Afrique Occidentale Française.* Paris: Larose, 1952.

Gravrand, H. *Visage africain de l'eglise: Une éxperience au Sénégal.* Paris: Editions de l'Orante, 1961.

Harrison, Christopher. *France and Islam in West Africa, 1860–1960.* Cambridge: Cambridge University Press, 1988.

Magassouba, Moriba. *L'Islam au Sénégal: demain les mollahs?* Paris: Karthala, 1985.

Marty, Paul. *L'Islam au Sénégal.* Vol. One: *Les personnages.* Vol. Two: *Les institutions.* Paris: Leroux, 1917.

———. *Les Mourides d'Amadou Bamba.* Paris: Leroux, 1913.

Monteil, Vincent. *L'Islam noir.* Paris: Seuil, 1964.

Robin, J. "L'évolution du mariage coutumier chez les musulmanes du Sénégal." *Africa* [London] 17 (3, 1947): 192–202.

Samb, Amar. *L'Islam et l'histoire du Sénégal.* Dakar: Hilal, 1974.

Senghor, Léopold. *Négritude et humanisme.* Paris: Seuil, 1964.

Silla, Ousmane. *Croyances et cultes syncrétiques des Lébous du Sénégal.* Dakar: Université de Dakar, 1967.

Sy, Cheikh Tidiane. *La confrérie sénégalaise des Mourides.* Paris: Présence Africaine, 1969.

Sylla, Assane. *La philosophie morale des Wolof.* Dakar: Sankoré, 1978.

Trimingham, J. Spencer. *Islam in West Africa.* London: Oxford University Press, 1959.

———. *A History of Islam in West Africa.* London: Oxford University Press, 1962.

Wane, Yaya. "Ceerno Muhamadu Sayid Baa, ou le soufisme intégral de Medina Gunass (Sénégal)." *Cahiers d'etudes africaines* 14 (56, 1974): 651–670.

III. ECONOMICS

Adams, Adrian. "The Senegal River Valley: What Kind of Change?" *Review of African Political Economy* 10 (September-December 1977): 33–59.

Amin, Samir. *Le monde des affaires sénégalaise*. Paris: Editions de Minuit, 1969.

————. *Neocolonialism in West Africa*. London: Penguin, 1973.

————. "The Development of the Senegalese Business Bourgeoisie." In Adebayo Adedji, ed. *Indigenization of African Economies* (London, 1981): 309–321.

Anson-Meyer, Monique. *Méchanismes de l'exploitation en Afrique: L'exemple du Sénégal*. La Rochelle: Editions Cujas, 1974.

Ba, Boubacar. *Commerce extérieur du Sénégal 1962–1970*. Dakar: Direction de la Statistique, 1971.

Ba, Sekou. *L'emploi des jeunes au Sénégal*. Dakar: Institut Africain de Développement Economique et de Planification, 1970.

Berg (Associates), Elliot. *Adjustment Postponed: Economic Policy Reform in Senegal in the 1980s*. USAID/Senegal: Dakar, 1990.

Brochier, Jacques. *La diffusion de progrès techniques en milieu rural sénégalais*. Paris: Presses Universitaires de France, 1968.

Club Nation et Développement au Sénégal. *Club Nation et développement au Sénégal*. Paris: Présence Africaine, 1972.

Copans, Jean. *Maintenance sociale et changement économique au Sénégal*. Bondy, France: ORSTOM, 1972.

Costa, E. "Problémes et politiques d'emploi au Sénégal." *Revue internationale du travail* 5 (1967): 461–497.

Cruise O'Brien, Rita. "Lebanese Entrepreneurs in Senegal: Economic Integration and the Politics of Protection." *Cahiers d'études africaines* 15 (57, 1975): 95–115.

————. ed. *The Political Economy of Underdevelopment: Dependence in Senegal.* London: Sage, 1979.

Dia, Mamadou. *L'économie africaine: études et problèmes nouveaux.* Paris: Presses Universitaires de France, 1957.

————. *Réflexions sur l'économie de l'Afrique noire, nouvelle édition revue et augmentée.* Paris: Présence Africaine, 1961.

Diagne, Pathé. *Sénégal: Crise économique et sociale et devenir de la démocratie.* Dakar: Sankore, 1984.

Diarassouba, Valy-Charles. *L'evolution des structures agricoles du Sénégal, déstructuration et restructuration de l'économie rurale.* Paris: Cujas, 1968.

Dieng, Amady Aly. "L'accumulation du capital et la répartition des revenues au Sénégal." *Présence africaine* 93 (1st Quarter, 1975): 25–57.

Diop, Papa A. "Senegal: The Battle to Create Employment." *ILO Bulletin* (Geneva) March-April (1970): 18–27.

Fougeyrollas, Pierre. *Modernisation des hommes: le cas du Sénégal.* Dakar: Flammarion, 1967.

Fouquet, J. *La traite des arachides dans le pays de Kaolack et des conséquences économiques, sociales et juridiques.* Saint-Louis: IFAN, 1958.

Gellar, Sheldon. *The Cooperative Experience and Senegalese*

Rural Development Policy, 1960–1980. Princeton: Princeton University, 1983.

————, R. Charlick and Y. Jones. *Animation Rurale and Rural Development: The Experience of Senegal.* Ithaca, NY: Cornell University Rural Development Committee, 1980.

Gerry, Chris. *Petty Producers and the Urban Economy: A Case Study of Dakar.* Geneva: International Labour Office, c. 1974.

Gersovitz, M. and Waterbury, J. *The Political Economy of Risk and Choice in Senegal.* London: Frank Cass, 1987.

Ladd, William and James McClelland. *Francophone Africa: A Report on Business Opportunities in Senegal.* Washington, DC: Overseas Private Investment Corporation, 1975.

Lakroum, Monique. "Les salaires dans le port de Dakar." *Revue française d'histoire d'outre-mer* 63 (3–4, 1976): 640–653.

Laville, Pierre. *Associations rurales et socialisme contractuel en Afrique Occidentale: Etude de cas: Le Sénégal.* Paris: Editions Cujas, 1972.

Ly, Abdoulaye. *L'emergence du néocolonialisme au Sénégal.* Dakar: Editions Xamle, 1981.

Mackintosh, Maureen. "The Political Economy of Industrial Wages in Senegal." In R. Cruise O'Brien, ed. *The Political Economy of Underdevelopment* (London: Sage, 1979): 156–174.

Mersadier, Yves. *Budgets familiaux africaines: Etude chez 136 familles de salairés dans trois centres urbains du Sénégal.* Saint-Louis: IFAN, 1957.

Niane, Bokar. *Le régime juridique et fiscale du code des investissements au Sénégal.* Dakar: Nouvelles Editions Africaines, 1978.

Pelissier, Paul. "L'arachide au Sénégal." *Problèmes agricoles au Sénégal.* Saint-Louis: IFAN, 1953.

Peterec, Richard J. *Dakar and West African Economic Development.* New York: Columbia University Press, 1967.

Pfefferman, Guy. *Industrial Labor in the Republic of Senegal.* New York: Praeger, 1968.

Rocheteau, Guy. "The Modernization of Agriculture: Land Utilization and the Preference for Consumption Crops in the Groundnut Basin of Senegal." In P. Cantrelle, ed. *Population in African Development* (Ordina: Editions Dolhain, 1974): 461–469.

———. *Pouvoir financier et indépendance économique en Afrique: le cas du Sénégal.* Paris: Karthala, 1982.

Skinner, Snider W. *Senegal's Agricultural Economy in Brief.* Washington, DC: Economic Research Service, U.S. Department of Agriculture, 1966.

Svejnar, J. "The Determinants of Industrial Sector Earnings in Senegal." *Journal of Development Economics* 15 (1984): 289–311.

Terrell, Katherine and Jan Svejnar. *The Industrial Labor Market and Economic Performance in Senegal.* Boulder, CO: Westview Press, 1989.

Thomas, Louis-Vincent, ed. *Prospective du développement en Afrique noire: Un scenario: Le Sénégal.* Paris: Presses Universitaires de France, 1978.

USAID. *An Overview of the Current USAID Program in Senegal.* USAID/Senegal: Dakar, 1990.

―――――. *Senegal Agricultural Sector Analysis.* Dakar: Agricultural Development Office of USAID/Senegal, 1991.

Van der Vaeren, Aguessy. "Les femmes commerçantes au détail sur les marchés dakarois." In P. C. Lloyd, ed. *The New Elites of Tropical Africa* (London, 1966): 244–255.

Vanhaeverbeke, André. *Rénumeration du travail et commerce extérieur: Essor d'une économie exportatrice et termes de l'échange des producteurs d'arachides au Sénégal.* Louvain: Centre de Recherches des Pays en Développement, 1970.

World Bank. *Senegal: Tradition, Diversification and Economic Development.* Washington, DC: World Bank, 1974.

―――――. *The World Bank and Senegal, 1960–1987.* Report #8041. Washington, DC: Operations Evaluation Department of the World Bank, 1984.

IV. HISTORY

A. *WORKS PUBLISHED BEFORE 1900*

Adanson, M. A. *A Voyage to Senegal, the Isle of Gorée and the River Gambia.* London: J. Nourse & W. Johnston, 1759.

Alfonce, Jean. *Les voyages aventureux du Capitaine Ian Alfonce, Sainctongeois.* Poitiers: Jean de Marnes, 1559.

Ancelle, J. *Les explorations au Sénégal et dans les contrées voisines depuis l'antiquité jusqu'à nos jours.* Paris: Maisonneuve et Leclerc, 1886.

Annales sénégalaises de 1854 à 1885, suivies de traités passés avec les princes de pays. Paris: Maisonneuve, 1885.

Aube, Théophile. "Trois mois de campagne au Sénégal." *Revue des deux mondes* (1863).

Azan, H. "Notice sur le Walo." *Revue maritime et coloniale* 9–10 (1863–1864).

Barbot, Jean. *A Collection of Voyages and Travels.* Vol. V.: *A Description of the Coasts of North and South Guinea.* Edited by A. Churchill. London: Churchill, 1732.

Bayol, Jean. "La Sénégambie." *Bulletin de la société des études coloniales et maritimes* 4 (1881): 122–126.

———. *Voyage en Sénégambie, 1880–1885.* Paris: L. Baudoin, 1888. Also published in *Revue maritime et coloniale* 95–96 (1887–1888).

Boilat, Abbé Pierre D. *Esquisses sénégalaises: physionomie du pays, peuplades, commerce, religions, passé et avenir, récits, légendes.* Paris: Bertrand, 1853.

Borgnis-Desbordes, A. *Sénégal et Niger: La France dans l'Afrique occidentale, 1879–1883.* Paris: Challamel, 1884.

Bouet-Willaumez, E. *Commerce et traite des noirs aux côtes d'Afrique.* Paris: Imprimèrie Nationale, 1848.

Boufflers, Stanislas J. *Correspondance inédité de la Comtesse de Sabran et du Chevalier de Boufflers (1778–1788).* Collected and published by E. de Magnien and Henri Prat. Paris: 1875.

Brosselard, Capitaine M. *Rapport sur la situation dans la vallée*

du Sénégal en 1886: Insurrection de Mahamadou Lamine.
Lille: Imprimérie de L. Danel, 1888.

Ça da Mosto, Alvise da. *Original Journal of Ça da Mosto.*
General History and Collection of Voyages and Travels,
Vol. II. Edited by Robert Kerr. Edinburgh: Ramsay, 1811.

—————. *Relation des voyages à la côte occidentale d'Afrique*
1455–1457. Publiés par Charles Schefer. Paris: Leroux,
1895.

Caillié, René. *Travels through Central Africa to Timbuctoo and*
across the Great Desert to Morocco, Performed in the Years
1824–1828. Vol. I. London: Colburn and Bentley, 1830.

Carrère, Frédéric and Paul Holle. *De la Sénégambie française.*
Paris: Firmin-Didot, 1855.

Corréard [n.f.n.], and Savigny [n.f.n.]. *Naufrage de la frégate 'La*
Méduse' faisant partie de l'expédition du Sénégal en 1816.
Paris: Emery, 1818.

Durand, Jean-Baptiste. *Voyage au Sénégal ou mémoires histor-*
iques, philosophiques et politiques sur les découvertes,
les établissements et le commerce des europééns dans les
mers de l'Ocean Atlantique. 2 vols. Paris: H. Agasse,
1803.

Faidherbe, Louis Léon Cesar. "Sénégal: Affaires politiques du
Fleuve." *Revue coloniale* 19 (1858).

—————. *Le Sénégal; la France dans l'Afrique occidentale.* Paris:
Hachette, 1889.

—————. "Notice historique sur le Cayor." *Bulletin de la société*
de géographie de Paris 4 (1883): 527–564.

————. *Notice sur la colonie du Sénégal et sur les pays qui sont en relations avec elle*. Paris: Imprimèrie Nationale, 1859.

Flize, L. "Le Bambouk." *Moniteur du Sénégal* 51–52 (1857): 3–5.

————. "Le Boundou." *Revue coloniale* 17 (1857): 175–178.

————. "Le Gadiaga." *Moniteur du Sénégal* 42 (1857).

————. "Le Ndiambour et le Gadiaga." *Revue coloniale* 17 (1857): 390–398.

Foret, Auguste. *Un voyage dans le Haut-Sénégal*. Paris: Challamel, 1888.

Frey, Colonel Henri. *Campagne dans le Haut Sénégal et dans le Haut Niger, 1885–86*. Paris: Plon, 1888.

Gafferel, Paul. *Le Sénégal et le Soudan français*. Paris: Delagrave, 1893.

Gallieni, Joseph. *Deux campagnes au Soudan français, 1886–1888*. Paris: Hachette, 1891.

Geoffroy de Villeneuve, René. *L'Afrique ou l'histoire des moeurs, usages et coutumes des Africains. Le Sénégal*. Paris: Neveu, 1814.

Gray, Major William and Staff Surgeon Dorchard. *Travels in Western Africa in the years 1818, 19, 20 and 21 from the River Gambia through Woolli, Boondoo, Galam, Kasson, Kaarta and Foolidoo to the River Niger*. London: J. Murray, 1825.

Hecquard, Hyacinthe. *Voyage sur la côte et dans l'intérieur de l'Afrique occidentale*. Paris: Bernard, 1855.

Labarthe, Pierre. *Voyage au Sénégal pendant les années 1784 et 85 d'après les mémoires de Lajaille.* Paris: Dentu An X, 1802.

Labat, P. Jean-Baptiste. *Nouvelle relation de l'Afrique occidentale contenant une description exacte du Sénégal et des pays situés entre le Cap Blanc et la rivière de Serrelione jusqu'à plus de 300 lieues en avant dans les terres.* 4 vols. Paris: Cavalier, 1728.

Lamartiny, J. L. *Etudes africaines: Le Boundou et le Bambouc.* Paris: Challamel, 1884.

Lejean, Guillaume. "Le Sénégal en 1859 et les routes commerciaux du Sahara." *Revue contemporaine* 11 (1859).

Mollien, Gaspard T. *Voyage dans l'intérieur de l'Afrique aux sources du Sénégal et de la Gambie, fait en 1818.* 2 vols. Paris: Courcier, 1820.

Park, Mungo. *Travels into the Interior Districts of Africa.* London: J. Murray, 1816.

Perrotet, M. "Voyage de Saint Louis, chef lieu du Sénégal à Podor fait en 1825." *Nouvelles annales des voyages et des sciences géographiques* 28 (Jan. à Juin): 1833.

Raffenel, Anne. *Nouveau voyage dans le pays des Nègres: suivi d'études sur la colonie du Sénégal et de documents historiques, géographiques et scientifiques.* 2 vols. Paris: Napoléon Chaix, 1856.

―――. *Second voyage de l'exploration dans l'intérieur de l'Afrique.* Paris: Bertrand, 1850.

―――. "Sénégal. Exploration du pays de Galam, du Boundou et

du Bambouck et retour par la Gambie." *Revue coloniale* 4 (1844): 136–218.

―――. *Voyage dans l'Afrique occidentale: Comprenent l'exploration du Sénégal et de la Gambie, executé en 1843 et 1844.* Paris: Bertrand, 1846.

Rançon, André. *Le Boundou: Etude géographie et d'histoire soudaniennes de 1681 à nos jours.* Bordeaux: Gounouilhou, 1894.

Roux, Capitaine Emile. *Notice historique sur le Boundou.* Saint-Louis: Imprimérie du Gouverneur, 1893.

Saugnier [n.f.n.] *Relations de plusieurs voyages à la côte d'Afrique, au Maroc, au Sénégal, à Gorée, à Galam, tiré des journaux de Saugnier, long temps esclave des maures.* Paris: Gueffier, 1791.

Schoelcher, Victor. *L'esclavage au Sénégal en 1880.* Paris: Librairie Centrale des Publications Populaires, 1880.

Verneuil, Victor. *Mes aventures au Sénégal: Souvenirs de voyage.* Paris: Librarie Nouvelle, 1858.

Walckenar, C. A. *Collection des relations de voyages par mer et par terre en différentes parties de l'Afrique depuis 1400 jusqu'à nos jours.* Paris: Le Fèvre, 1842.

B. *WORKS PUBLISHED SINCE 1900*

Amin, Samir. "La politique coloniale française à l'égard de la bourgeosie commerçante sénégalaise, 1820–1960." In C. Meillassoux, ed. *The Development of Indigenous Trade and Markets in West Africa* (London: Oxford University Press, 1971): 361–376.

Ba, Abdou Barri. "Essai sur l'histoire du Saloum et du Rip." *Bulletin de l'IFAN* 38 (4, 1976): 812–860.

Ba, Oumar. *La pénétration française au Cayor, 1854–1861.* Dakar: National Archives, 1976.

Ba, Tamsir Ousman. "Essai historique sur le Rip (Sénégal)." *Bulletin de l'IFAN* 19 B (July-October 1957): 564–591.

Barrows, Leland. "Faidherbe and Senegal: A Critical Discussion." *African Studies Review* 19 (1, April 1976): 95–117.

————. "General Faidherbe, the Maurel and Prom Company and French Expansion in Senegal." Ph.D. thesis, U.C.L.A., 1974.

————. "The Merchants and General Faidherbe: Aspects of French Expansion in Senegal in the 1850s." *Revue française d'histoire d'outre-mer* 61 (1974): 236–283.

————. "Some Paradoxes of Pacification: Senegal and France in the 1850s and 1860s." in B. Swartz and R. Dumett, eds. *West African Culture Dynamics* (The Hague, 1980): 515–544.

Barry, Boubacar. *Le royaume du Waalo, le Sénégal avant la conquête.* Paris: Maspero, 1972.

————. *Le Sénégambie du XVè au XIXè siècle: Traite négrière, Islam et conquête coloniale.* Paris: Harmattan, 1988.

————. "The Subordination of Power and the Mercantile Economy: The Kingdom of Waalo, 1600–1831." In R. C. O'Brien, ed. *The Political Economy of Underdevelopment* (London, 1979): 39–63.

Bathily, Abdoulaye. "La conquête française du Haut-Fleuve

(Sénégal), 1818–1887.'' *Bulletin de l'IFAN* 34 B (1, 1972): 67–112.

———. ''Guerriers, tributaires et marchands: le Gajaaga (ou Galam), 'le pays de l'or.' Le développement et la régression d'une formation économique et sociale sénégalaise (c. 8é-19é siècle).'' Thése d'Etat, Université de Dakar, 1985.

———. ''Imperialism and Colonial Expansion in Senegal in the Nineteenth Century, with particular reference to the Economic, Social and Political Developments of the Kingdom of Gajaaga.'' Ph.D. thesis, University of Birmingham, Centre for West African Studies, 1975.

———. ''Mamadou Lamine Drame et la résistance anti-impérialiste dans le Haut-Sénégal, 1885–1887.'' *Notes africaines* 29 (1970): 20–32.

———. *Les portes de l'or: Le royaume de Galam (Sénégal) de l'ère musulmane au temps de négriers (VIIIe-XVIIIe siècle).* Paris: Harmattan, 1989.

———. ''La traite atlantique et ses effets économiques et sociaux en Afrique: Le cas du Galam, royaume de l'hinterland sénégambien au dix-huitième siècle.'' *Journal of African History* 27 (2, 1986): 269–293.

Bathily, Ibrahima D. ''Notices socio-historiques sur l'ancien royaume Soninké du Gadiaga. Présentées, annotées et publiées par Abdoulaye Bathily.'' *Bulletin de l'IFAN* 31 B (1, 1969): 31–105.

Becker, Charles. ''Reflexions sur les sources de l'histoire de la Sénégambie.'' *Paideuma* 33 (1987): 147–165.

——— and Victor Martin. ''Kayor et Baol: Royaumes sénégalais

et traite des esclaves au XVIIIe siècle." *Revue française d'histoire d'outre-mer* 62 (1975): 270–300.

Behrman, Lucy. "The Islamization of the Wolof by the End of the Nineteenth Century." In D. McCall, et al., eds. *Boston University Papers on Africa,* Vol. IV. (New York: Praeger, 1968): 102–131.

————."French Muslim Policy and the Senegalese Muslim Brotherhoods." In D. McCall, et al., eds. *Boston University Papers on Africa,* Vol. V. (New York: Praeger, 1969–70): 185–208.

————. "The Political Significance of the Wolof Adherence to Muslim Brotherhoods in the Nineteenth Century." *African Historical Studies* 1 (1, 1968): 60–77.

Betts, Raymond F. *Assimilation and Association in French Colonial Theory, 1890–1914.* New York: Columbia University Press, 1961.

————. "The Establishment of the Medine in Dakar, Senegal, 1914." *Africa* [London] (April 1971): 144–153.

Blaise Diagne: sa vie, son oeuvre. Dakar: Nouvelles Editions Africaines, 1976.

Bomba, Victoria. "History of the Wolof State of Jolof until 1860." Ph.D. thesis, University of Wisconsin, 1969.

Boulègue, Jean. "Contribution à la chronologie du royaume du Saloum." *Bulletin de l'IFAN,* ser. B, 3–4 (1966): 657–662.

————. *Le Grand Jolof, XIIIe-XVIe siècle.* Paris: Karthala, 1987.

————. *Les luso-africains de Sénégambie au XVIè-XIXè siècle.* Dakar: Nouvelles Editions Africaines, 1972.

Boulègue, Marguérite. "La presse au Sénégal avant 1939." *Bulletin de l'I.F.A.N.* 27 B, (3–4, 1965): 715–754.

Brigaud, Felix. *Histoire traditonelle du Sénégal.* Saint-Louis, Senegal: Centre de Recherches et de Documentation du Sénégal, 1962.

Brooks, George. "Peanuts and Colonialism: Consequences of the Commercialization of Peanuts in West Africa, 1830–1870." *Journal of African History* 16 (1975): 29–54.

Camara, Camille. *Saint Louis du Sénégal: Evolution d'une ville en milieu africain.* Dakar: IFAN, 1968.

Charles, Eunice A. *Precolonial Senegal: The Jolof Kingdom, 1800–1890.* Boston: Boston University African Studies Center, 1977.

———. "Shaikh Amadu Ba and Jihad in Jolof." *International Journal of African Historical Studies* 8 (1975): 367–382.

Charpy, Jacques. *La fondation de Dakar.* Paris: Larose, 1958.

Chastanet, Monique. "Les crises de subsistance dans les villages soninke du cercle de Bakel de 1858 à 1945." *Cahiers d'études africaines* 23 (89–90, 1983): 5–36.

Chavane, Bruno A. *Villages d'ancien Tekrour.* Paris: Karthala, 1985.

Clark, Andrew F. "Economy and Society in the Upper Senegal Valley, 1850–1920." Ph.D. thesis, Michigan State University, 1990.

———. *Comparative Perspectives on Slavery: Pulaar Oral*

Traditions from Bundu, Senegambia. East Lansing, MI: Michigan State University Press, forthcoming.

———. "Oral Sources for the Socio-Economic History of the Upper Senegal Valley." *Raconteur: A Journal of World History* 2 (January 1991): 30–38.

Cohen, William B. "A Century of Modern Administration: From Faidherbe to Senghor." *Civilisations* (Brussels), 20 (1, 1970): 40–49.

———. *Rulers of Empire: The French Colonial Service in Africa.* Stanford: Stanford University Press, 1971.

Colvin, Lucie G. "International Relations in Precolonial Senegal." *Présence africaine* 93 (1st Quarter 1975): 215–230.

———. "Kajoor and its Relation with Saint-Louis du Sénégal, 1763–1801." Ph.D. thesis, Columbia University, 1972.

———. "Islam and the State of Kajoor: A Case of Successful Resistance to Jihad." *Journal of African History* 15 (4, 1974): 587–606.

———. "Theoretical Issues in Historical International Politics: The Case of the Senegambia." *Journal of Interdisciplinary History* 8 (Summer 1977): 23–44.

Coquery-Vidrovitch, Catherine. "L'impact des intérêts coloniaux: S.C.O.A. et C.F.A.O. dans l'ouest Africain." *Journal of African History* 16 (1975): 595–621.

Crowder, Michael. *Senegal: A Study in French Assimilation Policy.* London: Oxford University Press, 1962; revised ed., London: Methuen, 1967.

————. "West Africa and the 1914–18 War." *Bulletin de l'I.F.A.N.* 30 B (1, 1968): 227–247.

Cruise O'Brien, Rita. "France in Senegal in the Nineteenth Century: Coastal Trade in the Four Communes." *Tarikh* 8 (1969): 21–31.

Cultru, P. *Histoire du Sénégal du XVème siècle à 1870.* Paris: Larose, 1910.

————. *Premier voyage du Sieur de la Courbe fait à la côte d'Afrique en 1685.* Paris: Larose, 1913.

Curtin, Philip D. "The Abolition of the Slave Trade from Senegambia." In D. Eltis and J. Walvin, eds., *The Abolition of the Atlantic Slave Trade* (Madison: University of Wisconsin Press, 1981): 83–97.

————. "Chronology of Events and Reigns in the Upper Senegal Valley." *Bulletin de l'IFAN* 36 B (3, 1974): 525–558.

————. *Economic Change in Precolonial Africa: Senegambia in the Era of the Slave Trade.* Madison: University of Wisconsin Press, 1975.

————. "Jihad in West Africa: Early Phases and Interrelations in Mauritania and Senegal." *Journal of African History* 12 (1, 1971): 11–24.

————. "The Lure of Bambuk Gold." *Journal of African History* 14 (4, 1973): 623–631.

————. "Precolonial Trading Networks and Traders: The Diahanke." In C. Meillassoux, ed. *The Development of Indigenous Trade and Markets in West Africa* (London: Oxford University Press, 1971): 228–239.

————. "The Uses of Oral Tradition in Senegambia: Maalik Si and the Foundation of Bundu." *Cahiers d'études africaines* 15 (1975): 189–202.

————, ed. *Africa and the West: Intellectual Responses to European Culture.* Madison: University of Wisconsin Press, 1972.

————, ed. *Africa Remembered: Narratives of Slaves from the Era of the Slave Trade.* Madison: University of Wisconsin Press, 1967.

Delafosse, Maurice. *Haut-Sénégal-Niger.* 3 vols. Paris: Larose, 1912; new edition, 1972.

Delcourt, André. *La France et les établissements français au Sénégal entre 1713 et 1763.* Dakar: IFAN, 1952.

Demaison, André. *Faidherbe: Les grandes figures coloniales,* no. 9. Paris: Plon, 1932.

Deschamps, Hubert. *Méthodes et doctrines coloniales de la France.* Paris: Colin, 1953.

Diagne, Pathé. *Pouvoir politique traditionnel en Afrique occidentale: Essai sur les institutions politiques précoloniale.* Paris: Présence Africaine, 1967.

Diarra, Mamadou. *Le Sénégal, concession royale: Histoire de la colonie.* Dakar: Nouvelles Editions Africaines, 1973.

Diop, Cheikh Anta. *The African Origin of Civilization: Myth or Reality.* Trans. by Mercer Cook. New York: L. Hill, 1974.

————. *L'Afrique noire précoloniale: étude comparée des systèmes politiques et sociaux de l'Europe et de l'Afrique, de l'antiquité à la formation des états modernes.* Paris: Présence Africaine, 1960.

————. *Civilization or Barbarism.* Trans. by Y. Ngemi. Brooklyn, NY: Lawrence Hill Books, 1990.

————. *Nations nègres et cultures.* Paris: Editions Africaines, 1955.

————. *L'unité culturelle de l'Afrique noire: domaines du patri-arcat et du matriarcat dans l'antiquité classique.* Paris: Présence Africaine, 1959.

Diouf, Mamadou. *Le Kajoor au XIXè siècle: Pouvoir ceddo et conquête coloniale.* Paris: Karthala, 1990.

Echenberg, Myron. "Slaves into Soldiers: Social Origins of the *Tirailleurs sénégalais.*" In Paul Lovejoy, ed. *Africans in Bondage* (Madison: University of Wisconsin Press, 1986): 311–333.

Equilbecq, F. *La légende de Samba Guélâdio Diêgui, Prince du Fouta.* Dakar: Nouvelles Editions Africaines, 1977.

Fall, Boubacar and Mohamed Mbodj. "Travail forcé et migra-tions en Sénégambie." *Historiens-géographes du Sénégal* 3 (April 1988): 23–29.

Faure, Claude. "La garrison européene du Sénégal (1779–1858)." *Revue d'histoire des colonies* 8 (1920): 5–108.

Fisher, Humphrey. "The Early Life and Pilgrimage of al-Hajj Muhammad al-Amin the Soninke (d. 1887)." *Journal of African History* 11 (1, 1970): 51–70.

Founou-Tchuigoua, Bernard. *Fondements de l'économie de traite au Sénégal: la surexploitation d'une colonie de 1880 à 1960.* Paris: Editions Silex, 1981.

Galloway, Winnifred. "A History of Wuli from the Thirteenth to the Nineteenth Century." Ph.D. thesis, Indiana University, 1975.

Gentil, Pierre. *Les troupes du Sénégal de 1816 à 1890.* Vol. One: *Soldats au Sénégal, 1816–1865.* Dakar: Nouvelles Editions Africaines, 1978.

Girard, Jean. "Note sur l'histoire traditionelle de la Haute Casamance." *Bulletin de l'IFAN* 28 B (1–2, 1966): 540–554.

Gomez, Michael. "Bundu in the Eighteenth Century." *International Journal of African Historical Studies* 20 (1, 1987): 61–73.

Gonçalves, José. "Textes portugais sur les Wolofs au XVe siècle." *Bulletin de l'IFAN* 30 B (1968): 822–846.

Guèye, Mbaye. "L'affaire Chautemps (avril 1904) et la suppression de l'esclavage de case au Sénégal." *Bulletin de l'IFAN* 27 B (3, 1965): 542–559.

————. "La fin de l'esclavage à Saint-Louis et à Gorée en 1848." *Bulletin de l'IFAN,* 26 B (3–4, 1966): 637–656.

Hardy, Georges. *Une conquête morale: L'enseignement en A.O.F.* Paris: Larose, 1917.

————. *La mise en valeur du Sénégal de 1817 à 1854.* Paris: Larose, 1921.

Hargreaves, John D. "Assimilation in Eighteenth-Century Senegal." *Journal of African History* 6 (2, 1965): 177–184.

Hessling, Gerti. *Histoire politique du Sénégal: Institutions, droits et société*. Paris: Karthala, 1985.

Hilliard, Constance. "Zuhur al-Basatin and Ta'rikh al-Turubbe: Some Legal and Ethical Aspects of Slavery in the Sudan as seen in the Works of Shaykh Musa Kamara." In J. R Willis, ed. *Slaves and Slavery in Muslim Africa*, Vol. One: *Islam and the Ideology of Slavery* (London: Frank Cass, 1985).

Houdas, O. V. ed. and trans. *Ta'rikh al-Fettash*. 2 vols. Paris: Adrien-Maisonneuve, 1913–1914.

———. ed. and trans. *Ta'rikh al-Sudan*. 2 vols. Paris: Adrien-Maisonneuve, 1900.

Idowu, H. Oludare. "Assimilation in Nineteenth Century Senegal." *Bulletin de l'I.F.A.N.* 30 B (4, 1968): 1422–1447. Also published in *Cahiers d'études africaines* 9 (34, 1969): 194–218.

———. "Café au Lait: Senegal's Mulatto Community in the Nineteenth Century." *Journal of the Historical Society of Nigeria* 6 (1972): 271–288.

———. "The Establishment of Elective Institutions in Senegal, 1869–1880." *Journal of African History* 9 (2, 1968): 261–277.

Johnson, G. Wesley. *The Emergence of Black Politics in Senegal: The Struggle for Power in the Four Communes, 1900–1920*. Stanford: Stanford University Press, 1971.

———. "The Senegalese Urban Elite 1900–1945." In P. Curtin, ed. *Africa and the West* (Madison, 1972): 139–188.

Kamara, Sheikh Musa. "Histoire du Boundou." Trans. by Mustapha N'Diaye. *Bulletin de l'IFAN* 37 B (4, 1975): 784–816.

————. *La vie d'El Hajj Omar, 1797–1864*. Arabic text. IFAN Manuscripts, Fonds Shaykh Moussa Kamara, cahier 9. Also published as *La vie d'El Hajj Omar,* trans. by Amar Samb. Dakar: Editions Hillal, 1975.

————. *Zuhur al-Basatin fi Ta'rikh al-Sawadin.* (Fleurs des jardins sur l'histoire des noirs). Arabic text. IFAN manuscripts, Fonds Shaykh Moussa Kamara, cahiers 2–3.

Kane, Mustapha and David Robinson. *The Islamic Regime of Futa Toro*. East Lansing, MI: Michigan State University Press, 1984.

Kane, Oumar. "Le Fuuta Tooro des Satigi aux Almaami, 1512–1807." Thése d'Etat, Université de Dakar, 1987.

Kanya-Forstner, Alexander S. *The Conquest of the Western Sudan: A Study in French Military Imperialism*. London: Cambridge University Press, 1969.

Klein, Martin A. "Colonial Rule and Structural Change: The Case of Sine-Saloum." In R. C. O'Brien, ed. *The Political Economy of Underdevelopment* (London: Sage, 1979): 65–99.

————. "The Development of Senegalese Historiography." in B. Jewsiecki and D. Newbury, eds. *African Historiographies* (London: Sage, 1986): 215–223.

————. *Islam and Imperialism in Senegal: Sine Saloum, 1847–1914*. Stanford: Stanford University Press, 1968.

————. "Servitude among the Wolof and Sereer of Senegambia." In S. Miers and I. Koptoff, eds. *Slavery in Africa* (Madison: University of Wisconsin Press, 1975): 335–363.

————. "Social and Economic Factors in the Muslim Revolutions in Senegambia.'' *Journal of African History* 13 (1972): 419–441.

Leary, Fay. ''Islam, Politics and Colonialism: A Political History of Islam in the Casamance Region of Senegal, 1850–1914.'' Ph.D. thesis, Northwestern University, 1969.

Ly, Abdoulaye. *La compagnie du Sénégal de 1673 à 1696.* Paris: Présence Africaine, 1958.

————. *Un navire de commerce sur la côte sénégambienne en 1685.* Dakar: IFAN, 1964.

Ly-Tall, Madina. ''Le Haut-Sénégal et la Haut-Niger dans la politique française de la fin du XVIIè siècle au milieu du XVIIIè siécle: l'attrait de l'or du Bambouk et du commerce du Soudan.'' *Bulletin de l'IFAN* 43 B (1–2, 1981): 24–46.

Manchuelle, François. ''Slavery, Emancipation and Labour Migration in West Africa: The Case of the Soninke.'' *Journal of African History* 30 (2, 1989), 89–106.

Mark, Peter. ''Urban Migration, Cash Cropping and Calamity: The Spread of Islam among the Diola of Boulouf (Senegal), 1900–1940.'' *African Studies Review* 21 (2, 1978): 1–14.

Marty, Paul. ''L'établissement des Français dans le Haut-Sénégal (1817–1822).'' *Revue historique des colonies françaises* 18 (1925): 51–118; 210–268.

Maupoil, B. ''Notes concernant l'histoire des Coniagui-Bassari et en particulier l'occupation de leurs pays par les Français.'' *Bulletin de l'IFAN* 16 B (3–4, 1954): 378–389.

MBodj, Mohamed and Mamadou Diouf. ''Senegalese Historiography: Present Practices and Future Perspectives.'' In

B. Jewsiewicki and D. Newbury, eds. *African Historiographies* (London: Sage, 1986): 207–214.

McLane, Margaret. "Commercial Rivalries and French Policy on the Senegal River, 1831–1858." *African Economic History* 15 (1986): 39–67.

Michel, Marc. *L'appel à l'Afrique: Contributions et réactions à l'effort de guerre en A.O.F., 1914–1919*. Paris: Publications de la Sorbonne, 1982.

Moitt, Bernard. "Slavery and Emancipation in Senegal's Peanut Basin: The Nineteenth and Twentieth Centuries." *International Journal of African Historical Studies* 22 (1, 1989): 27–50.

Monteil, Vincent. *Esquisses sénégalaises*. Initiations et études africaines. No. 21. Dakar: IFAN, 1966.

———. "The Wolof Kingdom of Kayor." In D. Forde and P. Kaberry, eds. *West African Kingdoms* (London: Oxford University Press, 1967).

N'Diaye, Babacar and Matar Diouf. *Vie et oeuvre de Lamine Guèye, 1891–1968: Catalogue de l'exposition des archives*. Dakar: National Archives, 1987.

N'Diaye, F. "La colonie du Sénégal au temps de Briére de l'Isle, 1876–1881." *Bulletin de l'IFAN* 30 B (2, 1968): 463–512.

N'Diaye, Oumar. "Le Djolof et ses Bourbas." *Bulletin de l'IFAN* 28 B (3–4, 1966): 96–101.

Newbury, Colin. "The Formation of the Government General of French West Africa." *Journal of African History* 1 (2, 1960): 111–128.

————. "The Protectionist Revival in French Colonial Trade: The Case of Senegal." *Economic History Review* 21 (1968): 337–348.

Nyambarza, Daniel. "Le marabout El Hadj Mamadou Lamine d'après les archives françaises." *Cahiers d'études africaines* 9 (1969).

Oloruntimehin, R. Olatunji. "Muhammad Lamine in Franco-Tukolor Relations, 1885–87." *Journal of the Historical Society of Nigeria* 4 (3, 1968): 375–396.

————. "Senegambia-Mahmadou Lamine." In M. Crowder, ed. *West African Resistance: The Military Response to Colonial Occupation* (New York, 1971): 80–110.

Pasquier, Roger. "A propos de l'émancipation des esclaves au Sénégal en 1848." *Revue d'histoire d'outre-mer* 54 (1967): 188–208.

————. "Villes du Sénégal au XIXè siècle." *Revue française d'histoire d-outre-mer* 47 (1960): 387–426.

Pheffer, Paul E. "African Influence on French Colonial Railroads in Senegal." In G. W. Johnson, ed. *Double Impact* (Westport, CT, 1985): 31–49.

————. "Railroads and Aspects of Social Change in Senegal, 1878–1933." Ph.D. thesis, University of Pennsylvania, 1975.

Pulvenis, Claude. "Une épidemie de fièvre jaune à Saint-Louis-du-Sénégal, 1881." *Bulletin de l'IFAN* 30 B (1968): 1353–1373.

Quinn, Charlotte. *Mandingo Kingdoms of the Senegambia: Tradi-*

tionalism, Islam and European Expansion. Evanston, IL: Northwestern University Press, 1972.

Renault, François. *L'abolition de l'esclavage au Sénégal: l'attitude de l'administration française, 1848–1905.* Paris: Société Française d'Histoire d'Outre-mer, 1972.

————. *Libération d'esclaves et nouvelle servitude.* Dakar: Nouvelles Editions Africaines, 1975.

Ritchie, Carson. "Deux textes sur le Sénégal, 1673–1677." *Bulletin de l'IFAN* 30 B (1, 1968): 289–353.

Roberts, Richard. "Text and Testimony in the 'Tribunal de première instance,' Dakar, during the Early Twentieth Century." *Journal of African History* 31 (3, 1990): 447–463.

Robinson, David. "Abdul Qadir and Shaykh Umar: A Continuing Tradition of Islamic Leadership in Futa Toro." *International Journal of African Historical Studies* 6 (2, 1973): 286–303.

————. *Chiefs and Clerics: Abdul Bokar Kan and Futa Toro, 1853–1891.* Oxford: Clarendon Press, 1975.

————. "French 'Islamic' Policy and Practice in Late Nineteenth-Century Senegal." *Journal of African History* 29 (4, 1988): 415–435.

————. "Un historien et anthropologue sénégalais: Shaikh Musa Kamara." *Cahiers d'études africaines* 28 (109, 1988): 89–116.

————. *The Holy War of Umar Tal: The Western Sudan in the Nineteenth Century.* Oxford: Clarendon Press, 1985.

————. "The Islamic Revolution of Futa Toro." *International Journal of African Historical Studies* 8 (1975): 185–221.

————. "La mise en place d'une 'hegemonie' coloniale au Séné-gal." *Historiens-geographes du Sénégal* 3 (April 1988): 2–7.

————, P. Curtin and J. Johnson. "A Tentative Chronology of Futa Toro from the Sixteenth through the Nineteenth Centu-ries." *Cahiers d'études africaines* 12 (1972): 555–592.

Roche, Christian. *Histoire de la Casamance: Conquête et resis-tance.* Paris: Karthala, 1985.

Rousseau, R. "Le Sénégal d'autrefois: Etude sur le Cayor, cahiers de Yoro Dyao." *BCEHSAOF* 16 (1933): 237–298.

————. "Le Sénégal d'autrefois: Etudes sur le Oula, cahiers de Yoro Dyao." *BCEHSAOF* 12 (1929): 133–211.

————. "Le Sénégal d'autrefois: Etude sur le Toubé, papiers de Rawane Boy." *BCEHSAOF* 14 (1931): 334–364.

Saint-Martin, Yves. *L'empire toucouleur, 1848–1897.* Paris: Le Livre Africain, 1970.

————. *L'empire toucouleur et la France: Un demi-siècle de relations diplomatiques, 1846–1893.* Dakar: Université de Dakar, Faculté des Lettres, 1966.

————. *Le Sénégal sous la Seconde Empire.* Paris: Karthala, 1989.

————. *Une source de l'histoire coloniale du Sénégal: Les rapports de la situation politique, 1874–1894.* Dakar: Université de Dakar, Faculté des Lettres, 1966.

Sainville, Léopold. *Histoire du Sénégal depuis l'arrivée des Européens jusqu'à 1850 d'après les documents des archives françaises.* Saint-Louis: IFAN, 1972.

Sanneh, Lamine. "Slavery, Islam and the Jahanke People of West Africa." *Africa* 46 (1976): 80–97.

Sarr, Dominique. "Jurisprudence des tribunaux indigènes du Sénégal: Les causes de rupture du lien matrimonial de 1872 à 1946." *Annales africaines* 11 (1975): 143–178.

Saulnier, Eugene. *Une compagnie à privilège au XIXè siècle: La compagnie du Galam au Sénégal.* Paris: Larose, 1921.

Sinou, A. "Saint-Louis du Sénégal au début du XIXe: organisations spatiales et mutations sociales." *Cahiers d'études africaines* 29 (3–4, 1989).

Soh, Siré Abbas. *Chronique du Fouta Sénégalais.* Trans. by M. Delafosse and H. Gaden. Paris: Ernst Leroux, 1913.

Suret-Canale, Jean. *Afrique noire occidentale et centrale: L'ère coloniale, 1900–1945.* Paris: Editions Sociales, 1964.

———. *French Colonialism in Tropical Africa, 1900–1945.* New York: Pica, 1971.

Swindell, Ken. "Serawoollies, Tillibunkas and Strange Farmers: The Development of Migrant Groundnut Farming along the Gambia River, 1848–95." *Journal of African History* 21 (2, 1980): 93–104.

Thilmans, G. and A. Ravisé. *Protohistoire du Sénégal.* II: *Sintiou Bara et les sites du fleuve.* Dakar: IFAN, 1984.

Thilmans, Guy, C. Deschamps and B. Khayat. *Protohistoire du Sénégal: Recherches archéologiques.* Dakar: IFAN, 1980.

Touré, Oussouby. "Le réfus du travail forcé au Sénégal." *Cahiers d'études africaines* 24 (1, 1984): 25–38.

Umar Al-Naqar. "Tekrur: The History of a Name." *Journal of African History* 10 (3, 1969): 365–374.

Vaillant, Janet G. *Black, French, and African: A Life of Léopold Sédar Senghor.* Cambridge, MA: Harvard University Press, 1990.

Villard, André. *Histoire du Sénégal.* Dakar: Maurice Viale, 1943.

Webb, James. "The Trade in Gum Arabic: Prelude to French Conquest in Senegal." *Journal of African History* 26 (2, 1985): 149–168.

Witherell, Julian. "The Response of the Peoples of Cayor to French Penetration, 1850–1900." Ph.D. thesis, University of Wisconsin, 1964.

Wood, W. Raymond. "An Archaeological Appraisal of Early European Settlements in the Senegambia." *Journal of African History* 8 (1, 1967): 39–64.

Zuccarelli, François. "De la chefferie traditionelle au canton: évolution du canton colonial au Sénégal." *Cahiers d'études africaines* 13 (2, 1973): 213–238.

———. "Les maries de Saint-Louis et Gorée de 1816 à 1872." *Bulletin de l'IFAN* 35 B (3, 1973): 551–573.

———. "Le régime des engagés à temps au Sénégal de 1817 à 1848." *Cahiers d'études africaines* 2 (7, 1961): 420–461.

V. POLITICS AND GOVERNMENT

A. *GENERAL STUDIES*

Abelin, Philippe. "Domaine national et développement au Sénégal." *Bulletin de l'IFAN* 41 B (3, 1979): 508–538.

Adamolekum, Lapido. "Bureaucrats and the Senegalese Political Process." *Journal of Modern African Studies* (December 1971): 543–559.

Arnaud, Robert. *L'Islam et la politique musulmane française en Afrique occidentale française.* Paris: Larose, 1912.

Ba, Fama Hane, et al. "The Impact of Territorial Administrative Reform on the Situation of Women in Senegal." In *Rural Development and Women in Africa* (Geneva: International Labor Office, 1984).

Balans, Jean-Louis. *Autonomie locale et intégration nationale au Sénégal.* Paris: Karthala, 1975.

Barker, Jonathan. "Local Politics and National Development: The Case of a Rural District in the Saloum Region of Senegal." Ph.D. thesis, University of California at Berkeley, 1967.

———. "The Paradox of Development: Reflections on a Study of Local-Central Political Relations in Senegal." In M. Lofchie, ed. *The State of the Nations* (Berkeley: University of California Press, 1971): 47–63.

———. "Political Factionalism in Senegal." *Canadian Journal of African Studies* 7 (2, 1973): 287–303.

———. "Stability and Stagnation: The State in Senegal." *Canadian Journal of African Studies* 11 (1, 1977): 23–42.

Barry, Boubacar. "Neocolonialism and Dependence in Senegal, 1960–1980." in P. Gifford and W. Louis, eds., *Decolonization and African Independence* (New Haven: Yale University Press, 1988): 271–94.

Behrman, Lucy. *Muslim Brotherhoods and Politics in Senegal.* Cambridge: Harvard University Press, 1970.

————. ''Political Consolidation and Centre-Local Relations in Senegal.'' *Canadian Journal of African Studies* 4 (1, 1970): 101–120.

Blanchet, Gilles. *Elites et changements en Afrique et au Sénégal.* Paris: ORSTOM, 1983.

Casswell, N. ''Autopsie de l'ONCAD: La politique arachidière au Senegal, 1966–1980.'' *Politique africaine* 14 (1984): 39–73.

Copans, Jean. ''Paysannerie et politique au Sénégal.'' *Cahiers d'études africaines* 69–70 (1978): 241–256.

Cottingham, Clement. ''Clan Politics and Rural Modernization: A Study of Local Political Change in Senegal.'' Ph.D. thesis, University of California at Berkeley, 1969.

Coulon, Christian. ''L'Etat et l'Islam au Sénégal.'' *Annales africaines* (1984).

————. *Le marabout et le prince: Islam et pouvoir au Sénégal.* Paris: Pédone, 1981.

————. ''Les marabouts sénégalais et l'Etat.'' *Revue françaises de politiques africaines* 158 (1979): 15–42.

————. ''Political Elites in Senegal, I.'' *Mazawo* [Kampala] (June 1970): 9–22.

————. ''Political Elites in Senegal, II.'' *Mazawo* [Kampala] (December 1970): 29–37.

———— and D. B. Cruise O'Brien. "Senegal." In D. Cruise O'Brien, J. Dunn and R. Rathbone, eds. *Contemporary West African States* (Cambridge: Cambridge University Press, 1989): 145–164.

Creevey, Lucy. "Muslim Brotherhoods and Politics in Senegal in 1985." *Journal of Modern African Studies* 23 (4, 1985): 715–721.

Cruise O'Brien, Donal B. "Co-operators and Bureaucrats: Class Formation in a Senegalese Peasant Society." *Africa* 41 (1971): 263–278.

————. "Des bienfaits de l'inégalité: L'état et l'économic rurale au Sénégal." *Politique africaine* 14 (1, 1984).

————. "La filière musulmane: Confréries soufies et politique en Afrique noire." *Politique africaine* 1 (4, 1981): 7–30.

————. "Senegal." In John Dunn, ed. *West African States: Failure and Promise* (Cambridge: Cambridge University Press, 1978): 173–188.

Delavignette, Robert. *Freedom and Authority in French West Africa.* London: Oxford University Press, 1950.

Desouches, Christine. *Le Parti Démocratique Sénégalais.* Paris: Berger-Levrault, 1983.

Dia, Mamadou. "Le Président Dia trace un programme pour la politique d'indépendence." *L'unité africaine* (June 11, 1960).

————. *Le Sénégal trahi, marché d'esclaves.* Paris: SELIO, 1988.

Diagne, Pathé. *Sénégal: Crise économique et social et devenir de la démocratie.* Dakar: Sankore, 1984.

Diallo, Mamadou. *Galandou Diouf, homme politique sénégalais 1875–1941.* Dakar: Nouvelles Editions Africaines, 1972.

Diarra, Mamadou. *Justice et développement au Sénégal.* Dakar: Nouvelles Editions Africaines, 1973.

Diop, Alioune and C. A. Diop. *Culture et colonialisme.* Paris: La Nef de Paris, 1957.

Diop, Cheikh Anta. *Black Africa: The Economic and Cultural Basis for a Federated State.* Westport, CT.: L. Hill, 1976.

Diop, M. C. and M. Diouf. *Le Sénégal sous Abdou Diouf.* Paris: Karthala, 1990.

Diop, Majhemout. *Contribution à l'étude des problèmes politiques en Afrique noire.* Paris: Présence Africaine, 1959.

Diop, Ousman Blondin. *Les heriters d'une indépendance.* Dakar: Nouvelles Editions Africaines, 1982.

Diouf, Abdou. *Rapport de politique générale: Le PS, moteur du sursaut national.* Dakar: Publications de Parti Socialiste, 1984.

Fall, Ibrahima. *Sous-développement et démocratie multipartisane: L'experience sénégalaise.* Dakar: Nouvelles Editions Africaines, 1977.

Fall, Mar. "L'état sénégalais et le renouveau récent de l'Islam: Une introduction." *Mois en Afrique* 219/220 (1984): 154–159.

————. "Le multipartisme et l'union nationale au Sénégal?" *Mois en Afrique* 217/218 (1984): 31–37.

————. *Sénégal: L'état de Abdou Diouf ou les temps des incertitudes.* Paris: Harmattan, 1986.

Fatton, Robert. *The Making of a Liberal Democracy: Senegal's Passive Revolution, 1975–1985.* Boulder, CO: Lynne Rienner, 1987.

Foltz, William J. *From French West Africa to the Mali Federation.* New Haven: Yale University Press, 1965.

————. "Senegal." In James Coleman and C. Rosberg, Jr., eds. *Political Parties and National Integration in Tropical Africa* (Berkeley: University of California Press, 1970): 16–64.

Gautron, Jean-Claude and Michel Rougevin-Baville. *Droit public au Sénégal.* Paris: Editions Pedone, 1970.

Gellar, Sheldon. "State-Building and Nation-Building in West Africa." In S. Eisenstadt and S. Rokkan, eds. *Building States and Nations: Models, Analyses, and Data Across Three Worlds,* Vol. 2 (Beverly Hills, 1973): 384–426.

————. *Structural Changes and Colonial Dependency: Senegal, 1885–1945.* Beverly Hills: Sage, 1976.

Jalloh, Abdul A. *Political Integration in French-Speaking Africa.* Berkeley: Institute of International Studies, University of California, 1973.

Johnson, G. Wesley. "The Ascendancy of Blaise Diagne and the Beginning of African Politics in Senegal." *Africa* [London] 34 (1966): 235–252.

————. "The Development of Local Political Institutions in Urban Senegal." In Arnold Rivkin, ed. *Nations by Design: Institution-Building in Africa* (New York, 1968): 208–227.

Lo, Magatte. *Sénégal: L'heure du choix.* Paris: Harmattan, 1985.

Ly, Abdoulaye. *L'état et la production paysanne ou l'état et la révolution au Sénégal 1957–58.* Paris: Présence Africaine, 1958.

Markowitz, Irving L. *Léopold Sédar Senghor and the Politics of Négritude.* New York: Atheneum, 1969.

————. "The Political Thought of Blaise Diagne and Lamine Guèye: Some Aspects of Social Structure and Ideology in Senegal." *Présence africaine* 72 (1969): 21–38.

————. "Traditional Social Structure: The Islamic Brotherhoods and Political Development in Senegal." *Journal of Modern African Studies* (April 1970): 73–96.

Milcent, Ernest. *Au carrefour des options africaines: Le Sénégal.* Paris: Centurion, 1965.

————. "Senegal." In G. Carter, ed. *African One-Party States* (Ithaca: Cornell University Press, 1962): 87–148.

————, and Monique Sordet. *Léopold Sédar Seghor et la naissance de l'Afrique moderne.* Paris: Seghers, 1969.

Morgenthau, Ruth Schactner. *Political Parties in French-Speaking West Africa.* Oxford: Clarendon Press, 1964.

N'Diaye, M. B. *Panorama politique du Sénégal.* Dakar: Nouvelles Editions Africaines, 1986.

Nzouankeu, Jacques M. *Les partis politiques sénégalaises.* Dakar: Editions Clairafrique, 1984.

Quellien, Alain. *La politique musulmane dans l'Afrique Occidentale Française.* Paris: Larose, 1910.

Robinson, Kenneth. "Senegal: The Elections to the Territorial Assembly." In W. McKenzie and K. Robinson, eds. *Five Elections in Africa* (New York, 1960).

Robson, Peter. "Problems of Integration between Senegal and Gambia." In A. Hazelwood, ed. *African Integration and Disintegration* (London, 1967): 115–128.

————. "The Problems of Senegambia." *Journal of Modern African Studies* 3 (1965).

Schumacher, Edward. *Politics, Bureaucracy and Rural Development in Senegal.* Berkeley: University of California, 1975.

Senghor, Léopold. *Les fondements de l'Africanité ou Négritude et Arabicité.* Paris: Présence africaine, 1967.

————. *Liberté I: Négritude et Humanisme.* Paris: Seuil, 1964.

————. *Liberté IV: Socialisme et planification.* Paris: Seuil, 1983.

————. *Nation et voie africaine du socialisme.* Paris: Présence Africaine, 1961.

————. *On African Socialism,* trans. by Mercer Cook. New York: Praeger, 1964.

————. *Pierre Teilhard de Chardin et la politique africaine.* Paris: Seuil, 1962.

Silla, Usmane. "Les partis politiques au Sénégal." *Revue française d'études politiques africaines* (April 1968): 78–94.

Sow, Fatou. *Les fonctionnaires de l'administration centrale du Sénégal.* Dakar: IFAN, 1967.

Terrisse, André. "Aspects du malaise paysan au Sénégal." *Revue française d'études politiques africaines* 55 (July 1970): 79–91.

Traoré, Bakory. "Evolution de partis politiques au Sénégal depuis 1946." In B. Traoré, M. Lo, and J. L. Alberts, eds. *Forces politiques en Afrique noire.* Paris: Presses Universitaires de France, 1966.

Zuccarelli, François. *Un parti politique africain: l'Union Progressiste Sénégalaise.* Paris: Pichon et Durand-Auzias, 1971.

B. *EXTERNAL AFFAIRS*

Biarnès, Pierre. "La diplomatie sénégalaise." *Revue française d'études politiques africaines* 149 (1978): 62–78.

Bourgi, Albert. *La politique française de coopération en Afrique: Le cas du Sénégal.* Paris: Pichon et Durand-Auzias, 1979.

Colvin, Lucie G. "International Relations in Precolonial Senegal." *Présence africaine* 93 (1975): 215–230.

Dia, Mamadou. *African Nations and World Solidarity.* New York: Praeger, 1961.

Mortimer, Edward. *France and the Africans, 1944–1960: A Political History.* New York: Walker and Company, 1969.

Parker, Ron. "The Senegal-Mauritania Conflict of 1989: A

Fragile Equilibrium.'' *Journal of Modern African Studies* 29 (1, 1991): 155–71.

Senghor, Léopold. *La poésie de l'action, conversations avec Mohamed Aziza.* Paris: Editions Stock, 1980.

Skurnik, W.A.E. *The Foreign Policy of Senegal.* Evanston, IL: Northwestern University Press, 1972.

Thiam, Doudou. *The Foreign Policy of African States.* New York: Praeger, 1965.

Tunteng, P. Kiven. ''External Influences and Subimperialism in Francophone West Africa.'' In P. Gutkind and I. Wallerstein, eds. *The Political Economy of Contemporary Africa* (Beverly Hills: Sage, 1976): 212–231.

White, Dorothy. *Black Africa and DeGaulle: From the French Empire to Independence.* University Park: Pennsylvania State University Press, 1979.

VI. SCIENCE

A. *ENVIRONMENT AND GEOGRAPHY*

Adam, J. G. ''Les pâturages naturels et postculturaux du Sénégal.'' *Bulletin de l'IFAN* 38 A (2, 1966): 456–537.

Ba, Alioune and Ndiacé Diop. ''Les nouveaux enjeux dans la vallée du fleuve Sénégal.'' *Historiens-géographes du Sénégal* 2 (March 1987): 79–94.

Ba, Cheikh. *Les Peul du Sénégal: Etude géographique.* Dakar: Nouvelles Editions Africaines, 1986.

Batude, Fernand. *L'arachide au Sénégal.* Paris: 1941.

Berhault, J. *Flore du Sénégal.* 2nd edition. Dakar: Editions Clairafrique, 1967.

Chamard, Philippe Claude. *Le Sénégal: Géographie.* Dakar: Nouvelles Editions Africaines, 1973.

Church, R. J. Harrison. *West Africa: A Study of the Environment and of Man's Use of It.* London: Oxford University Press, 1957.

La désertification au sud du Sahara. Colloque de Nouakchott, 17–19 December 1973. Dakar: Nouvelles Editions Africaines, 1976.

Diop, Moussa. "L'elevage au Sénégal." *Historiens-géographes du Sénégal* 3 (April 1988): 30–36.

Guiraud, Xavier. *L'arachide sénégalaise.* Paris: 1937.

Kane, Alioune. "Le bilan de l'eau sur le bassin versant du fleuve Sénégal." *Historiens-géographes du Sénégal* 2 (March 1987): 13–21.

Mauny, Raymond. *Tableau géographique de l'ouest africain au moyen age.* Dakar: IFAN, 1961.

Moral, Paul. "Le climat du Sénégal." *Revue de géographie de l'Afrique occidentale* (Dakar) 1–2 (1965): 49–70 and 3 (1966): 26–35.

Niasse, Madiodio. "L'amenagement du lac de Guiers: Prelude a l'après-barrage." *Historiens-géographes du Sénégal* 2 (March 1987): 37–48.

Pélissier, Paul. *Les paysans du Sénégal: Les civilisations agraires du Cayor à la Casamance.* Saint-Yrieux: Imprimerie Fabrègue, 1966.

―――. *La région arachidière: Etude régionale.* 2 vols. Dakar: Grande Imprimérie Africaine, n.d.

Peterec, Richard. *The Port of Ziguinchor: The Direct Ocean Outlet for Casamance (Senegal).* New York: Columbia University, Division of Economic Geography, 1962.

―――. *The Position of Kaolack (Senegal) and Other Ports of the Saloum Estuary in West African Trade.* New York: Columbia University, Division of Economic Geography, 1962.

―――. *Saint-Louis du Sénégal: The Natural Ocean Outlet for the Senegal River Valley.* New York: Columbia University Press, 1966.

Seck, Mansour. "Etude des principaux factuers agrométéorologiques au Sénégal." *L'agronomie tropicale* 25 (3, 1970): 241–276.

Sénégal, Ministère du Plan et de la Cooperation. *Atlas pour l'aménagement du territoire.* Dakar: Nouvelles Editions Africaines, 1977.

Thomas, Benjamin. "Railways and Ports in French West Africa." *Economic Geography* 33 (January 1957): 1–15.

Toure, Kiba. *Environment: Les problèmes de la détérioration et de la protection de la nature dans le département de Vélingara.* Dakar: Nouvelles Editions Africaines, 1976.

B. *MEDICINE AND PUBLIC HEALTH*

Cantrelle, P. and H. Leridon. "Breast-Feeding, Child Mortality and Fertility in a Rural Zone of Senegal." *Population Studies* 25 (1971): 505–533.

Kamara, Shaikh Musa. *Husuulul-aghraad fii shiffa'il-amraad.* (L'obtention des buts sur le remède des maladies ou la médecine indigène.) Arabic text. IFAN manuscripts, Fonds Shaykh Mousa Kamara, cahier 18.

Lacombe, B. and J. Vaugelade. "Mortalité au sevrage, mortalité saisonnière. Un exemple: Fakao (Sénégal)." *Population* 2 (1969): 339–343.

Menes, Robin. Syncrisis: The Dynamics of Health. Vol. XIX: *Senegal.* Washington, DC: U.S. Department of Health, Education and Welfare, June 1976.

Snyder, Francis. "Health Policy and the Law in Senegal." *Social Science and Medicine* 8 (1974).

U.S. Walter Reed Army Hospital. *Health Data Publications: Republic of Senegal.* No. 26. Washington, DC: June 1965.

ABOUT THE AUTHOR

ANDREW F. CLARK (A.B., Columbia University; M.A., Ohio University; Ph.D., Michigan State University) is Assistant Professor of African History at the University of North Carolina at Wilmington, where he also teaches courses in Middle Eastern and global history. Dr. Clark has spent several years in Senegal, initially as a Peace Corps volunteer (1978–1981), and later on grants from the Fulbright-Hays Dissertation Abroad Program (1986–1988) and the National Endowment for the Humanities Translations Program (1991). He is fluent in French, Arabic, Pulaar (Fulfulde) and Wolof. He has presented papers to numerous professional organizations and has published several articles in professional journals. Dr. Clark is preparing two book-length manuscripts for publication, *Comparative Perspectives on Slavery: Oral Traditions from Bundu, Senegambia* (Michigan State University Press), and *From Frontier to Backwater: Economy and Society in the Upper Senegal Valley, 1850–1920*.

FOR REFERENCE

NOT TO BE TAKEN FROM THIS ROOM

GAYLORD			PRINTED IN U.S.A.